TAHITI: ISLAND
OF LOVE

TAHITI: ISLAND OF LOVE

by

ROBERT LANGDON

Fourth Edition

PACIFIC PUBLICATIONS
Sydney

First published in 1959 by Cassell and Company Ltd., London, W.C.1.

Ace Books paperback edition published in 1960 by the Harborough Publishing Co. Ltd., London, W.C.1.

This fourth edition, 1972, and third edition, 1968, published by Pacific Publications (Aust.) Pty. Ltd., Technipress House, 29 Alberta Street, Sydney, N.S.W. 2000.

National Library of Australia card number and ISBN 0 85807 006 5

Printed by North Shore Stationery and Printing Pty. Ltd., Artarmon, N.S.W., 2064.

CONTENTS

LIST OF ILLUSTRATIONS

ACKNOWLEDGEMENTS

MY thanks are due to:
    Messrs. Calmann-Levy, Paris, for permission to publish an abridged version of Pierre Loti's '*Le Mariage de Loti*' ('The Marriage of Loti').

Mr. Harold Dean Cater, Tarrytown, New York, for permission to quote extracts from two letters of Henry Adams, published in Mr. Cater's book, *Henry Adams and his Friends*, Boston, 1947.

Messrs. Sidgwick & Jackson, Ltd., London, and McClelland & Stewart, Ltd., Toronto, for permission to quote extracts from the poems 'The Soldier' and 'Tiare Tahiti' in *The Collected Poems of Rupert Brooke*.

Sir Geoffrey Keynes and Mr. Christopher Hassall, London, literary trustees of Rupert Brooke, for permission to quote extracts from six of Brooke's letters published in Arthur Stringer's book, *Red Wine of Youth*, New York, 1948.

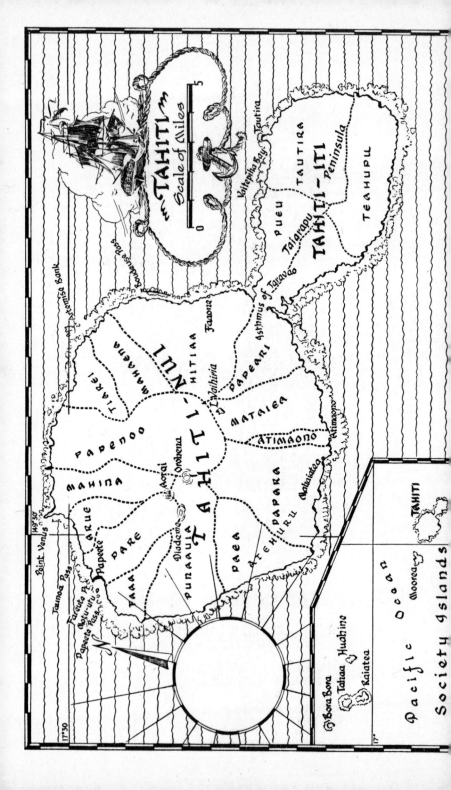

TAHITI
Scale of Miles

0 — 5

Boudeuse Pass

Point Venus   145°30'

Taunoa Pass
Nobu-utu Pass
Taaputapu Pass
Papeete

TAAA
PUNAAUIA
PAEA
ATEHURU
PAPARA
Mahaiatea
Atimaono

PARE
ARUE
MAHINA
Aorai
Orohena
Diadema
PAPENOO
TIAREI
MAHAENA
HITIAA

TAHITI-NUI

MATAIEA
PAPEARI
Papenoo

Vaihiria
Vaihiria
Faaone

Isthmus of Taravao
PUEU
TAUTIRA

Vaitepiha Bay   Tautira

Taiarapu
Peninsula

TAHITI-ITI

TEAHUPU

Atimaono

17°30'
17°

Antonise Bank

Pacific   Ocean

Bora Bora
Tahaa Huahine
Raiatea

Moorea   TAHITI

Society Islands

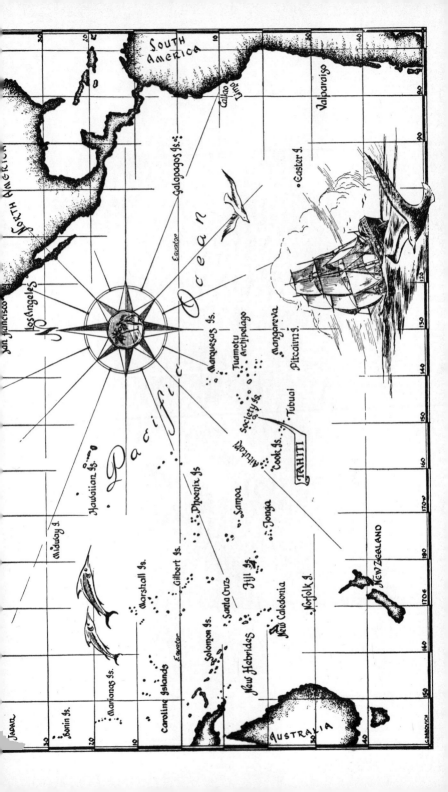

INTRODUCTION

TAHITI is the most famous island in the South Seas. Everyone has heard of its lovely, brown-skinned Polynesian girls (nobody ever seems to bother about the men), who dance the hula-hula on the edge of sleepy, palm-girt lagoons against a backdrop of superbly beautiful scenery. Everyone knows that in Tahiti there is unique sex-freedom; that the climate is mild and langorous; and that there is no need to work, as Nature provides with tropical prodigality. This is the picture that is conjured up whenever the name, Tahiti, is mentioned. Thanks largely to novels, magazine articles, films and tourist advertisements, Tahiti has become everyone's idea of Paradise.

Yet although Tahiti is far-famed, few people know why it has become as famous as it is. This is hardly surprising as Tahiti's varied and colourful story has never been told before in a single book.

I have attempted to tell the story in the following pages. My book is not a history of Tahiti. It might best be described as a chronological narrative of the events which have made the island famous. Naturally, there is a good deal of history in the book. But where events in Tahiti made no particular stir in the outside world, I have gone into them only sufficiently to make later, more famous episodes intelligible. Sometimes the story wanders far from Tahiti itself. This occurs where it seemed to me that events elsewhere, connected with Tahiti, played their part in furthering the island's fame, or where it was necessary to introduce or round off the story of some particular event.

The idea of writing this book grew on me gradually. In 1953, I visited Tahiti as a fireman on a New Zealand passenger-freighter. I was returning from Canada to my home in Australia after six years of travel and adventure in various parts of the world. I had wanted to go to Tahiti for a long time. I had read about it in Somerset Maugham's *The Moon and Sixpence* and a number of other books, and I had come to regard it as the supreme mecca of all travel. My first sight of the island's astonishing peaks in the dim light of a January dawn more than fulfilled my expectations. I had a feeling, in fact, of religious awe. It seemed to me that God must have created Tahiti as a final masterpiece to impress mere earthlings with the magnificence of his handiwork. As we sailed along the reef seeking the entrance to Papeete lagoon, I found myself asking many questions. Who had discovered this astounding island? How had it become French? What were the Chinese doing there? And so forth.

During my all-too-brief stay at the island, I tried to obtain the answers to these questions. But the natives I asked did not seem to know much about their history and seemed to care even less. I was none the wiser when I came away. But my glimpse of Tahiti had whetted my curiosity, and when I returned to Australia I looked around for a book which would tell me what I wanted to know. To my astonishment, I found that there was no book in any language which adequately answered my questions. To satisfy my curiosity, I had to go to the original sources. I read the narratives of the early explorers and the journals of the first missionaries, and as the fascinating story of Tahiti began to unfold itself to me, I started to make notes for this book.

The task of finding all the material I needed was a much more arduous one than I at first imagined. The literature on Tahiti is amazingly vast. Tens of millions of words have been written about it. The information I needed was buried in hundreds of different, and often unexpected, places—narratives of voyages, books of philosophy, biographies, magazines, scientific journals, encyclopedias, books of poetry, guide-books, playbills, Admiralty records, manuscript letters, missionary journals, anthropological works, government reports, British Foreign Office documents, consular correspondence, parliamentary papers, Hansards, newspapers, novels, travel books, year books, books on art, etc. For the chapter called 'The Romance of Atimaono', for example, I read every newspaper published in Tahiti between 1862 and 1875, all the British consular correspondence, numerous travel books, and a great deal of other material. Fortunately, I was able to find all the information I needed for the book in Australia. The Mitchell Library, Sydney, is a treasure house of literature on Tahiti, and my thanks are due to its staff for their

2

never-failing assistance. I also wish to thank the staffs of the National Library, Canberra, and the South Australian Public Library, Adelaide, for much valuable help. To Dr. Bengt Danielsson, Swedish anthropologist and Kon-Tiki raftsman, I am indebted for reading the manuscript and making many helpful comments. And I have to thank Mr. G. Dabovich, of Adelaide, for his excellent maps of Tahiti and the Pacific.

A few words here about Tahiti and its inhabitants will help to make the story in the following pages more vivid and intelligible.

To begin with, it should be said that Tahiti is the most beautiful island in the South Seas. It is a lofty, green island, almost classical in shape—being in the form of a figure '8' lying on its side. The larger circle of the '8', which is known as Tahiti-nui, or Big Tahiti, is a mass of jagged peaks of volcanic origin which rise up to 8,000 feet above the sea. Tahiti-iti, or Little Tahiti, is connected with the larger circle by a low, narrow isthmus; and the whole island is about 140 miles around. The mountains of the two circles are surrounded at the coast by a low belt of rich, alluvial soil, which is the only inhabited portion of the island. This belt is covered by prolific vegetation. At a distance of one or two miles from the shore is a reef of coral which rings the island like a necklace. The reef is broken wherever the numerous mountain streams enter the sea, but only a few of the gaps are wide enough or deep enough to admit ships to the peaceful, glassy lagoons within. Twelve miles west of Tahiti-nui is the picturesque island of Moorea.

Many writers have attempted the almost impossible task of describing the astonishing spectacle of Tahiti when first seen from the sea after a voyage of many days on the seemingly endless and empty expanse of the Pacific. No writer has succeeded better than Herman Melville.

Seen from the sea, [he said] the prospect is magnificent. It is one mass of shaded tints of green, from beach to mountain-top; endlessly diversified with valleys, ridges, glens and cascades. Over the ridges, here and there, the loftiest peaks fling their shadows, and far down the valleys. At the head

3

of these, the waterfalls flash out in the sunlight as if pouring through vertical bowers of verdure. Such enchantment, too, breathes over the whole that it seems a fairy land, all fresh and blooming from the hand of the Creator. Upon a nearer approach, the picture loses not its attractions. It is no exaggeration to say, that to a European of any sensibility, who, for the first time, wanders back into these valleys—away from the haunts of the natives—the ineffable repose and beauty of the landscape is such that every object strikes him like something seen in a dream; and, for a time, he almost refuses to believe that scenes like these should have a commonplace existence . . .

The climate of Tahiti is mild. The average maximum temperature during the rainy season is about 85° F., and the average minimum 75°. In the dry season, the temperature ranges from about 80° F. in the day to 60° at night. At the time of its discovery, the island produced breadfruit, coconuts, bananas, sweet potatoes, sugar-cane, and several other fruits and vegetables that were not known to the Europeans. Many others have since been introduced.

The people of Tahiti are Polynesians. They seem to be descended from two, and possibly three, distinct races. No one is sure where they came from originally, but it seems possible that one race migrated from South America, one from what is now British Columbia, via Hawaii, and one from Melanesia. There had been a good deal of inter-breeding before the Europeans arrived.

In the old times, there was no supreme chief in Tahiti. The island was divided between two families—the Tevas and the Tus (later known as the Pomares). The heads of these families were known as 'arii rahi', or 'great chiefs' and they appointed lesser members of their families to rule over their various districts. If any one of the chiefs, great or small, tried to extend his power, the others united to overthrow him. This was a matter which the early European visitors never understood.

The people believed in a variety of gods, from whom the chiefs claimed to be descended. The most powerful chiefs were so sacred that anything they touched became their property. To

4

avoid dispossessing their subjects, they were therefore carried on the shoulders of retainers. The son of a ruling family took over his father's government at birth, but the father ruled as regent until his son came of age.

The gods of the Tahitians were worshipped in elaborate ceremonies. The temples of worship were known as '*maraes*' and were solidly constructed of coral blocks.

Another matter which baffled the early visitors was the native manner of replying to questions. When the Tahitians were asked the name of their island, they replied: 'Otaheite,' which meant 'It is Tahiti.' As the Europeans thought that the 'o' was part of the name, the island was incorrectly known for many years as 'Otaheite'. Similar mistakes were made over such names as Tu, Purea, Reti, Turu, and Mai, which were written down as Otoo, Oberea, Ereti, Aotourou, and Omai.

The Tahitian language does not use the following consonants: b, c, d, g, j, k, l, q, s, w, x, y, and z. The pronunciation of the vowels is as in Spanish or Italian—a—ah; e—e (in egg); i—ee; o—o (in cot); u—oo.

NOTE TO THE FOURTH EDITION

I have taken advantage of this new edition to extend my story of Tahiti from the end of 1967 to the beginning of 1972. I have also retained the slightly modified title of the third edition as the original title apparently misled some readers.

The original title, *Island of Love*, was derived from the explorer Bougainville's name for Tahiti, which was La Nouvelle Cythere, or The New Cythera. Cythera, an island in the Mediterranean, was the birthplace of Cytherea, the Greek goddess of love. So Bougainville's name for Tahiti actually meant the New Island of Love. Anyone who reads the ample literature on Tahiti will agree that this was, and still is, an appropriate name. However, I should not have expected anyone to grasp the significance of my title without an explanation; and I have modified it now to ensure that anyone who buys the book before reading it will be in no doubt that it is about Tahiti, and not necessarily about love.

PART I

THE NOBLE SAVAGE

1. TWO THEORIES

T HE story of Tahiti really began in late September, 1513, when Vasco Nuñez de Balboa discovered the Pacific. Balboa called his discovery 'The Great South Sea' and took possession of it in the name of the King of Spain.

The first navigator to cross the new ocean was Ferdinand Magellan, who entered it in 1515 by way of the strait that now bears his name. Magellan sailed for ninety-eight hungry days before reaching land and did not sight a single island south of the equator. His followers for the next 250 years had little better luck. Their ships were at the mercy of the winds and currents, which generally steered them away from the land they so eagerly sought. Yet enough islands were discovered to provide geographers with material for an ingenious theory. This was that the islands of the South Sea were really the edge of a vast continent that must necessarily exist to balance the land masses of the Northern Hemisphere.

Charles de Brosses, of France, gave the southern continent idea a great boost in 1756 when he published his *Histoire de Navigations aux Terres Australes*. De Brosses believed that the Terres Australes covered an area of eight to ten million square miles, and he guessed that they were staggeringly rich in fruits, minerals, fish, etc. The discovery of this land, he said, was 'the grandest, noblest, most useful enterprise a sovereign could undertake', and he warned his countrymen that unless France acted quickly the valuable continent would fall into British hands.

As it was, it was Britain that made the first move to discover it. De Brosses's theory had a particular fascination for King George III, who ordered Commodore John Byron, the poet's grandfather, to go in search in HMS *Dolphin*. Byron sailed from England in June, 1764, but returned without making any significant discoveries. King George was not discouraged. He immediately ordered the *Dolphin* to go out again—this time under Captain Samuel Wallis—and it was on this voyage that Tahiti was discovered.

Meanwhile, another theory was sweeping Europe that was destined to receive tremendous impetus with the discovery of Tahiti. This was the 'noble savage' theory of the Swiss philosopher, Jean Jacques Rousseau, who believed that the ills of civilization could be cured if man returned to his primitive state. Rousseau expounded his theory in a *Discourse on Inequality*, which was first published in 1754, and he elaborated it later in the *Social Contract*. In the first book, he drew a portrait of his ideal man, the 'noble savage'. This man, he said, 'had neither houses, huts, nor any kind of property; everyone lived where he could; and the sexes united without design, as accident, opportunity or inclination brought them together'.

Rousseau's 'noble savages' wore no clothes because they felt no need for them. For the same reason, they built no houses, fenced no fields, and sowed no seeds. Neither did they form families, tribes, or nations. They enjoyed the perfect freedom of the undomesticated brute, and their equality with other men was complete.

From this point, Rousseau argued that the inequality of Europe had come about because man had passed from the happy, primitive state to the unhappy complexity of society. To be happy, it was therefore necessary to become a 'noble savage' again. Rousseau, in other words, was promulgating his revelation of the primitive liberty, equality, and fraternity of mankind. It was the gospel of democracy—the gospel of revolutionary change.

Rousseau clothed his ideas in such forceful and persuasive terms that they became as familiar in his day as Communism is today. Rousseauism was in the air.

2. ISLAND OF GIRLS

CAPTAIN WALLIS discovered Tahiti on June 19, 1767.
He had left England in the *Dolphin* to search for the southern continent on August 22, 1766, sailing in company with HM Sloop *Swallow*. The *Swallow* was commanded by Captain

Philip Carteret, who had been Byron's first lieutenant on the previous voyage.

The two ships entered the Straits of Magellan on December 17 after a tedious Atlantic crossing due to the wretched sailing qualities of the *Swallow*. Worse was to come. The weather in the straits was foul; both ships had narrow escapes from shipwreck; and on one occasion the *Swallow* was given up for lost. The two ships battled with the elements for four months before passing the western opening of the straits. But on the following day—April 11, 1767—the *Dolphin* lost sight of the *Swallow* in a fog, and the vessels did not meet again.

The most interesting account of the *Dolphin*'s subsequent voyage is contained in the journal of the master, George Robertson. Robertson was man of above-average education, although his spelling and grammar were erratic. His journal lay in the Public Record Office, London, for nearly 180 years before being published by the Hakluyt Society in 1948.

Robertson said that after leaving the Straits of Magellan the *Dolphin* sailed north-west and then west along latitude 20° S. She passed through the Tuamotu Archipelago and encountered a number of islands that had not been seen before. In the middle of June, the *Dolphin* reached the island of Mehetia, where some refreshments were obtained although a landing was not made.

'At this time,' Robertson said, 'we hade our Capt. and first Lieut, very Bade, and a great many of our Men Extreemly bade in the Scurvey and oyther complaints, and those who did duty was all very weakly. This was our case when it was Determined to bear away from this Island (Mehetia), where we all saw great plenty of refreshments, and nothing to keep us from shearing of them but a few Indians with Spears, Sticks and perhaps some Stones. But thanks be to God, we soon after got what we wanted Most.'

On June 18, the *Dolphin* steered westward for some high land that had been sighted from Mehetia. At 6 a.m. next day, she had come within fourteen leagues of it. 'This made us all rejoice and fild us with greatest hopes Imaginable,' Robertson said. 'We now lookt upon ourselves as relived from all our distresses as we was almost certain of finding all sorts of refreshments on this great Body of Land. . . . We now supposed we saw the long wishd for Southern Continent, which has been often talkd of, but never seen by any Europeans.'

As the *Dolphin* came nearer to this fascinating land—which turned out to be Tahiti—a thick fog came down and obscured everything from sight. A thunderous surf could be heard pounding on the reef. When the fog cleared up, the easternmost point of land was only two leagues away. A hundred canoes were then seen paddling out between the breakers and the ship.

When the canoes came within pistol shot, the paddlers lay to, looked at the ship with great astonishment, and held 'a sort of council of war'. The *Dolphin*'s sailors made all the friendly signs they could think of, and tried to entice some of the natives aboard by showing them trinkets. The natives replied by holding up banana leaves, paddling round the ship, and laughing and talking a great deal. After one of them had made a speech lasting fifteen minutes, the canoes came closer and some of the natives ventured aboard.

The sailors made signs to them to bring off food in exchange for cloth, knives, beads, and other trinkets which they showed them. Some of the sailors 'grunted and cryd lyke a Hogg' and pointed to the shore; others 'crowd lyke cocks' to indicate that poultry was wanted. The natives caught on quickly and some got into their canoes to bring off the desired goods. Others, however, began to pull at the iron stanchions and iron ring ball and seemed to be unwilling to leave the ship without some iron work. They became a little surly, in fact, and the Englishmen were obliged to fire a nine-pound shot over their heads to frighten them. This had the desired effect. The natives promptly jumped overboard and swam to their canoes. One of them gave the first example of the local love for impudent pilfering by snatching a midshipman's 'gold laced Hatt' as he jumped. The sailors shouted and pointed their muskets at him, but the native had yet to learn the destructive terrors of gun-powder and took no notice.

After this encounter with the natives, the *Dolphin* bore away to the westward to seek a place to anchor in.

> All the way that we run allong the shore [Robertson said] we saw the whole coast full of Canoes. The country hade the

most Beautiful appearance its posable to Imagin. From the shore side, one, two and three miles back, their is a fine Leavel country that appears to be all laid out in plantations, and the regular built Houses seems to be without number. They appeared lyke long Farmers Barns and all seemed to be all very neatly thatched, with Great Numbers of Cocoa Nut Trees and several oyther trees that we could not know the names of. The Interior part of this country is very Mountainous, but their is beautiful valeys between the Mountains. . . . This appears to be the most populoss country I ever saw—the whole shore side was lined with men, women and children all the way that we saild allong.

The *Dolphin* worked to windward all night, and when daylight came the barge and cutter were hoisted out to sound for an anchorage. They found one in Matavai Bay, about ten miles eastward of a sandy spit that Captain Cook later named Point Venus. The *Dolphin* came in and anchored, and was immediately surrounded by canoes bearing coconuts, fruit, fowls, and some 'fine fatt Young Pigs'. The sailors began to trade. But the Tahitians behaved 'very insolently', and some took the sailors' nails and toys without giving anything in return. Some 'carried their insolence so high' that they struck some of the *Dolphin*'s men. An unpleasant scene threatened to develop, and one of the marines fired at a native and killed him. After that, the natives traded honestly. It was only necessary to point a musket or a spy-glass at them and they would 'return the nails or give Value'.

Robertson said that the 'market price' for a 20 lb. hog on this day—June 22—was a twenty penny nail. A roasting pig could be had for a tenpenny nail, and fowls and fruit for a string of beads. Most of the natives, however, preferred nails.*

Next day, John Gore, the gunner, was sent off with a boat's crew to get water. The Englishmen were still diffident about landing and tried to get the natives to fill their casks without going ashore. When they could not prevail on them to do this by fair means, they pointed their muskets at them. But this only made the natives laugh. It was then that the natives brought

---

* In the eighteenth century, nails were sold at so many pence per hundred. Thus, tenpenny nails cost 10d a hundred.

'a good many fine young Girls' to the waterside—some of 'a light coper collour, oythers a mulatto, and some almost if not alto-geather White'. This new sight attracted the Englishmen's 'fance a good dale'. The natives observed it and made the girls play 'a great many droll, wanton tricks'. But the Englishmen 'very prudently referd going ashore' until they 'turnd better aquanted' with the native temper.

Later that day, the *Dolphin* shifted her anchorage in Matavai Bay after being briefly aground on a reef which is still known as the Dolphin Bank.

At sunrise next morning, about three hundred canoes came off and lay round the ship to trade. By 8 a.m. the number had grown to five hundred, carrying about four thousand men. Most of the canoes contained 'fair young Girls' who played the same 'droll and wanton tricks' of the previous day. But when the English-men crowded to the gunwales to see them, they noticed that each canoe contained a great number of stones.

It was soon evident that 'an onset' was near at hand. At a signal from a large double canoe, friendly trading suddenly broke up and the *Dolphin* was bombarded by stones. The sentries were ordered to open fire to frighten the assailants, but this only inspired them to more intensive onslaught. The Englishmen therefore 'applyd to the Great Guns and gave them a few round and Grape shot, which struck such terror amongs the poor un-happy croad that it would require the pen of Milton to describe it'. By noon, not a single canoe was to be seen in the water nor ten people along the shore.

The few natives who ventured out to the ship next morning were ceremoniously obsequious and very anxious to make friends. This emboldened the Englishmen to make their first landing on Tahitian soil, and on June 26, Tobias Furneaux, the second lieu-tenant, hoisted a pennant on a long pole and took possession of the island in the name of King George III. But the natives were again hostile on the following morning, and this induced Captain Wallis to send an armed party ashore with axes and saws to dis-able their canoes. From then on, the Tahitians did everything they could to be friendly and hospitable.

When Furneaux went ashore for water during the afternoon, many natives came to meet him waving banana leaves and bringing peace offerings. Among the natives were several handsome young girls. The Englishmen 'could not help feasting their Eyes with so agreeable a sight', and when this was observed by some of the old men, 'several of the Young Girls was drawn out'. Robertson said that 'the old men made them stand in Rank, and made signs for our people to take which they lyked best, and as many as they lyked. And for fear our men hade been Ignorant and not know how to use the poor young Girls, the old men made signs how we should behave to the Young women. This all the boat's crew seemd to understand perfectly well, and begd the Officer would receive a few of the Young Girls on board. At the same time, they made signs to the Young Girls that they were not so Ignorant as the old men suposed them. This seemd to please the Old men Greatly when they saw our people merry, but the poor young Girls seemd a little afraid but soon after turn'd better aquanted.'

When the watering party returned to the *Dolphin*, 'the sailors swore they neaver saw handsomer made women in their lives', and they declared to a man that they would rather live on two-thirds' allowance than 'lose so fine an opportunity of getting a Girl apiece'. This news made all the others 'madly fond of the shore'. Even the sick who had been on the doctor's list for weeks declared that 'a Young Girl would make an Excelent Nurse', and they felt certain of 'recovering faster under a Young Girl's care nor all the Doctor would do for them'.

The Englishmen soon had the opportunity of becoming 'better aquanted' with the Tahitian belles. Each day, a number of the sick were taken to rest in a tent on a small island near the *Dolphin*'s anchorage and it was not long before the native girls ventured over to see them. Robertson said that the 'honnest hearted tars received them with great chearfulness and made them some little presents which gaind their hearts'. The girls, in turn, gave the men a signal 'which they would have willingly obayed hade they not been immediately orderd on board'.

Meanwhile, trading parties from the *Dolphin* had been doing a brisk trade in pigs, fowls, and fruit in exchange for ear-rings, nails, and beads. But soon 'a new sort of trade took up most of their attention' although Robertson thought 'it might properly

15

be called the old trade'. It was begun, he said, by one of the marines—'a Dear Irish boy'—who got a severe thrashing from the liberty men for 'not beginning in a more decent manner—in some house or at the back of some bush or tree'. Robertson added that 'Pady's Excuse was the fear of losing the Honour of having the first'.

By July 9, 'the price of the old trade' had been fixed at 'a thirty penny nail each time'. But the liberty men were dealing 'so largely in that way' that the gunner became afraid of losing his trade in island produce. Robertson took the matter up with the doctor, the purser, and Furneaux, and the last two said that the only thing to do was to keep the liberty men on board. But the doctor affirmed that such a course 'would ruin their health and constitution' because 'anything that depresses the mind and spirits of men must Sertainly hurt them'. His opinion was 'plainly confirmed' when several men were sent for and threatened with stoppage of leave. There was 'a visable change in their Countenance', and it was therefore resolved to try to prevent the liberty men from taking toys and nails with them.

All went well for the next ten days or so. But on July 21, as Robertson was ordering the liberty men into the boats, the carpenter came and told him that 'every cleat in the Ship was drawen and all the Nails carryed off'. At the same time, the boatswain said that most of the hammock nails had been drawn, and that two-thirds of the men had to lie on the deck for want of nails to hang their hammocks on. Robertson immediately stopped the liberty men and called all hands. He told them that no one could go ashore until he learned who had drawn the nails and cleats and what they were being used for. None of the seamen would own up, although they all said that they knew why the articles had been taken. Robertson later learned from a midshipman that for some days past, the girls had raised their prices from a twenty or thirty penny nail to a forty penny nail, and that some had even gone as high as a seven-inch or nine-inch spike.

That evening, Robertson heard 'a great murmuring amongst the people' as they were preparing their suppers in the galley. As it was dark, he crept for'ard to see if he could learn who the nail-thief was. 'At last I found out,' he said, 'that most of them was concerned, and several said they hade rather receive a dozen lashes nor have their Liberty stopt.' He also heard them hold a trial among themselves in which six were condemned for 'spoiling the old trade by giving large Spick nails when oythers hade only a Hammock nail'. But two of the seamen cleared themselves 'by proving that they got double value for the Spicks'. Next morning, it was proved that a seaman called Francis Pinckney had drawn one of the cleats, and the captain ordered him to 'run the gauntlet' three times around the ship. The men were warned that a much more severe punishment would be meted out if any more nails or cleats were stolen.

On July 22, 'a strong well-made woman', whom the Englishmen knew as Queen Oberea, came on board for the second time. She was treated to breakfast in the captain's cabin, and Robertson later gave her a 'ruffled shirt'. The queen wanted to see if Robertson was tattooed like her own people and would not believe that his skin was white until she felt it. She began to feel his legs and thighs 'to know if they hade the strength they seemd to have' and was greatly pleased when Robertson picked her up and carried her round the cabin with one arm. The queen eyed him 'all round' and 'began to be very merry and cheerful'. 'And if I am not mistaken by her Majesty's behaviour afterwards,' Robertson said, 'this is the way the Ladys here trys the men before they admit them to be their Lovers.'

During the latter part of the morning, Robertson and a midshipman accompanied the queen ashore. The Queen pressed them to stay to dinner, and when Robertson declined, she whispered something to an old woman. 'This woman,'' Robertson said, 'made me understand with very plain Signs that I should have her Daughter to sleep with. When that hade not the desired Effect, the old Lady pointed to two very handsom Young Ladys and made me understand that the Young Gentleman and I should have *them* to sleep with.' Robertson, however, again declined, but made them understand that he would come again some time. This pleased them very much, and the queen took his arm to accompany him to the water's edge. On the way, she made him call in at each house where he shook hands with the old people and was 'very merry with the Young'. At the last house, Robertson found two of the handsomest girls he had seen on the island. One, in particular, he said, 'was fully as fair and hade as good features as the Generality of Women in England, and hade she been drest after the English manner, I am certain no man would have thought her of another country'.

On July 26, Captain Wallis announced that the *Dolphin* would sail next day. Queen Oberea came on board to entreat him to stay for ten more days. But tears and pleading were of no avail. Wallis would not even allow her to stay on board overnight. So the queen went ashore in a new flood of tears and 'made a long speech to her people which seemed to make them very sad'.

Early next morning, when the launch was sent ashore for the last replenishment of water, it was found that the queen and her subjects had slept on the beach all night so that they could watch the *Dolphin* sail. The queen came out to the ship in a canoe and bade a fond farewell to everyone. Robertson said that 'she wept and cryd with as mutch tenderness and Affection as any Wife or Mother could do at parting with their husbands or children'. An hour or so later, the *Dolphin* made sail and steered westward towards the neighbouring island of Moorea. The beautiful and friendly island of Tahiti was soon out of sight.

The remainder of the *Dolphin*'s voyage was not particularly notable. Wallis had none of the qualities needed on a voyage of exploration, and he made no serious attempt to search for the elusive southern continent. After sighting and naming three new islands near Tahiti and one to the west of Samoa, the *Dolphin* headed quickly homewards. She anchored in the Downs on May 25, 1768.

Meanwhile, the Dolphin's miserable consort, the *Swallow*, had unexpectedly survived the perils of the Straits of Magellan, and Captain Carteret had made a number of interesting discoveries. Among these was the rocky islet of Pitcairn—later to become famous as the refuge of the *Bounty* mutineers and their Tahitian wives.

An account of the voyages of the *Dolphin* and *Swallow* was published in London in 1773. It was edited by a high-falutin' literary gentleman called Dr. John Hawkesworth. Hawkesworth combined the journals of Robertson and Wallis for his version of the *Dolphin*'s voyage, but he 'improved' their descriptions to suit his own Rousseauistic philosophy and the genteel tastes of the British reading public. He naturally paid considerable attention to the episodes dealing with Tahiti, and the result was that his book appealed to a much wider public than that normally interested in geographical matters. A second edition was called for within three months.

3. *VOILA LES FEMMES!*

EIGHT months after Captain Wallis's departure from Matavai Bay, Tahiti was visited by two French ships under Captain Louis Antoine de Bougainville. Bougainville was on a twofold mission for the French Government. He had been ordered to hand over the Falkland Islands to Spain and to proceed to the East Indies by crossing the Pacific within the tropics.

His two ships, the *Boudeuse* and *Etoile*, passed through the Straits of Magellan on January 26, 1768. Tahiti came in sight on April 2, and as it seemed a likely place for provisions, Bougainville steered towards it with all sails set. He anchored inside the reef at Hitiaa on April 6.

> The aspect of this coast [Bougainville wrote] offered us the most enchanting prospect. We hardly believed our eyes. As we came nearer the shore, the number of islanders surrounding our ships increased. The canoes were so numerous that we had much to do to warp in amidst the crowd of boats and the noise. All these people came crying 'tayo,' which means 'friend,' and gave a thousand signs of friendship. They all asked nails and ear-rings of us. The canoes were full of females, who, for agreeable features, are not inferior to most European women; and who, in point of beauty of body, might with much reason vie with them all. Most of these fair females were naked, for the men and the old women that accompanied them had stripped them of the garments which they generally dressed themselves in.

The glances which they gave us from the canoes seemed to discover some degree of uneasiness, notwithstanding the innocent manner in which they were given—perhaps because nature has everywhere embellished their sex with a natural timidity, or perhaps because even in those countries where the ease of the golden age is still in use, women seem least to desire what they most wish for.

The men, who were more plain, or, rather, more free, soon explained their meaning very clearly. They pressed us to choose a woman and to come ashore with her; and their gestures, which were nothing less than equivocal, denoted in what manner we should form an acquaintance with her.

It was very difficult amidst such a sight to keep at their work 400 young French sailors who had seen no women for six months. Despite all our precautions, a young girl came on board and placed herself upon the quarter deck near one of the hatchways, which was open to give air to those heaving at the capstan below it. The girl carelessly dropped the cloth which covered her and appeared to the eyes of all beholders much as Venus showed herself to the Phrygian shepherd—having, indeed, the celestial form of that goddess. Both sailors and soldiers endeavoured to come to the hatchway, and the capstan was never hove with more alacrity than on this occasion. But at last our cares succeeded in keeping these bewitched fellows in order, though it was no less difficult to keep the command of ourselves. . . .

There was one man, however, whose cares were not onerous enough to keep him in order. This was Bougainville's cook, who slipped ashore with an island maiden, but soon returned more dead than alive. He said that he had hardly set foot on shore before he was surrounded by a crowd of natives who undressed him from head to foot. After 'tumultuously examining' every part of his body, they returned him his clothes, brought his girl to him, and desired him 'to content those desires which had brought him on shore with her'. But all their persuasive arguments had no effect, and the poor cook was brought back on board still a virgin as far as Tahiti was concerned.

Bougainville's narrative of his ten-day stay on the island often became rapturous. Everywhere he went, he was greeted with the greatest hospitality and friendship. He was enchanted by the island's beauty, and fascinated by the native's pleasure-loving, carefree ways, and by their custom of offering pretty girls to visitors. Although it became known that the native name for the island was Tahiti, Bougainville dubbed it 'La Nouvelle Cythère' because it reminded him of the Greek goddess of love.

> Here Venus is the goddess of hospitality [he wrote]. The very air the people breathe, their songs, their dances . . . all conspire to call to mind the sweets of love, and all engage to give themselves up to them. Thus accustomed to live continually immersed in pleasure, the people of Tahiti have acquired a witty and humorous temper, which is the offspring of ease and joy. They likewise contracted from the same source a character of fickleness which constantly amazed us. Everything strikes them, but nothing fixes their attention. Amidst all the new objects which we presented to them, we could never succeed in making them attend for two minutes to any one. It seems as if the least reflection is a toilsome labour for them, and that they are still more averse to the exercises of the mind than those of the body. I shall not, however, accuse them of want of understanding. The skill and ingenuity in the few necessary instances of industry . . . would be sufficient to destroy such an assertion.

Writing of the island's beauty, Bougainville said he often though he was 'transported into the Garden of Eden'. The lofty, jagged mountains did not make Tahiti 'gloomy and wild', but 'served only to embellish it'. The little mountain streams, besides providing the inhabitants with water, also served 'to adorn and heighten the charm of the plains'. As for the 'rich productions of Nature', they, inevitably, were 'in that beautiful disorder which it was never in the power of Art to imitate'.

Bougainville was equally impressed by the beauty of the men. 'I never saw men who were better made or whose limbs were more proportionate,' he wrote. 'In order to paint a Hercules or a

Mars, one could nowhere find more beautiful models. Nothing distinguishes their features from those of the Europeans; and if they were clothed, lived less in the open air and were less exposed to the sun at noon, they would be as white as ourselves.'

Bougainville's stay in Tahiti was too brief for him to make detailed observations. But he noted among other things that there were only three quadrupeds—dogs, hogs, and rats; that pearls were the only rich articles of commerce; and that there were none of the troublesome insects that were usually the plague of tropical countries. 'The climate is so healthy that none of our people fell sick,' he said.

There was only one thing about the island that Bougainville found disagreeable. This was the native passion for thieving. 'Even in Europe itself,' he wrote, 'one cannot see more expert filchers than the people of this country.' Nevertheless, Bougainville believed that stealing was 'not usual amongst themselves' and that it was only their curiosity for European objects which 'excited the violent desires in them'.

Before leaving the island on April 15, the Frenchmen took formal possession by burying an inscribed oak plank and a bottle containing a list of the ships' officers. Their departure was a moving one. Embraces were exchanged all round and many tears were shed. Before they cleared the reef, where they lost several anchors, Ereti, the chief of Hitiaa, came aboard to ask Bougainville to take a young man called Aotourou back to Europe. Bougainville consented, and sailed away 'no less surprised at the sorrow of the natives' on his departure than at 'their affectionate confidence' on his arrival.

During the next few weeks, he discovered a number of new islands in the Samoan group. From there he passed through Melanesia to the Solomons, where one of the largest islands still bears his name. Bougainville returned to France on March 16, 1769, after a voyage of 2½ years. As he was the first Frenchman to circumnavigate the world, he was received with extravagant acclaim. But he did not enjoy the limelight alone. Aotourou, the Tahitian youth, was almost as popular. To people of culture, he was the very kind of 'noble savage' that they had been reading about for the past fifteen years. Everything he did became the subject of gossip in salons and cafés. Rich women like the Duchess of Choiseul loaded him with favours, and Aotourou acquired a passion for opera and a great appreciation of French wine and food. But being a good Tahitian, his '*grande passion*' was for the ladies '*auxquelles il se livre indistinctement*'. His stay in France lasted a year, at the end of which a ship was fitted out at Bougainville's expense to take him home. But Aotourou did not live to see his native shores again. He died of smallpox off the island of Mauritius, and the voyage to Tahiti was abandoned.

Meanwhile, Bougainville was busily preparing his *Voyage Round the World* for the press. It was published in Paris in 1771 and was translated into English the following year. The narrative had an enormous success. Every cultured person in Europe was eager to read about the island where free love appeared to be the rule and where everyone seemed to live according to the gospel of Jean Jacques Rousseau. Bougainville's descriptions were fully confirmed by M. Philibert de Commerçon, the expedition's botanist, in a long article in the *Mercure de France*. Hawkesworth's versions of Wallis's voyage and the subsequent voyage of Cook provided further confirmation, and even the sceptics were satisfied. 'When the French and English are in agreement,' Voltaire said in a letter to the Chevalier de Lisle, 'we can be sure they have not deceived us.'

The early descriptions of Tahiti gave philosophers a new slant on the whole question of morals and western ethics. Denis Diderot, the disciple of Rousseau, wrote a *Supplement au Voyage de Bougainville* in which he argued that European laws were noxious and unnatural, and that constancy in marriage was immoral. Although the *Supplement* was considered too provocative for publication in the author's lifetime, Diderot was able to hint at much the same thing in his contributions to the *Encyclopedia*. Other French writers said, in effect, that Tahiti offered the strongest possible proof that Rousseau was right. They said that the Tahitian way of life showed that European society had no real support in reason or experience, and that its absurd conventions were contrary to the natural rights and innate virtue of man. It therefore followed that European society should be abolished.

The conclusions of these writers were taken up by other propagandists, and the clamour for the overthrow of the old regime grew louder. It culminated on July 14, 1789, with the fall of the Bastille,* which marked the decisive moment of the French Revolution. This epoch-making revolution changed the face of France and the whole world. It ushered in an era of democracy, nationalism, and socialism which has not yet reached its end.

Historians have been prone to overlook Tahiti's contributory part in touching off the French Revolution. It was undoubtedly an important one.

4. VENUS OBSERVED

TAHITI's third visitor was Lieutenant James Cook, who anchored in Matavai Bay in HMS *Endeavour* on April 13, 1769, on the first of his three famous voyages to the Pacific. Cook had been sent to Tahiti to observe the transit of the planet Venus across the sun. Accurate observations of this once-in-a-century phenomenon were expected to simplify the determination of longitude at sea. Expeditions organized by the Royal Society had been sent to various parts of the world, but Cook's was the only one to the southern hemisphere and was therefore of special importance. Tahiti had been chosen as the most suitable spot for its observations on the enthusiastic recommendation of Captain Wallis.

Cook's expedition consisted of eighty-four officers and seamen, and eight civilians. The civilians included Joseph Banks, a young botanist and future president of the Royal Society; Dr. Daniel Solander, an eminent Swedish naturalist; and Mr. Charles Green, assistant to the Astronomer Royal. Banks, who had just inherited a large fortune, spent £10,000 on scientific equipment for the voyage. This prompted a contemporary scientist to write that 'no people ever went to sea better fitted for the purpose of natural history'.

* Since Tahiti became a French colony in 1880, Bastille Day (July 14) has been the island's national day. The day marks the beginning of the gayest festivities of the year, which sometimes go on for a fortnight. Dancing, singing, wrestling, canoe-racing and other sports are a feature of them.

The *Endeavour* left England in the middle of August, 1768, and arrived at Tahiti, via the Horn, seven weeks before the transit of Venus was expected. Crowds of natives greeted the ship with the now customary friendship and enthusiasm and immediately recognized four of the officers who had visited the island with Wallis.

Cook's first act was to post up a list of rules to regulate trading with the natives. To prevent a repetition of the *Dolphin*'s chaotic trade in nails, he ordered that 'no sort of iron or anything made of iron' was to be given for anything but provisions. He also exhorted his men to treat the natives with 'all imaginable humanity' and to use every fair means of cultivating their friendship. In the main, this policy was carefully observed. The natives appreciated it, and quickly came to know the Englishmen affectionately by their 'Tahitianized' surnames—Tute (Cook), Opane (Banks), Tolano (Solander), and so forth.

Cook soon fixed on the NE point of Matavai Bay for his observations. He obtained permission from the chiefs to erect tents and a fort there, and for the next few weeks the Englishmen made careful preparations for the great day. These preparations were nearly ruined on the night of May 2 when a native pilferer stole the quadrant, which was an essential piece of equipment. There was a hectic scramble in search of the culprit, and although the instrument was eventually retrieved with the aid of a chief, it was only after it had been removed from its box and taken to pieces. This, of course, did not improve its working order, and Cook subsequently blamed the theft for some inaccuracy in his observations.

The day for the observations was warm, calm, and cloudless. Cook and Green observed every phase of the transit from the fort at Point Venus, while two other parties double-checked their readings from points several miles away on either side. Their programme was a complete success, but the results were of little value in improving the determination of longitude for it was subsequently found that the readings taken in Tahiti and elsewhere had been vitiated by an unforeseen optical distortion.

Cook's expedition stayed in Tahiti for three months, during which a careful examination of the island was made. Cook was indefatigable in learning what he could of the native religion, laws, and customs, and in making accurate surveys of the island;

25

while Banks devoted his great energies to studying the island's plants. Generally speaking, Cook was favourably impressed by what he saw of the native life, but there were a couple of unpleasant facets which his predecessors had overlooked. One was the custom of offering human sacrifices to the Eatuas, or gods; and the other was the custom of infanticide practised by members of the Areoi Society. Cook said that the Areoi Society counted 'more than one half of the better sort of inhabitants' among its members, and that these had 'entered into a resolution of enjoying free liberty in love without being troubled or disturbed by its consequences'. 'They mix and cohabit together with the utmost freedom,' he said, 'and the the children who are so unfortunate as to be thus begot are smothered at the moment of their birth. Many of these people contract intimacies and live together as man and wife for years, in the course of which all the children that are born are destroyed.' Cook also noted that the natives had acquired venereal disease through their freedom in love with the earlier European visitors.

On leaving Tahiti on July 13, 1769, Cook sailed westward and discovered the islands of Huahine, Raiatea, Tahaa, and Bora Bora. He named them the Society Islands 'because they lay contiguous to one another'; planted seeds to benefit future navigators; and took possession in the King's name. In the next few weeks, he followed the second part of his instructions by sailing south and then east in search of the southern continent. This course eventually brought him to New Zealand, which had remained unvisited since Tasman's voyage in 1642. Cook spent six months making a careful survey of the New Zealand coast before sailing to the unexplored east coast of Australia, which he picked up at a point south of Sydney. After several days at Botany Bay, the *Endeavour* proceeded northwards until reaching a passage between the mainland and New Guinea which was named after the ship. The expedition arrived home via Batavia and the Cape of Good Hope on July 12, 1771.

Cook's voyage was easily the most important that had been made to the Pacific since the pioneering expedition of Magellan. Besides the extraordinary amount of surveying and exploratory work performed, Cook had considerably narrowed the search for the southern continent. But these achievements were of no great moment to the public of his day. What they wanted were more descriptions 'à la Bougainville' of the alluring women and 'noble savages' of Tahiti.

Dr. John Hawkesworth, who was given the journals of Cook and Banks to edit for publication, saw that the public was well served. His version of the *Endeavour*'s voyage (which appeared in a three-volume edition in 1773 with the voyages of Byron, Wallis, and Carteret) minimized the geographical achievements and made the most of the slightest hint of a Tahitian love affair among Cook's men. Hawkesworth also converted the homely styles of Cook and Banks into pompous, Johnsonian English; sprinkled classical allusions liberally throughout; and added numerous rose-coloured reflections of his own. He thus succeeded in continuing the glamorous South Sea literary tradition started by Bougainville, and the story of the *Endeavour*'s voyage was a great success.

The public was particularly amused by Hawkesworth's hint that Banks had had a passionate love affair with Queen Oberea. One jester quipped that 'while the crew of the *Endeavour* were subduing the hearts of Queen Oberea's Maids of Honour by dint of ten-penny nails, the fascinating Banks had obtained the gracious consideration of the Queen herself'. Another jester, with a gift for doggerel verse, made a small fortune out of a poem which pictured the queen as Banks's deserted lover. The poem went through at least five editions in the course of a year. It was humorously entitled: 'An Epistle from Oberea, Queen of Otaheite, to Joseph Banks, Esq., translated by T. Q. Z. Esq., professor of the Otaheite language in Dublin and of all the languages of the undiscovered islands in the South Sea.' The first verse ran thus:

I Oberea from the Southern main,
Of slighted vows, of injur'd faith complain.
Though now some European maid you woo,
Of waist more taper, and of whiter hue;
Yet oft with me you deign'd the night to pass,
Beyond yon bread-tree on the bending grass.
Oft in the rocking boat we fondly lay,
Nor fear'd the drizzly wind, or briny spray.

Banks was naturally furious about these aspersions on his character, but as there was no law of libel in those days, there was nothing he could do about them. Meanwhile, Cook (who had been promoted to the rank of captain) had gone off to the South Sea on a second voyage, and he did not see a copy of Hawkesworth's version of his first voyage until July, 1775. He indicated his annoyance when he wrote to the editor of his second voyage: 'With respect to the amours of my people at Otaheite and other places, I think it will not be necessary to mention them at all.'

5. VIVA ESPAÑA!

Nᴇᴡs of British activities in Tahiti caused grave concern to the Spanish Government. From Balboa's time onwards, the Spaniards had regarded the Pacific as their own private preserve, and they looked on the possibility of a British settlement in Tahiti as a potential threat to their rich South American dominions. As soon as Captain Wallis returned, the Spanish Ambassador in London wrote to the Minister of State in Madrid giving details of the *Dolphin's* voyage.

My dear sir,
The Dolphin ship of war, of whose whereabouts we have been ignorant for more than a year and a half has returned to this port. Capt. Wallace, who was in command of her, had audience of the Sovereign the day before yesterday. It is said that he has been round the world, and a host of jumbled-up details of the voyage are being bruited about. The public prints aver that he has discovered some islands in the South Sea in the latitude of 20 degrees S; but as the longitude is not stated, one cannot know their true position. If we may put faith in the gazettes, he has given the name of King George's Land to the principal one, which is large and fertile and very thickly peopled . . .

I send Your Excellency the *Gazetteer* of yesterday and today so that you may see what is stated of this new discovery; but until we have other more positive information, we ought not to take much account of what the newspapers of this country say.

If the British Government should be thinking of sending out a colony to this island (where, as I am assured, they have left no one), it would add to the reasons we have for complaining of its procedures. The injury that may result to us from their settlement will be greater or less . . . in proportion to the distance of the island from our mainland. In any case, it is most unfortunate that it should be in the South Seas where ships of that nation used formerly not to go.

As I know how important this subject is, I will use all possible means of procuring the information we need for communication to Your Excellency so that you may notify me of any step you may wish me to take . . .

London: May 27, 1768

The Prince of Masserano

Four weeks later, Masserano sent another letter to Madrid enclosing an account of Tahiti written by a seaman of the *Dolphin*, who had been bribed with the promise of a job in the Spanish Navy. Tahiti's position was given as 17° 30′ S., and 154° W. This information was temporarily pigeon-holed, for the Spaniards took no further action over Tahiti until Captain Cook's return. The Spanish Government then decided to send an expedition to the island to see what the British were up to.

A letter dated October 9, 1771, instructed the Viceroy of Peru, Señor Don Manuel de Amat y Jimient, to make immediate preparations 'for searching out the island of Otaheite by any practical means' and to report on its 'physical features and other circumstances' at the first opportunity.

In less than a year, Amat had commissioned the 22-gun frigate *Aguila* for the voyage under Captain Don Domingo de Boenechea. Boenechea was instructed to 'investigate Tahiti's conformation, fertility, habitable extent, proportions, outline, longitude and latitude'; be careful not to maltreat the natives; refuse to allow any women on board his ship; and bring back four or five intelligent Tahitian youths for instruction in the Spanish language and the Catholic religion. Boenechea was also told to enter a protest, by word of mouth and in writing, if any foreigners had formed a colony on the island.

The *Aguila* sailed from Callao on September 26, 1772, with two priests who were charged with 'rescuing the natives from their wretched idolatry'. She arrived at Tahiti on November 8, where she had the misfortune to go aground on a coral patch (later called the Artemise Bank) six days later. This incident, however, did not impede Boenechea's investigations, which he carried out faithfully according to the Viceroy's instructions. A notable feature of the Spaniards' stay was the correctness of their behaviour towards the Tahitian women. Boenechea said that although the natives 'tendered their women to us quite freely, they showed much surprise at the non-acceptance of such offers'.

The *Aguila* stayed in Tahiti (which Boenechea renamed 'Isla de Amat') until December 20, when she sailed for the Chilean port of Valparaiso. Three natives who were taken off the island were later sent to Lima and lodged in the Viceroy's palace. There, according to Amat, they were 'clothed and entertained in more than commonplace decency', for it was his wish that they should eventually be returned to their native island 'conscious of the benefits of civilized society'.

6. THE NOBLE SAVAGE IN ENGLAND

CAPTAIN COOK visited Tahiti on two occasions in the course of his second great voyage to the Pacific, during which he discovered numerous new islands and proved almost beyond doubt that the southern continent did not exist. His first Tahitian sojourn lasted from August 17 to September 1, 1773; and his second from April 22 to May 14, 1774. Both visits were prompted by the need for fresh provisions, and both were marked by the cordial hospitality of the natives. Captain Cook was a great favourite. He was kind, sympathetic, and thoughtful. He did everything he could to understand and conform to the native customs. But above all, he had the qualities of a great chief. He was a tall, well-built man, whose air of command demanded respect. These were qualities that the natives appreciated, and they dubbed him accordingly 'Arii Tute'— 'Cook, the chief'.

Although Cook's sojourns in Tahiti were relatively minor incidents in his three-year voyage, they were easily the most interesting to the reading public of Europe. Once whetted, the public's appetite for literature on the island of love was insatiable. As usual, a man was on hand to provide what the public craved for. This man was George Forster, one of the botanists of the expedition, whose father (also a member of the expedition) had translated Bougainville's narrative into English. George Forster's book, *A Voyage Round the World in the Sloop, Resolution*, was in the glamorous Bougainville vein, and it had a great vogue. But the interest in it was a mere bagatelle compared with the interest in Omai.

Omai was a real, live 'noble savage' who was brought back to England by Captain Tobias Furneaux, commander of the sloop *Adventure*, which sailed as consort to Cook's *Resolution*. Omai was a young man, probably in his early twenties. Although he was born in Tahiti, he was living on the island of Huahine when Captain Furneaux picked him up. His education in the *Adventure* was mainly in the hands of a cultured young officer, Lieutenant James Burney. He could not have had a better tutor. Burney was the son of Dr. Thomas Burney, a famous musician, and brother of Fanny Burney, whose novel *Evelina* was one of the most popular books of the late eighteenth century. By the time he reached England on July 14, 1775, Omai had learned a little English and knew something of English manners and customs.

He was a sensation almost from the moment he arrived. As one writer has said, he answered 'the cry of England for a representative in a state of nature'. It was not long before articles about him appeared in the magazines; and within a month, Fanny Burney was writing in her diary that 'the present Lyon of the times . . . is Omy, the native of Otaheite'.

Although Omai moved in a new world of unfamiliar faces, strange customs, and formal manners, he always seemed to be at

31

home. He went to the opera, visited country houses, dined at banquets, walked through the streets, and attended the House of Lords, as if he had been used to them all his life. Even when Lord Sandwich presented him to King George III, he acted with complete assurance. 'How do, King Tosh?' he said, with a deferential bow. Then he listened politely to the King's address of welcome, and accepted the gift of a sword without hesitation or awkwardness.

Omai's behaviour naturally excited widespread admiration. 'His address is uncommonly courteous and polite, and even carries with it the air of some breeding,' one writer said. Crusty Dr. Samuel Johnson thought there was 'so little of the savage in Omai' that when he saw him dining one day with Lord Mulgrave, he was 'afraid to speak to either lest (he) should mistake one for the other'. Fanny Burney went even further. 'Omai,' she said, 'with no tutor but Nature ... appears in a new world like a man who had all his life studied the Graces and attended with unremitting application and diligence to form his manners, and to render his behaviour politely easy and thoroughly well-bred. . . . Indeed, he seems to shame education, for his manners are so extremely graceful, and he is so polite, attentive and easy, that you would have thought he came from some foreign court. . . . I think this shows how much more Nature can do without art than art with all her refining, unassisted by Nature.'

Fanny Burney was well qualified to judge. She met Omai at her father's house four months after his arrival in England. She had been ill in bed for three days, and when she came downstairs she was 'very much wrapt up and quite a figure'.

> I found Omai [she said] seated on the great chair and my brother next to him talking Otaheite as fast as possible. Mama and Susy and Charlotte were opposite. As soon as there was a cessation of talk, Jem introduced me, and told him I was another sister. He rose and made a very fine bow and then seated himself again. But when Jem went on and told him that I was not well, he again directly rose and muttered something about the fire in a very polite manner . . . insisting upon my taking his seat. He would not be refused. He then drew his chair next to mine, and looking at me

with an expression of pity, said: 'Very well tomorrow-morrow?' I shook my head. 'No?' he said. 'O very bad.'

Fanny said that as Omai had been to court, he was dressed 'very fine'. He wore a suit of Manchester velvet lined with white satin, lace ruffles, and the handsome sword that the King had given him. He was tall and very well made; much darker than Fanny expected; but he had 'a pleasing countenance'.

At dinner, Fanny had the honour of sitting next to him. He ate heartily and 'committed not the slightest blunder at table'. Neither did he do anything awkwardly or ungainly. When he found by the turn of conversation and some wry faces that a joint of beef was not roasted enough, he took great pains to assure Mrs. Burney that he liked it. 'Very dood, very dood,' he said politely two or three times. Even when the servant brought him porter in mistake for another drink, he was 'too-well bred to send it back'.

When the coach came for Omai at six o'clock and the servant announced, 'Mr. Omai's servant,' the gentle savage was not so rude as to make an immediate move to go. He kept his seat for about five minutes longer and then rose to get his hat and sword. Finding his host engaged in conversation with a Mr. Strange, he did not choose to interrupt him 'nor to make his compliments to anyone else first'. He waited until Dr. Burney had finished, and then went up to him and made 'an exceeding fine bow'. This done, he made separate bows to everyone else and went out with Jem to his coach.

The fascinating Omai provided the Burneys with a topic of conversation for months after. They compared his manners most favourably with those of Mr. Stanhope* who had 'all the advantages of Lord Chesterfield's instructions' and had been taught 'all possible accomplishments from an infant'. Stanhope, in fact, was considered to be 'a mere pedantic booby' alongside the untutored Omai.

Omai created equally favourable impressions elsewhere. At

* Philip Stanhope (1732–1768) was the illegitimate son of Lord Philip Dormer Stanhope Chesterfield. During his youth, Lord Chesterfield wrote him numerous letters on the 'graces' and correct behaviour in society. The letters were published in 1774—the year of Omai's visit—and created considerable interest in fashionable circles. They are still obtainable in an edition of the Everyman Library.

Christmas, 1774, he spent several weeks at Hinchinbroke, the country residence of Lord and Lady Sandwich, where he was the centre of attraction. The glittering company was particularly amused by his conversation.

'What do you like best about London?' a pretty lady asked him.

'The great hog that carries people,' Omai replied instantly. 'English hogs very fine. Only this month, Lord and Lady Sandwich show me a great hog that gives coconut milk. Very dood. No climb trees—only put hand under and squeeze.'

'How do you like tea?' asked the beautiful Lady Carew.

'Very well, not very ill,' Omai replied.

'And how do you like Lady Carew?' asked Lady Townshend.

'Very nice, not very nasty,' the gentle savage answered amid much merriment.

'Would you take a pinch of snuff, sir?' Lord Townshend enquired, proffering his box.

'No tank you, sir. Me nose be no hungry.'

But Omai did not limit himself to amusing the company with his verbal sallies. In the tea room, he gallantly handed round cake and bread and butter to the ladies. He listened with rapt attention when Dr. Boyce played the Old Hundredth Psalm for the first time. And he made himself useful by cooking a shoulder of mutton in the native manner by enveloping it in leaves and burying it in hot coals in the ground. In short, the 'amazing Omai'—'this lyon of lyons' as Fanny Burney now called him—captured all hearts.

A 'lyon of lyons' was naturally a desirable subject for a portrait, and Omai was painted by at least four artists during his stay in England. Sir Joshua Reynolds, the most famous and fashionable artist of his time, painted three canvases of him. Others were done by Sir Nathaniel Dance, William Hodges, and William Parry.

The portraits of the lesser-known artists were realistic in detail. Dance's portrait, for example, showed Omai in a long robe of white 'tapa'* cloth, holding a wooden Tahitian head-rest in one hand and a native bag and fan in the other. It was a representation of Omai as he was.

Reynolds's portraits, on the other hand, were highly idealized.

* 'Tapa'—A cloth made from the bark of the paper mulberry tree.

They showed Omai as devotees of Rousseau wished him to be. Every device was used to make him look noble. In the two best-known portraits, Omai was dressed in a robe of 'tapa', but Reynolds added the exotic detail of a Mohammendan turban. In one picture, which showed only the head and shoulders, the turban was adorned with plumes of the Indies and a jewelled Arabian crescent. The other picture was a full-length portrait. It represented Omai standing gracefully before a palm tree with a silver stream in the background at right lit up by the light of a tropical moon. If Omai had been wearing a floral loin-cloth instead of a robe, the portrait would serve as a modern tourist poster advertising the romantic South Seas.

Omai stayed in England for two days short of two years. During the latter part of his stay, he lived alone in lodgings at Warwick Street, receiving a pension from the King. When he called on the Burneys unexpectedly in December 1775, his English had much improved, although his pronunciation sometimes made him unintelligible. Omai began immediately to talk of Fanny's brother who was then in America.

'Lord Sandwich write one, two, tree monts ago,' he said, counting on his fingers, 'Mr. Burney come home.'

'He will be very happy to see you,' Fanny said.

Omai bowed. 'Mr. Burney very dood man.'

'Have you seen the King lately?' Fanny asked.

'Yes; King George bid me—"Omy, you go home." Oh, very dood man, King George.'

Omai then said how happy he was at the thought of seeing his native land again, but, at the same time, he would be sorry to leave his friends in England. The conversation then turned to Lady Townshend.

'Very pretty woman, Lady Townshend,' Omai said. 'I drink tea with Lady Townshend in one, two, tree days. Lord Townshend my friend. Very pretty woman, Lady Townshend. Very pretty woman, Mrs. Crewe. Very pretty woman, Mrs. Bouverie. Very pretty woman, Lady Craven. When they wish to see me, they write and bid me—"Mr. Omy, you come, dinner, tea, or supper"—then I go.'

Omai's partiality for the ladies provoked a good deal of malicious comment in London. 'Here he is honoured with the smiles and favours of red and white goddesses,' one gossip said. 'Though his clime is fertile and healthful, and the women beautiful and numerous, yet he cannot resign this paradise of earth without showing the keenest and severest emotions.' This sort of talk provided an anonymous versifier with a theme for a profitable poem. On the eve of Omai's departure for Tahiti with Captain Cook in July, 1776, the poet came out with *Omiah's Farewell: Inscribed to the Ladies of London*. One of the verses ran thus:

> Well may Omiah with regret depart,
> Well may he show the feelings of his heart,
> Well may he prove the weakness of his mind,
> But who is brave who leaves his heart behind?

The poem went on to compare feminine customs of adornment in England and Tahiti, and it suggested that the Tahitian women would soon change their ways:

> Is it not strange, the ladies of my shore,
> Whom heaven favours and whom you adore—
> That they should use their paints with such disgrace
> And give the tail what they deny the face?
> Here painted faces bloom on ev'ry strum,
> In Otaheite—we tattow the bum,
> But such a custom shall no more appear,
> Such charms in future shall not grace the rear.
> The blooming cheek shall now with all prevail,
> No future beauty shall tattow her tail.

While many people in England were laughing over these graceless lines, other more serious minds were wondering whether Omai had really benefited from his glimpse of civilization. Dr. Johnson thought not; and William Cowper, the poet, had the idea that his taste of western culture would make him dissatisfied with his native land. In his poem, 'The Task', Cowper wrote:

> . . . And having seen our state,
> Our palaces, our ladies, and our pomp

Of equipage, our gardens, and our sports,
And heard our music; are thy simple friends,
Thy simple fare, and all thy plain delights
As dear to thee as once? And have thy joys
Lost nothing by comparison with ours?

Yet one thing was certain. Omai did more to glamourize and advertise Tahiti than all the Bougainvilles, Hawkesworths, and Forsters could ever do. Nine years after his departure, he inspired one of the most successful stage shows of the eighteenth century—'Omai, or a Trip Around the World'. This show was presented at the Theatre Royal, Covent Garden, over fifty times. It brought the house down every night. Four years later, there was still sufficient interest in England's 'noble savage' for a French writer to produce a 950-page book called the *Narrations d'Omai*, which purported to be a life of the hero written by himself.

What was the secret of Omai's success? A modern writer, T. B. Clark, has explained it very clearly.

> Omai was the most agreeable specimen of a man in a state of nature the English people had ever seen. Whereas Eskimos, Indians and English peasants had all failed in the Graces, Omai displayed them like a peacock. . . . To Polynesians of his day, form and ceremony were all-important. Tabus and observances governed every move they made from the morning bath to the evening meal. . . . Omai, having been apprenticed to a priest, was doubly aware of the subtleties of form and ceremony. . . . The secret of Omai's great success lies in the fact that he caught in (the Englishmen's) ceremonies the true religion of the eighteenth century—wealth, vanity and convention . . . A man was respected by his fellows in proportion to the fineness of his dress and manner. It did not take Omai long to realize this.

7. SPANIARDS AGAIN

O MAI had not yet reached England when the Spanish Government decided to send a second expedition to Tahiti to 'foster friendly relations with the Indians', make a more intensive survey of the island, and set up 'some mark or inscription' to indicate its discovery by emissaries of Spain. Instructions to this effect were sent to Viceroy Amat, in Lima, on October 26, 1773.

Amat immediately commissioned the *Aguila* to make a new voyage under her old commander, Captain Don Domingo de Boenechea. The *Aguila* sailed from Callao on September 20, 1774. Embarked in her were two Franciscan friars, Fray Geronimo Clota and Fray Narciso Gonzalez, who were to be left on the island to christianize the natives. The friars were to be assisted by a young marine called Maximo Rodriguez, who was to act as interpreter. Rodriguez had picked up the rudiments of Tahitian on the *Aguila*'s first voyage and had improved his knowledge by association with the three Tahitian youths whom Boenechea had brought back to Lima. Two of these youths (one had died in Lima) were also embarked in the *Aguila*. Amat told the Spanish Government that the youths had been 'well-informed and instructed' and should 'prove of much assistance to the missionaries'.

The *Aguila* sailed with a small trading vessel, the *Jupiter*, which carried stores, an altar, and a portable house for the missionaries. Amat gave the officers and missionaries a list of a hundred questions to help them get accurate information about the island. Some of the questions were rather odd:

(1) Are there any giants or pygmies, and how tall are they?
(2) Find out what the priests pray and in what posture.
(3) Find out whether the Demon they call 'tupapau' reveals himself to them very often, and whether, as is alleged, his apparitions are most frequent when the moon is on the wane.

(4) Make sure as to the truth or otherwise of the alleged apparition of the Devil in the form of a shark, and whether he helps them, as is said, to regain the shore when their canoes founder.

The *Aguila* and *Jupiter* came in sight of Tahiti in the second week of November, 1774, and anchored at Vaitepiha Bay on November 27. The Spaniards were greeted with great cordiality. Vehiatua, the chief of the district, and Otoo, the chief of Pare who was paying him a visit, showed 'inexpressible satisfaction' when told that the friars and their interpreter were to be left on the island. They agreed to provide men and anything else that was necessary for the construction of the mission house.

A site for the house was chosen on November 29 and work on it began immediately. It was ready for occupation on the last day of the year. Next day, 'an infinite number of Indians' collected to watch the Spaniards erect a cross in front of the house to signify 'the indisputable right' of the King of Spain to 'all the islands adjacent to his dominions.' The cross was inscribed thus:

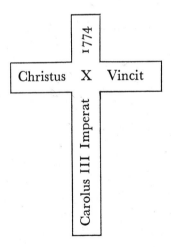

After the cross had been erected, the chiefs promised to protect the friars and to provide them with food if their own food ran out. The Spaniards then drew up a convention with the chiefs. This said that the King of Spain desired to 'befriend and instruct

39

their people' so that they would be 'superior to all who dwelt in similar ignorance'. In the name of the King, they offered to provide tools and implements to protect the chiefs against their enemies. They said they would visit them frequently in the King's ships so long as they did what they had promised. At this, the Spanish account continued, the chiefs 'manifested a lively satisfaction'. 'They loudly declared that they acknowledged His Majesty as King over Tahiti and all its lands—the terms of the convention being greatly to their liking.'

This being settled, the *Aguila* and *Jupiter* weighed anchor and sailed, on January 7, for the near-by island of Raiatea. As soon as they were gone, the natives began a programme of uproarious public festivities, which, Rodriguez said, 'became prolonged into a continuous orgy'. The two friars were not left in peace for a single hour of the day or night. All the natives were eager to inspect the mission house, and such large crowds jostled around it that the friars were afraid of being hurt. They therefore locked themselves in the house 'in a state of eternal apprehension and watchfulness', which caused the natives to taunt them with opprobrious names. 'Old gaffers,' they shouted, 'fools . . . shellfish . . . thieves.' These insults, which were accompanied by roars of laughter, were difficult enough for the sensitive friars to bear. But matters were made worse when one of the natives who had been to Lima deserted from the mission house and joined in the revels of his own people. The friars then had to cook their own meals, carry barrels of water, and do 'other menial offices not proper to their status'.

The prospect of the friars doing any useful work was none too rosy when the *Aguila* and *Jupiter* unexpectedly returned on January 20. The reason for their return was the sudden grave illness of Captain Boenechea, who had deputed the command of the *Aguila* to Senior Lieutenant Don Thomas Gayangos. The friars immediately complained to Gayangos of the 'many indignities' they had suffered while the frigate had been away. They asked that two men be left with them to do their cooking, etc. Gayangos obliged them by detailing one ordinary seaman, Francisco Perez, to look after them.

On January 26, Boenechea died. He was buried on shore with full naval honours next day, and Gayangos sailed early on the

28th. The natives gave him an affectionate farewell and urged him repeatedly to come back.

The Franciscan missionaries and their two assistants, Perez and Rodriguez, were left on Tahiti for nearly a year, but they made no converts. This was hardly surprising for it would be difficult to imagine two priests who were less equipped for gaining the respect or even the goodwill of a Polynesian community. Their journals show them to have been narrow-minded, peevish, illiberal and pusillanimous. They hardly ever dared to venture out of the mission house, and they made no attempt to learn the Tahitian language. Perez made things worse for them by being unruly and causing trouble with the natives. Rodriguez, the interpreter, was the only member of the mission who got along well with the natives. His knowledge of the language and his tolerance of native customs earned him the confidence of chiefs and commoners alike. He roamed freely throughout the island noting in a diary details of everything he saw. The natives knew him affectionately as Marteemo, which was the nearest they could get to Maximo, his Christian name.

On November 3, 1775, the *Aguila* again anchored at Vaitepiha Bay. Her commander on this occasion was Captain Don Cayetano de Langara. Langara wrote to the friars that he had stores for them. But the friars replied that they had decided to return to Lima. 'We are left unprotected and are in imminent danger of losing our lives,' they said. 'Our Lord God not only commands us in His most holy law not to take our own lives, but also not to expose ourselves to the risk of losing them.' Langara did not seem convinced by this argument, but after further correspondence he agreed to take the friars off. Most of the livestock which had been left on the island on the previous voyage was rounded up and taken aboard. One of the junior officers told the chiefs, through Rodriguez, that the friars were returning to Lima to report progress to the King, and that new missionaries would be brought to the island within a year or so. The chiefs agreed to keep the mission house in good repair during the interval, and the *Aguila* sailed on November 12.

Soon after her return to Callao, Amat, the Viceroy, was retired from his post at his own request after a long and energetic reign. His successor did not share his enthusiasm for expeditions to Tahiti, nor was the local treasury able to finance them. Although the King of Spain issued repeated commands that the Tahitian mission should be resumed, his orders were never carried out. It was over one hundred years before the next Spanish expedition visited Tahiti, but by that time the island had fallen into the hands of another power.

Only one copy of the valuable diary that Maximo Rodriguez kept in Tahiti is known to exist. This was found by pure chance in 1908 in the library of the Royal Geographical Society, London, by an English scholar, Bolton Glanvil Corney, who later translated it and had it published by the Hakluyt Society. Rodriguez's daughter had given the diary to Captain Robert Fitzroy, commander of H.M.S. *Beagle*, in Lima in 1835.

In 1912, Corney also found a unique Tahitian stone bowl that Rodriguez had brought from Tahiti. The bowl, after many vicissitudes, had found its way into the National Archæological Museum of Madrid. But all knowledge of its history and country of origin had long been forgotten.

8. THE LAST OF CAPTAIN COOK

THE Spaniards had been gone from Tahiti exactly eight months when Captain Cook arrived at the island for the last time. He was making his third and final voyage to the Pacific. The primary object of the voyage was to find out whether there was a north-west passage between the Pacific and the Atlantic. A secondary object was to return 'the amazing Omai' to his home island. The expedition consisted of two ships—HMS *Resolution* and HMS *Discovery*. The latter was commanded by Captain Charles Clerke.

The two ships anchored at Vaitepiha Bay on May 12, 1777, after visiting various Polynesian islands to the west where Omai proved a valuable interpreter. A number of natives came off to the *Resolution* before she was properly moored, among whom was Omai's brother-in-law and some old acquaintances. Cook said there was nothing either 'tender or striking' in their meeting with their long-lost friend. On the contrary, there was 'perfect indifference' on both sides until Omai took his brother-in-law to his cabin and gave him a few red feathers. This changed the whole complexion of things. The brother-in-law begged that they might be friends and sent ashore to get Omai a hog. Omai's other friends crowded into the cabin in the hope of getting some red feathers too. 'Such,' said Cook, 'was Omai's first reception among his countrymen. I own I never expected it would be otherwise. But still I was in hopes that the valuable cargo of presents, with which the liberality of his friends in England had loaded him, would be the means of raising him into consequence, and of making him respected and even courted by the first persons throughout the extent of the Society Islands. This could not but have happened had he conducted himself with any degree of prudence. But instead of it, I am sorry to say that he paid too little regard to the repeated advice of those who wished him well, and suffered himself to be duped by every designing knave. . . .'

Cook stayed at Vaitepiha Bay until August 23 taking on water and repairing his ships. While he was there, he inspected the cross and mission house which the Spaniards had erected. To make sure that there should be no doubt about England's prior discovery of the island, he had the cross taken down and an inscription carved on the opposite side to the Spanish one. The inscription was—'Georgius Tertius Rex, Annis 1767, 1769, 1773, 1774, 1777.'

On leaving Vaitepiha Bay, Cook sailed to his other anchorage at Matavai Bay. There he put ashore three cows, a horse, a mare, and some sheep, geese, and ducks, which had been brought from England for the benefit of the Tahitians. 'Having thus disposed of these passengers,' Cook said, 'I found myself lightened of a very heavy burthen. The trouble and vexation that attended the bringing of this living cargo thus far is hardly to be conceived. But the satisfaction that I felt in having been so fortunate as to fulfil His Majesty's humane design in sending such valuable animals to supply the wants of this worthy nation sufficiently recompensed me for the many anxious hours I had passed before this subordinate object of my voyage could be carried into execution. . . .' Cook also planted some melons, pineapples, potatoes and shaddock trees for his native friends.

43

On the morning of August 27, a native came from Vaitepiha Bay with a report that two Spanish ships had anchored there the night before. To confirm his story, he produced a piece of new blue cloth which he said he had obtained from one of the ships. Cook immediately sent a boat party to Vaitepiha Bay to verify the report, the native informer going with them. In the meantime, he had the guns mounted and the decks of his two ships cleared for action in case war had been declared between England and Spain since he had left home. It turned out, however, that the native had imposed on him. The Tahitians were merely curious to know what would happen if ships of the two nations should meet.

During Cook's stay at Matavai, John Webber, who accompanied the expedition as artist, drew a portrait of Otoo, the chief of the district. When the portrait was finished Otoo asked what it was for. Cook said he wanted it as a souvenir. Otoo replied that he would like one too. So Webber painted a portrait of Cook, which was given to Otoo. The chief promised faithfully to keep it.

It was Cook's desire that Omai should be settled at Matavai under Otoo's protection. But Cook said that he behaved so imprudently that he soon lost the friendship of Otoo and of every other person of note in Tahiti. It was therefore decided to take him back to Huahine where Captain Furneaux had picked him up in 1774. Before they sailed for that island, Otoo told Cook that if the Spaniards should return, he would not let them stay at Matavai as that land belonged to the Englishmen. 'This shews,' Cook said, 'with what facility a settlement might be made at Otaheite, which, grateful as I am for repeated good offices, I hope will never happen.'

The *Resolution* and *Discovery* sailed for Huaheine via Moorea on September 29. On board, according to the unpublished journal of Lieutenant James Burney, were a number of Tahitian girls who had apparently provided the English sailors with solace during their stay. Huahine was reached on October 13. There the ships' carpenters built Omai a house, in which he was soon installed with a large number of European possessions. Cook gave a very full description of Omai's settlement and domestic arrangements. He said that the history of Omai would probably interest 'a very numerous class of readers more than any other occurrence of the voyage'.

On leaving Huaheine, Cook steered for the north-west coast of America. En route he discovered five islands of the Hawaiian group which he named the Sandwich Islands in honour of the First Lord of the Admiralty. The mainland of America was sighted in March, 1778. The next few months were spent exploring the coast from Oregon northwards, through Bering Strait right up to Icy Cape. As there was no sign of an ice-free passage to the Atlantic, Cook decided to return to Hawaii.

The *Resolution* and *Discovery* reached Hawaii in late November. The natives were celebrating a great victory when they arrived and mistook the Englishmen for the god, Lono, and his immortal company. Divine honours were offered, and Cook accepted them. But trouble began when it became apparent that the entertainment of a god was an extremely expensive affair, and quarrels became frequent after one of Cook's sailors was buried ashore. To everyone's relief, Cook decided to quit the islands. But he was back again within a few days to make repairs to the *Resolution*'s foremast. More trouble began immediately. One of the ship's cutters was stolen, and Cook put ashore in a boat to capture one of the chiefs and hold him as hostage until the cutter was returned. As the boat party reached the shore, the natives crowded round and pelted it with stones. After several shots were fired, Cook turned to give orders to the boat party. As he did so, he was stabbed in the back and he fell dead with his face in the water. Thus ended the life of England's most famous navigator. He was fifty-one.

The command of the expedition then passed to Captain Clerke, who took the *Resolution* and *Discovery* to the Kamchatka Peninsula of Siberia, where he died on August 22, 1779. Clerke was succeeded by Captain John Gore, a veteran of four Pacific voyages, who brought the two ships safely home to England via the Cape of Good Hope and the Orkney Islands at the end of 1780. This brought the great era of Pacific exploration to a close. Although dozens of small islands still remained to be discovered, Cook and others (but mainly Cook) had visited every Pacific land mass of any size. This stupendous achievement was very largely due to Captain Wallis's discovery of Tahiti thirteen short years before.

45

The convenient situation of Tahiti in mid-Pacific; its friendly and amorous inhabitants; and its abundance of supplies made it the ideal stopping place for the revictualling of ships and the refreshments of crews. Tahiti, in fact, can truthfully be said to have been the focal point of Pacific exploration. Almost every major discovery was made from its shores. For this reason, and for others described in earlier chapters, Tahiti acquired a pre-eminence among the islands of the Pacific which it has not lost to this day.

9. A CHANCE VISITOR

ELEVEN years passed after Cook's departure from Tahiti before the next ship called at the island. This was the convict transport vessel, *Lady Penrhyn*, which dropped anchor in Matavai Bay on July 10, 1788. The *Lady Penrhyn* was one of Governor Arthur Phillip's First Fleet of eleven ships which brought out the 'foundation members' for the Australian convict settlement at Botany Bay. She left England under Captain William Sever on May 13, 1787, and arrived at Port Jackson on January 26, 1788. On the way to Macao three months later, an outbreak of scurvy enfeebled almost everyone on board and contrary winds blew the vessel hundreds of miles off course. Captain Sever therefore decided to make for Tahiti when he fell in with the south-east trade wind on July 7.

On arrival at Matavai Bay, hundreds of natives were on Point Venus and round the beach waving pieces of cloth and making signs for the visitors to come ashore. One of the few fit men on board at this time was Lieutenant John Watts, who had visited Tahiti previously in the *Resolution*. Watts found that Otoo was still living and that he carried Webber's portrait of Cook wherever he went. But great numbers of the natives had been carried off by venereal disease which they had caught from the crews of the *Resolution* and *Discovery*.

When it was learned that no ships had called at the island

since 1777, it was resolved to conceal Cook's death—with the idea, no doubt, of ensuring the continued respect of the natives. Captain Sever made a present in Cook's name to the chief, Hitihiti, who informed the Englishmen that Omai had died in Huahine a long time before. As the iron utensils which the natives had obtained from earlier visitors were practically exhausted, refreshments were bought very cheaply for hatchets, knives, nails, gimlets, files, and scissors.

After a stay of twelve days, the *Lady Penrhyn*'s scrofulous crew had recovered so much that Captain Sever decided to set sail again. Otoo was very sad about it, and begged the Englishmen to come to Tahiti more often. The *Lady Penrhyn* cleared the Society Islands towards the end of July. The lonely atoll of Tongareva was discovered on August 8 and was named after the ship. It is still marked as Penrhyn Island on many maps as a reminder of an otherwise forgotten voyage to the eastern South Pacific.

PART II

THE SAGA OF THE *BOUNTY*

10. MUTINY IN THE *BOUNTY*

Tahiti's reputation as an earthly paradise was already firmly fixed at the time of the *Lady Penrhyn*'s visit, but an event was then preparing which was destined to give it an even greater vogue. This was the celebrated voyage of HMS *Bounty*.

The voyage of the *Bounty* was the result of a petition to King George III by English merchants in the West Indies asking that the breadfruit tree be transplanted from Tahiti. Cook and others had spoken highly of the breadfruit as a substitute for bread, and the merchants believed that it would lessen the costs of feeding their negro slaves. One of the leading petitioners was a Mr. Duncan Campbell, whose niece had married William Bligh, master of the *Resolution* on Cook's last voyage. Campbell had a number of large plantations in Jamaica, was well connected in Government circles, and was the owner of several ships. He employed Bligh as commander of two or three of these ships when Bligh was on half-pay from the Navy after the *Resolution*'s voyage.

It was on one such ship that Bligh first sailed with a dark young man called Fletcher Christian. Christian, who came from a good family in Cumberland, had been recommended to Bligh by a mutual friend and sailed in the capacity of midshipman. After their first voyage together, Christian spoke of Bligh with great respect. He said that although he had had his share of labour with the common men, Bligh had been kind in showing him the use of his charts. He also observed that Bligh was very passionate, and he therefore took some credit in knowing how to humour him. Bligh and Christian were making their second voyage together when the King, on the enthusiastic recommendation of Sir Joseph Banks (now president of the Royal Society), granted the petition of the West Indian merchants. When they returned, Campbell was waiting to tell Bligh the good news and to offer him the command of the breadfruit expedition. Meanwhile, one of Campbell's ships, the *Bethia*, was being refitted for the voyage at Deptford under Banks's botanical eye. Banks had suggested to the Admiralty that the vessel should be renamed HMS *Bounty*.

Bligh received his appointment to the *Bounty* on August 16, 1787. For the next few months, he was busy taking on stores and signing on his crew. The latter presented no difficulties, as the prospect of visiting voluptuous Tahiti brought a flood of applications for the voyage. Bligh, in fact, was in the unusual position for those days of being able to choose his men instead of having to accept what the press-gang gave him. Fletcher Christian and John Norton, two old shipmates, were signed on respectively as master's mate and quartermaster; William Peckover, an able-seaman in Cook's *Endeavour*, was taken on as gunner; and David Nelson, the botanist on the *Resolution*'s last voyage, was appointed to the same job in the *Bounty*. Others got their jobs more through friendship and influence than because of their qualifications. Among these were two midshipmen—Peter Heywood and George Stewart. Heywood was the fifteen year-old son of the Deemster of the Isle of Man, where Bligh had married; and Stewart was a native of the Orkney Islands, where Bligh had received kind treatment at the end of the *Resolution*'s voyage. Thomas Ellison, an able seaman, was signed on on the recommendation of Duncan Campbell. The other members of the *Bounty*'s crew were:

John Fryer, master.
William Elphinstone, master's mate.
Charles Churchill, master-at-arms.
Thomas Huggan, surgeon.
John Mills, gunner's mate.
William Cole, boatswain.
James Morrison, boatswain's mate.
William Purcell, carpenter.
Charles Norman, carpenter's mate.
Thomas McIntosh, carpenter's mate.
Joseph Coleman, armourer.
Thomas Hayward, John Hallett, and Edward Young, midshipmen.
Peter Linkletter, quartermaster.
George Simpson, quartermaster's mate.
Lawrence Lebogue, sailmaker.

Mr. Samuel, clerk.

Robert Lamb, butcher.

William Brown, gardener.

John Smith and Thomas Hall, cooks.

Robert Tinkler, boy.

Thomas Burkett, Matthew Quintal, John Sumner, John Millward, William McCoy, Henry Hillbrandt, Alexander Smith, John Williams, Isaac Martin, Richard Skinner, Matthew Thompson, William Muspratt, Michael Byrne, Thomas Ledward (a qualified surgeon), and James Valentine—able-seamen.

The *Bounty* did not carry a corps of marines to enforce discipline as was customary in the navy in those days; nor did she carry a purser. The enforcement of discipline was in the hands of Churchill, the master-at-arms; and Bligh undertook the profitable purser's duties himself with the assistance of his clerk.

Thus manned and completely fitted to carry the breadfruit, the *Bounty* sailed from Spithead on December 23, 1787. Three days out from England, she ran into a heavy sea which broke away the spare yards and spars, stove in the boats, washed several casks of beer overboard, and spoiled a large quantity of bread. This initial mishap made it necessary to put into Teneriffe, and apparently made Bligh niggardly and even unscrupulous with the provisions.

At Teneriffe, the ship's cheeses were ordered to be aired on deck. When two were found to be missing from their cask, Bligh claimed they had been stolen. Henry Hillbrandt, the cooper, maintained on the contrary that the cask had been opened while the *Bounty* lay in the Thames, and that the cheeses had been taken to Bligh's house on Mr. Samuel's order. This caused Bligh to threaten Hillbrandt with 'a damned good flogging' if he didn't hold his tongue, and then to order the allowance of cheese to be stopped for all officers and men until the deficiency was made good.

Several days later, there was further trouble when Bligh ordered each man to be served with two pounds of decaying pumpkin instead of two pounds of bread. When the men complained about this, Bligh flew into a violent passion and dared any one of them to refuse it. 'You damned infernal scoundrels,' he roared, 'I'll make you eat grass or anything you can catch before

I have done with you.' This was not all. When the men complained that they were getting short weight of beef and pork, Bligh declared that he was 'the fittest person to judge of what was right or wrong'. And he added that he would severely flog the first person who complained again. This threat, however, did not prevent 'frequent murmurings among the officers about the smallness of their allowance'.

Whether these murmurings were justified or not, Bligh showed that he had the welfare of his men at heart in other respects. On January 10, 1788, he divided the crew into three watches— giving the command of the third watch to Fletcher Christian. 'I have always considered this is a desirable regulation,' Bligh wrote later, 'and I am persuaded that unbroken rest not only contributes much to the health of the ship's company, but enables them more readily to exert themselves in cases of sudden emergency.'

In the early days of February, the *Bounty* ran into so much bad weather that everything became wet and covered in mildew. Solicitous for his crew's health, Bligh had the ship 'aired below with fires and vinegar'. And he took advantage of every interval of dry weather to open all the hatchways and clean the ship, and to have the crew's wet clothing washed and dried.

On February 17, the *Bounty* came up with a homeward-bound whaler, by which Bligh despatched a letter to Duncan Campbell. 'We are all in good spirits,' he wrote, 'and my little ship fit to go around half a score of worlds. My men are all active, good fellows, and what has given me much pleasure is that I have not been obliged to punish anyone. My officers and young men are all tractable and well-disposed, and we now understand each other so well that we shall remain so the whole voyage, unless I fall out with the surgeon, who I have trouble to prevent from being in bed for fifteen hours out of the twenty-four.'

Bligh's happy outlook continued during the next few weeks, and on March 2, he gave Christian a written order to act as lieutenant. On March 10, however, he had to inflict his first flogging when Fryer, the master, reported Matthew Quintal for insolence and contemptuous behaviour.

Towards the end of the month, the *Bounty* began her attempt to round Cape Horn and so pass into the Pacific. But violent winds and heavy seas prevented much progress. Soon the ship 'began to complain' and had to be pumped every hour. The decks became so leaky that Bligh gave up his great cabin to accommodate the seamen with wet berths. In these trying conditions, a number of the crew fell sick, but the others carried on 'with alacrity and spirit'. Their behaviour—according to James Morrison, the boatswain's mate—'merited the entire approbation of the officers and Mr. Bligh's thanks in a public speech'.

Bligh's determination to enter the Pacific via the Horn did not give way until after a full month of vain battling. Then, 'having maturely considered all circumstances', he had the helm put up to bear away to the Cape of Good Hope, to the great joy of everyone on board. With favourable winds, the *Bounty* made a speedy passage and reached the Cape on May 24, 1788. Here an extensive overhaul took place, as the ship had been continuously at sea for four months. While at the Cape, Bligh wrote another letter to Duncan Campbell in which he said that his men were in good health and good humour. He attributed this to dancing to the fiddle on the forehatch from six to eight each night, and to the excellence of the food he had provided. 'I assure you that I have not played the purser with them,' he wrote, 'for profits was trifling to me while I had so much at stake.'

Only one unpleasant incident occurred at the Cape, and that was the punishment of Able-Seaman John Williams, who got six lashes for 'neglect in heaving the lead'. On July 1, the *Bounty* was ready to sail to Tasmania. She anchored in Adventure Bay on August 21. Here she stayed for fourteen days taking in wood and water. During this time, Bligh had trouble with William Purcell, the carpenter. Purcell refused to assist in loading water on the ground that it was 'not in his line'. So Bligh ordered food to be stopped until he became more amenable to discipline.

The next people to get on the wrong side of Bligh were Fryer, the master, and Huggan, the surgeon. On the voyage from Tasmania to Tahiti, these two officers quarrelled with him several times, refused to eat in his cabin, and stopped speaking to him except on duty. Fryer made matters worse by refusing to sign two of the ship's expense books unless Bligh signed his certificate of good behaviour. As the books had to be signed before the captain and warrant officers could receive their pay, Bligh felt that the matter should be aired before the whole ship's company. He therefore ordered all hands to be called, mentioned the master's refusal to sign, and read the Articles of War and Officers' Instructions. Fryer was then ordered to sign the books or to express his reasons for not complying at the foot of the page. Fryer took up the pen. 'I sign in obedience to your orders,' he said, 'but this may be cancelled hereafter.'

Around about this time—on October 9, to be exact—James Valentine, an able-seaman, died of an asthmatic complaint. Sixteen days later, the *Bounty* came in sight of the island of Mehetia. Here Bligh issued orders that on reaching Tahiti, no one was to say that Captain Cook was dead, and no one was to tell the natives the purpose of the *Bounty*'s visit.

At 4 a.m. next morning, the *Bounty* reached Point Venus. She was soon surrounded by a large number of canoes filled with natives shouting 'tayo' (friend), and asking whether the visitors had come from 'Pretanie' or Lima, Peru. But as soon as they saw Bligh and Nelson, the botanist, there were many inquiries after Captain Cook, Sir Joseph Banks, and many other former friends.

With the natives as well disposed as ever, Bligh was soon able to obtain permission to collect the breadfruit. But the botanist found that the trees were at a stage of their growth which made them unsuitable for immediate transplanting. This made it necessary to stay at the island much longer than had been expected—over five months, as it turned out.

Many students of the *Bounty* believe that this long stay was largely responsible for the mutiny which afterwards occurred. The members of the crew had little to do but surrender themselves up to the island's delights, and this had a disastrous effect on discipline and attention to duty. Bligh had frequent cause to complain. On November 3, when the natives stole the gudgeon of the rudder belonging to the large cutter, Bligh noted in his journal that such thefts were 'mostly owing to the negligence of our own people'.

On December 5, when Bligh ordered the carpenter to cut a large stone for the natives to grind their hatchets on, he was astonished to hear the carpenter's reply. 'I will not cut the stone,' the carpenter said, 'for it will ruin my chisel, and though there may be a law to take away my clothes, there is none to take away my tools.' Purcell's insubordination, which had previously cost him stoppage of food, this time earned him a stretch of confinement to his own cabin.

The next incident that incurred Bligh's wrath took place on the night of January 5, 1789, when three men deserted in the ship's cutter. 'Had the mate of the watch been awake,' Bligh wrote in his journal, 'no trouble of this kind would have happened. . . . Such neglectful and worthless petty officers, I believe, never were in a ship as are in this. No orders for a few hours together are obeyed by them, and their conduct in general is so bad, that no confidence or trust can be reposed in them; in short, they have driven me to everything but corporal punishment, and that must follow if they do not improve.' Corporal punishment followed very quickly. Morrison said that the day after the deserters' escape, Midshipman John Hayward was put in irons for eleven weeks for sleeping on watch.

A week or so later, Bligh was angered to learn that a number of sails had been allowed to rot and accumulate mildew in the sail-room. His officers were blamed again. 'If I had any officers to supersede the master and boatswain or was capable of doing without them,' he wrote, 'they would no longer occupy their respective stations.'

Then on March 7, Bligh complained that 'verbal orders in the course of a month were so forgotten' that the officers would 'impudently assert that no such thing or directions were given'. 'I have therefore been under the necessity,' he said, 'of writing out what, by decent young officers, would be complied with as the common rules of the service.'

Meanwhile, the three deserters—Churchill, Muspratt, and Millward—had been brought back on board and given a good flogging and a spell in irons. Bligh, however, seemed to be enjoying himself. In the account of his stay that he wrote up afterwards, he spoke of pleasant rambles ashore through 'delightfully shaded' breadfruit groves; of jokes played on the natives; of the 'obliging manners' of the Tahitian women; of his 'drollery and good humour' when playing with the native children; of the 'mirth and jollity' of his constant visitors on board; and of the riotous *heivas* and wrestling matches ashore. Generally speaking, Tahiti was a wonderful place for captain and crew alike.

But the time drew near for the *Bounty*'s departure. And if Bligh had been too lenient with his men during the preceding five months, he now became excessively severe. According to Morrison, he claimed possession of all goods that were brought aboard, and he even issued privately owned foodstuffs as the official ration. When the men complained about this, he shut their mouths with his customary threats.

Yet Morrison said that 'everyone seemed in high spirits, and began to talk of home as though they had just left Jamaica . . . so far onward did their flattering fancies waft them'. Thus, on April 4, 1789, the *Bounty* weighed anchor and steered towards the leeward islands of the Society group. On board were 1,015 breadfruit trees and a large number of other plants which had been collected at the suggestion of Sir Joseph Banks. Thomas Ledward was now acting as surgeon—Huggan, the original occupant of that post, having drunk himself to death.

By April 6, the *Bounty* had left the Society group and the island of Aitutaki, and was heading westward for the Tonga group. Namuka was reached on April 23. Here Bligh and the crew bought quantities of coconuts from the natives who came off to the ship, and Christian was sent ashore for wood and water. On shore, however, the natives proved so hostile that Christian had to return on board without fulfilling his mission. Bligh promptly abused him as a 'cowardly rascal' and demanded whether he was afraid of a bunch of naked savages while he had weapons in his hand.

'God damn your blood,' he cried, 'why didn't you fire? You, an officer!'

'The arms are of no use, sir,' Christian replied respectfully, 'while your orders prohibit their use.'

Four days later, when the *Bounty* was at sea again, Bligh came on deck and fancied he missed some of his coconuts that had been piled between the guns. He claimed that they had been stolen and that they could only have been taken with the knowledge of the officers. The officers were summoned on deck and questioned, but each denied any knowledge of the thefts.

'Then you must have stolen them yourselves,' Bligh roared, and turning to Christian, he asked how many coconuts he had bought for his own use.

'I do not know, sir,' Christian replied, 'but I hope you do not think me so mean as to be guilty of stealing yours.'

'Yes, you damned hound, I do,' Bligh shouted. 'You must have stolen them from me or you would be able to give a better account of them.'

Then he turned to the other officers.

'Damn you, you scoundrels, you are all thieves alike, and combine with the men to rob me. I suppose you will steal my yams next. But I will sweat you for it, you rascals! I'll make half of you jump overboard before you get through Endeavour Straits.'

This threat was followed by an order to the clerk to 'stop the villains' grog' and to reduce their issue of yams next day to half a pound. 'And if they steal them,' Bligh added, 'I'll reduce them to a quarter.'

Later that day, Bligh abused Christian again, and Christian came away from his cabin with tears in his eyes. Purcell, the carpenter, stopped him and spoke.

'What is the matter, Mr. Christian?'

'Can you ask me and hear the treatment I receive?'

'Do not I receive as bad as you do?' Purcell asked.

'But you have your warrant to protect you and can speak again,' Christian said. 'If I should speak to him as you do, he would probably break me, turn me before the mast, and perhaps flog me. And if he did, it would be the death of us both, for I am sure I should take him in my arms and jump overboard with him.'

'Never mind,' Purcell said, 'it is but for a short time longer.'

'I would rather die ten thousand deaths than bear this treatment,' Christian replied. 'I always do my duty as an officer and as a man ought to do, yet I receive this scandalous usage. It is more than flesh and blood can stand. In going through Endeavour Straits, I am sure the ship will be a Hell.'

That same afternoon, Christian made a desperate resolve to leave the ship. He gave away all his Tahitian curiosities, tore up his letters, and made a raft by lashing a plank to the two masts of the launch. After dinner, he took a piece of pork that had been left over and hid it until the appropriate moment in his cot. He also obtained a supply of nails from the carpenter which he intended to use in trade with the natives of whatever island he landed on. He planned to escape early in the evening but there were too many people on deck, attracted by a volcano on the nearby island of Tofua. The time slipped by. Midnight came and went. But still the opportunity to slip overboard unobserved did not present itself. At 3.30 a.m., Christian gave up, and retired to bed to get some rest before taking over his watch at four o'clock. When Midshipman Stewart called him at that hour, he seemed 'much out of order', and Stewart—knowing his intention— urged him strongly to abandon it.

'When you go, Mr. Christian,' he said, 'we are ripe for anything.'

Ripe for anything . . . ripe for anything. Stewart's words kept repeating themselves in Christian's mind as he went on deck.

The time was certainly ripe for seizing the ship. Midshipman Hayward, Christian's mate of the watch, was asleep on the arms chest, and Hallett, the other midshipman, had not come on deck.

Christian called Quintal and Martin, the two able-seamen on duty, and broached the idea of mutiny. Quintal and Martin were behind the idea at once, and quickly got Churchill, Smith, McCoy, and Williams to join them. The next move was to obtain arms. This they did by borrowing the armourer's key to the arms chest on the pretext that they wanted a musket to shoot a shark. Meanwhile, three other seamen—Burkett, Sumner and Mills—had joined the mutineers; and Hayward had been awakened from his nap on the arms chest and sent to another part of the ship. Two of the mutineers were told to stand watch over the cabins of Fryer, the master, and Nelson, the botanist, while the others dealt with Captain Bligh.

It was still dark when Christian, Churchill, Mills, and Burkett crept into Bligh's cabin and hauled him out of bed. They threatened him with instant death if he made the least noise; tied his hands behind his back; and dragged him roughly on deck. Bligh ignored their threats and demanded to know the reason for their violence. His only answer was a round of abuse for not holding his tongue.

Cole, the boatswain, Purcell, the carpenter, and Samuel, the clerk, were then allowed to come on deck. Cole was ordered to hoist out the launch, and Hayward, Hallett, and Samuel were told to get into it.

'What is the meaning of all this?' Bligh demanded of his captors who were standing over him abaft the mizen mast with muskets cocked and bayonets fixed.

'Hold your tongue, sir, or you are dead this instant,' one of the mutineers shouted.

'Damn his eyes, blow his brains out,' cried another.

'What is the meaning of all this, I say?' Bligh repeated.

'Can you ask, Captain Bligh?' Christian replied quietly. 'Can you ask when you know you have treated us officers and all these poor fellows like Turks?'

Bligh looked around in desperation.

'This is a serious affair, Mr. Young,' he said to one of the midshipmen who had just come on deck.

'Yes,' said Young, who had taken sides with the mutineers. 'It is a serious affair to be starved. I hope this day to get a belly full.'

By this time, Churchill had ordered eighteen of the officers and men to get into the boat, and he now told Christian that they were only waiting for Captain Bligh.

'Come, Captain Bligh,' Christian ordered, 'your officers and men are now in the boat and you must go with them. If you attempt to make the least resistance, you will instantly be put to death.'

'Is this a proper return for my many instances of friendship?' Bligh asked.

Christian appeared much disturbed and answered with emotion.

'That, Captain Bligh, that is the thing. I am in Hell, I am in Hell.'

'Consider, Mr. Christian,' Bligh said appealingly. 'I have a wife and four children in England, and you have danced my children on your knee.'

'You should have thought of them sooner yourself, Captain Bligh. It is too late to consider now. I have been in Hell for weeks past with you.'

And without further ceremony, Bligh was forced into the boat, where he found his companions had been given some twine, canvas, lines, sails and cordage, a 28-gallon cask of water, 150 lb. of bread, some wine and rum, a compass, and a quadrant. The boat was then veered astern by a rope. A few pieces of pork, some clothes and cutlasses were thrown down as additional equipment. Coleman, McIntosh, and Norman called out to Bligh to remember that they had been kept on board against their will.

Finally, after Bligh had been thoroughly ridiculed and abused by the mutineers, the boat was cast adrift in the open ocean. It was so heavily laden that the water was lapping its gunwales.

11.   RETURN OF THE *BOUNTY*

THE twenty-five men who remained in the *Bounty* consisted of two parties: those who had taken an active part in the mutiny, and those who had not. In the first group were:

Fletcher Christian, acting lieutenant.

Edward Young, midshipman.

John Mills, gunner's mate.

Charles Churchill, master-at-arms.

William Brown, gardener.

Thomas Burkett, Matthew Quintal, John Sumner, John Millward, William McCoy, Henry Hillbrandt, Alexander Smith, John Williams, Thomas Ellison, Isaac Martin, Richard Skinner, and Matthew Thompson, able-seamen.

The non-mutineers were:

Peter Heywood and George Stewart, midshipmen.

James Morrison, boatswain's mate.

Joseph Coleman, armourer.

Charles Norman, carpenter's mate.

Thomas McIntosh, carpenter's crew.

William Muspratt and Michael Byrne, able-seamen.

Christain's first act as the new commander of the vessel was to change course and steer for the island of Tubuai, about three hundred miles south of Tahiti. Those on board were then divided into two watches—Christian taking charge of one, and Midshipman Stewart, the other. The breadfruit and other plants were thrown overboard at Christian's order, and Christian moved into Captain Bligh's cabin.

The *Bounty* had been sailing on her new course for some days when Morrison hit on a plan for retaking the vessel on reaching port. He discussed the plan with some of the others, but Christian got wind of it and took measures to prevent it. He took the key to the arms chest from Coleman, and moved the chest into his own cabin where Churchill made his bed on it. He also armed the members of his party with a brace of pistols, kept Captain Bligh's pistol in his own pocket, and gave orders to his men to make sure that three people were always present in any conversation.

So things went on until May 28, when the *Bounty* reached Tubuai and anchored in a sandy bay. The natives were hostile, and twelve were killed in a bloody skirmish that took place on the first day. Nevertheless, Christian decided that Tubuai would be a suitable place for a settlement after hogs, goats, and poultry had been acquired from Tahiti.

The return journey to Tahiti began three days later. On the way, Christian gave orders that no one was to tell the natives the name of the island where they intended to settle; and he threatened to shoot anyone who tried to desert. He also distributed the articles of trade amongst all hands and told them to make the best market they could as it would probably be their last opportunity.

On June 6, the *Bounty* anchored in Matavai Bay. The natives flocked around in the usual large numbers and asked what had happened to the plants and the rest of the crew. Christian had the answer pat. He said that the *Bounty* had encountered Captain Cook at the island of Aitutaki; that Cook was forming an English colony there; that Bligh, Nelson, and the others had stayed behind to help him after the launch and breadfruit trees had been unloaded; and that Cook had ordered the *Bounty* to return to Tahiti to trade for further stores and livestock.

This answer was sufficient to deceive the natives and no further questions were asked. Christian, however, made doubly sure of procuring the things he wanted by entertaining the chiefs on board and plying them with wine and arrack.

The *Bounty* remained in Tahiti until June 16, by which time the mutineers had taken aboard 460 pigs, fifty goats, a bull and a cow, a few dogs and cats, and a number of fowls. On the return voyage to Tubuai, the mutineers were accompanied by nine Tahitian men, eight women, and nine children, many of whom hid themselves on board until the *Bounty* was at sea. Among the natives was the chief, Hitihiti.

Tubuai was reached after a rough passage of seven days. The *Bounty* anchored in the same harbour as before, which the mutineers had christened 'Bloody Bay'. The natives on this occasion did not prove troublesome and the livestock was landed without difficulty. The mutineers then hauled the *Bounty* on shore and proceeded to build a fort with walls eighteen feet thick at the base and twelve feet thick at the top. The walls were to be surrounded by a deep and wide moat, which would be crossed in the approved fashion by a drawbridge.

The Herculean labour on this construction was still going on on August 9 when the *Mercury*, an English merchant brig commanded by Captain John Henry Cox, approached Tubuai from the west.

12. A CLOSE SHAVE

THE story of Christian and his band of followers might have ended very differently if the winds blowing from the west on August 9, 1789, had been a little stronger. In that case, the *Mercury* would probably have reached Tubuai before nightfall and the mutineers' hide-out may very well have been discovered. As it was, it was 8 p.m. before the vessel came abreast of the island and passed within a quarter of a mile of it. 'We perceived several lights on shore,' said Lieutenant George Mortimer in his narrative of the *Mercury*'s voyage, 'and fired two guns to draw the attention of the inhabitants, but night prevented us from seeing them.'

Four days later, the *Mercury* anchored at Matavai Bay. The

natives were as friendly as ever, and Otoo produced Webber's portrait of Captain Cook. On the back of this, in Bligh's handwriting, was an inscription saying that the *Bounty* had left Tahiti on April 4. Mortimer was therefore mystified to learn that the *Bounty* had subsequently returned to the island under the command of the chief officer. A native who offered to sell him a club said that the officer's name was Titreano, and that Titreano had brought the club from a place called Tootate. The native added that Titreano had returned to Tahiti about two months after the *Bounty* first sailed, and that Bligh had been left at Tootate. This story was corroborated by Otoo and other chiefs, who said that Titreano had sailed only fifteen days before the *Mercury*'s arrival, and that he had returned to Tootate with several Tahitian families.

Mortimer could not then guess 'where Tootate could be or who they meant by Titreano', but he observed that a number of clubs he purchased were 'different from those of Otaheite and the adjacent island, but very similar to the weapons of the Friendly Islands'. He reported these facts to the Admiralty when he returned to England in June, 1790.

Mortimer's account of the *Mercury*'s stay in Tahiti contained no other item of relevant to this story except that 'a desperate fellow called Brown', who had cut another sailor across the face with an old razor, was left on the island at his own request. The *Mercury* sailed for Hawaii and the north-west coast of America on September 2.

13. THE LAST OF THE *BOUNTY*

MEANWHILE, things at Tubuai had not been running smoothly. On August 25, some of the mutineers had been stripped of their clothes by the natives; and a few days later, others had complained about the difficulty of getting women. When Christian refused to head an armed party to bring women to the camp by force, the men refused to do any work and demanded more grog. When this was also refused, the men broke into the spirit room and helped themselves.

By September 10, it was obvious to Christian that he had lost his authority, so he called all hands to ask them what they wanted to do. Sixteen of the twenty-four voted to return to Tahiti (where they could 'get Weomen without force'), and the other eight elected to remain with Christian. This being settled, Christian made the following speech:

'Gentlemen,' he said, 'I will carry and land you wherever you please. I desire no one to stay with me, but I have one favour to request—that you will grant me the ship, tie the foresail, give me a few gallons of water, and leave me to run before the wind. I shall land on the first island the ship drives to. I have done such an act that I cannot stay at Otaheite. I shall never live where I may be carried home to disgrace my family.'

Immediate preparations were then made to refloat the *Bounty*, which was ready for sea on September 17. Most of the livestock was rounded up and taken aboard, but only after another bloody encounter with the Tubuaians in which sixty-six natives were killed.

As the *Bounty* was leaving the island, she ran into a tremendous squall and lost the spare gaff of the driver and all her spare topgallant yards. She reached Tahiti without further incident on the morning of September 23. There the natives helped to land the equipment of those who intended to remain on shore and, by evening, everything had been taken off. Christian, however, promised to stay a day or two longer in case anything had been forgotten, but it was found next morning that he had already put to sea. When last seen, the *Bounty* was standing to the north-west on a wind. Those who had gone with Christian were Edward Young, John Mills, William Brown, John Williams, Isaac Martin, Matthew Quintal, William McCoy, and Alexander Smith. Also on board were a number of Tahitian and Tubuaian men and women.

Those remaining in Tahiti were Peter Heywood, George Stewart, James Morrison, Charles Norman, Thomas McIntosh, Joseph Coleman, Charles Churchill, Richard Skinner, Thomas Ellison, Henry Hillbrandt, Thomas Burkett, John Millward, John Sumner, Matthew Thompson, William Muspratt, and Michael Byrne.

These men immediately split up and went to live with former friends—some going to Pare, and some remaining at Matavai. Those at Matavai were soon joined by John Brown, of the *Mercury*, but they found him 'a dangerous kind of man' and resolved to have as little to do with him as possible.

Early in November, half a dozen of the mutineers agreed to a suggestion by Morrison that they should try to build a boat in which they could sail to England via the East Indies. A plan for a schooner with a deck length of thirty-five feet was laid down. For the next seven months, the boat builders were busily occupied in cutting planks, making ironwork, and using their ingenuity in finding substitutes for the tools, materials, and equipment they lacked. Meanwhile Churchill, who had contrived to become chief of Tiarapu, was murdered by Thompson after a quarrel. And Thompson, in turn, was murdered by the Tiarapuans to avenge the loss of their chief.

On July 5, 1790, the schooner was launched and named the *Resolution*. The mutineers then began the task of making casks and salting hogs for the long voyage to Batavia. This task was interrupted a number of times in the next few months when rebellions broke out against Otoo's authority. On each occasion, Otoo asked the mutineers to help him, and on each occasion the rebels were put to rout by the mutineers' guns.

Late in November, six of the mutineers, with Morrison in command, set sail in the schooner for the East Indies, but lack of water or distrust of Morrison's navigational powers soon occasioned their return. By this time, the rainy season had begun in full force, and it was decided to beach the *Resolution* until the new year.

It was not until March 21, 1791, that the vessel was taken out for another voyage. On that day, Morrison, McIntosh, Millward, and Hillbrandt set sail from Matavai to take part in a native war at Tiarapu. They put into Papara three days later to pick up Burkett, Sumner, Muspratt, and Brown. While there, a friend of Hitihiti's arrived in haste to tell them that a ship had anchored at Matavai on March 23, and that those who remained behind—Stewart, Heywood, Coleman, and Skinner—had been placed in irons on board. The messenger added that an armed boat party was then on its way down the coast in search of those in the

Resolution; that the boat was being piloted by Hitihiti; and that Hitihiti had sent word in advance so that the mutineers would know how to act.

The mutineers decided that the best plan was to put to sea and avoid seeing the armed party's boat.

14. PANDORA'S BOX

THE ship that had anchored at Matavai Bay was HMS *Pandora*, a 24-gun frigate commanded by Captain Edward Edwards. She had been sent from England towards the end of 1790 for the express purpose of finding and arresting the mutineers. Her despatch followed Bligh's return to England after a voyage of appalling hardship from Tofua to Timor. Only one man was lost on this gruelling, 3,000-mile voyage in an open boat; but six others died after reaching the East Indies. The eleven survivors returned home by various vessels—Bligh, himself, landing at the Isle of Wight on March 14, 1790.

Within three days Bligh was presented to the King, and through the newspapers, the story of his adventures and sufferings was soon widely known. Two months after his arrival, a play entitled, *The Pirates, or Calamities of Captain Bligh*, was produced at the Royalty Theatre, London. The playbills claimed that the show exhibited 'a full account of his voyage ... the attachment of the Otaheitan women to, and their distress at parting from, the British sailors ... and an exact representation of the seizure of Captain Bligh in the cabin of the *Bounty* by the pirates'. All this, the playbills said, had been 'rehearsed under the immediate instruction of a Person who was on board the *Bounty* storeship'.

Meanwhile, Bligh, with the help of James Burney, Omai's former mentor, was preparing his *Narrative of the Mutiny on Board HMS 'Bounty'*. It was published in mid-year. In it, Bligh condemned everyone who had stayed in the *Bounty* with more or less equal severity, and took care that nothing could suggest that he had been responsible for the mutiny in any way.

The publication of the book probably helped to persuade the Admiralty to send out the *Pandora* to bring the mutineers to punishment. The only clue the naval lords could give Captain Edwards was that the mutineers were probably at Tootate, which was probably in the Friendly Islands. They told him, however, to call at Tahiti just in case the mutineers had been attracted back by—what Bligh called—'the allurements of dissipation'.

The Lords of the Admiralty showed great wisdom. Before the *Pandora* had dropped anchor, Coleman, the *Bounty*'s armourer and a non-mutineer, had clambered aboard, dripping wet after a long swim from shore. He was soon followed by two other non-mutineers, Midshipmen Stewart and Heywood. These two had learned from a native that John Hayward, their *Bounty* shipmate, was on board as lieutenant. But when they asked to see him, Hayward (the man who had slept on the arms chest while the plot for mutiny was hatched) received them very coolly and pretended to be ignorant of their affairs. Heywood and Stewart were looked on, in fact, as 'piratical villains' and were ordered to be clapped in irons. Richard Skinner received the same treatment when he came on board during the afternoon.

When Captain Edwards learned the whereabouts of the other mutineers, he sent Lieutenants Corner and Hayward to arrest them in the launch and pinnace, with Hitihiti acting as guide. But the mutineers, under Morrison, had already put to sea, and the two lieutenants returned at nightfall empty-handed. Sixteen days passed—sixteen days of hide-and-seek on land and sea—before Morrison & Co. were rounded up. They were brought on board with their hands tied behind their backs, and were confined in irons, with the others, under the half deck. Two seamen and a midshipman with pistols and bayonets were placed over them as sentinels. Next day, handcuffs were put on them for extra security. The prisoners were forbidden to speak among themselves in the Tahitian language, and were likewise forbidden to speak to their native friends who brought off supplies.

A few days later, Captain Edwards had the prisoners transferred to a round house which had been erected for their reception on the quarter deck. This place, which was promptly nicknamed 'Pandora's Box', was only eighteen feet wide at the bulkhead and eleven feet long at the deck. The entrance to it was by the scuttle at the top about twenty inches square. Two sentries were placed on top, while another walked across by the bulkhead. No one was allowed to speak to the prisoners except the master-at-arms, and his conversation was limited to the subject of provisions. Morrison said that the heat in 'Pandora's Box' was so intense that the sweat of the prisoners frequently ran to the scuppers in streams. The hammocks issued were full of vermin, which could not be avoided except by lying on the bare deck. Added to all this were 'two necessary tubs which were constantly in the place', and which helped to render the prisoners' situation 'truly disagreeable'.

This was bad enough, but it was not long before the prisoners' situation was made even more uncomfortable. One night, McIntosh happened to slip his leg out of the extra large shackle which fettered him, and the result was that Captain Edwards ordered all leg-irons to be 'reduced to fit close'. Larkin, the first lieutenant, also adopted a barbaric method of trying the handcuffs for size. He would set his foot against a prisoner's chest and haul at the manacles with all his might. If the manacles came off—even if they brought some skin with them—they were reduced so that there was no possibility of turning the wrists in them. 'The handcuffs are not intended to fit like gloves,' Larkin said, when the prisoners complained that their wrists were becoming swollen.

The prisoners' Tahitian wives frequently came out to the ship and created heart-rending scenes below the stern which were 'sufficient to evince the truth of their grief and melt the most obdurate heart'. Some had their children with them—four girls and two boys had been born to the mutineers—and some were pregnant. In typical Polynesian fashion, they rent the air with bitter lamentations and cut their heads with sharks' teeth until the water around their canoes was red with blood. These carryings-on eventually got on Captain Edwards's nerves, and he gave orders that the sorrowing wives were to be kept away from the ship.

On May 19, the *Pandora*—with Brown, of the *Mercury*, as an extra member of the crew—was ready for sea. The mutineers' schooner, *Resolution*, had been fitted out to accompany her as a tender.

Captain Edwards shaped his course to Raiatea, Tahaa, and Bora Bora, and then to Aitutaki. Not finding any trace of

Christian and his party on those islands, he continued westward to Palmerston Island. There, the crew of the *Resolution* discovered a spar marked 'Bounty's driver yard', which made Edwards think that the missing mutineers were not far away. A minute examination of Palmerston Island was therefore carried out, but Christian & Co. were not to be found. (The spar, in fact, had floated up from Tubuai after being lost in the violent squall on the day of the *Bounty*'s departure.)

On May 29, the *Pandora* proceeded to the Samoan group, where she parted company with the *Resolution* in a heavy thunderstorm. By this time, Edwards's hopes of finding the missing mutineers had dwindled considerably, and his search for them in Samoa, Tonga, Rotuma, the Santa Cruz group, and the Louisiade Archipelago of the Solomons was little more than cursory. The Great Barrier Reef near the northern tip of Australia was reached on August 28. A calamity occurred there the same night.

At half past seven, while Edwards was searching for the entrance to Endeavour Straits, the *Pandora* struck a submerged reef and was badly holed. Within ten minutes, she had shipped four feet of water and, twenty minutes later, eight feet. With the ship in danger of being battered to pieces, Edwards ordered all guns on one side to be thrown overboard in an effort to lighten her. When this was done, the *Pandora* was driven over the reef and settled in fifteen fathoms of water. All hands were then called to man the pumps, and three of the prisoners—Coleman, Norman, and McIntosh—were released from irons to help. The others, imagining that the vessel was about to sink, wrenched themselves out of their shackles and pleaded with the captain to be given a chance to save their lives. Edwards was merciless. He ordered their irons to be replaced and posted two extra sentinels over them with orders to shoot anyone who tried to unfetter himself again.

In this condition the mutineers spent the night, while the *Pandora*'s crew sweated desperately at the pumps. It was evident before daylight, however, that the *Pandora* would soon sink, so the order was given to abandon ship. The four boats were hoisted out and a small quantity of provisions hastily thrown into them. It was now half past six; the hold was full of water and the decks were awash. With each passing minute, the *Pandora* slipped further into her watery grave. Many of the seamen had already jumped overboard, but nobody paid the slightest heed to the fettered occupants of 'Pandora's Box'. Even when young Peter Heywood entreated the captain to have mercy on them as he passed over their prison to make his own escape, their plight was ignored. By this time, the ship was lying on her broadside with the port bow completely under water.

The prisoners had practically resigned themselves to death when the master-at-arms—either by accident or design—let the keys to the round house slip through the scuttle, which he had opened the moment before. The prisoners were thus able to begin liberating themselves. The boatswain's mate suddenly appeared to help them. He said he would set them free or go to the bottom with them. All but four had been unfettered when the ship went down. Those drowned were Stewart, Sumner, Skinner, and Hillbrandt.

The ten who escaped supported themselves on planks and other debris until they were picked up by the *Pandora*'s boats and taken to a sandy cay about three miles away. When everyone was mustered, it was found that thirty-one of the *Pandora*'s crew of 110 had been drowned besides the four mutineers. A survey of the provisions showed that there were only enough for a daily ration per man of two small glasses of water and one of wine, and two to three ounces of bread.

During the next three days, Captain Edwards had the *Pandora*'s four boats prepared for a voyage to Timor. Meanwhile, the mutineers were miserably treated. Most of them had escaped from the wreck without a stitch of clothing on, and Edwards refused even to lend them a sail to make a tent to protect their skins from the fierce sun. In this plight, they found that the only way to avoid being roasted alive was to dig 'graves' at the water's edge and bury themselves in them up to the neck!

On August 31, the four boats were launched for the long voyage to Timor—three or four mutineers being placed in each. The next fourteen days were a nightmare of scarcely bearable hunger, sunburn, and thirst, but Edwards's goal was reached without loss of life.

In Timor, the mutineers were confined in a castle for three weeks, during which they plaited straw hats and sold them for clothes. On October 6, the whole party sailed for Samarang in a Dutch East Indiaman. On reaching this port three weeks later, they were amazed to find the mutineers' schooner, *Resolution*, which had been lost in the storm off Samoa four months before. Edwards promptly sold this unexpected windfall and bought clothing and other necessaries for his crew. Nothing, however, was given to the 'pirates' who had built the little schooner.

From Samarang, the Englishmen proceeded to Batavia where they were split up and taken in four vessels to the Cape of Good Hope. Edwards and some of the mutineers then transferred to HMS *Gorgon*, which landed them at Portsmouth on June 19, 1792. The remaining mutineers reached home with Lieutenant Hayward a few weeks later.

A Court Martial inquiry into the mutiny on the *Bounty* was held on HMS *Duke* from August 12 to August 18. Of the ten mutineers tried, Norman, Coleman, McIntosh, and Byrne were acquitted; Burkett, Ellison, and Millward were condemned to death and hanged from the yard-arm; Muspratt was condemned but pardoned on a point of law; and Heywood and Morrison were condemned but pardoned by the King. This meant that of the forty-six men who sailed in the *Bounty* from Spithead on December 23, 1787, only nineteen survived to live in England as free men—Bligh, eleven members of his boat party, and the seven who escaped with their lives from the Court Martial. Of the twenty-seven others, eight died of illness, one was killed by natives at Tofua, two were murdered in Tahiti, four were drowned, and three were hanged. This left nine still to be accounted for.

The story of the fate of the vanished nine is the subject of another, much later, chapter, for it was many years before their lonely hide-out was discovered.

15. THE OLD ORDER CHANGETH

WHILE the drama of the *Bounty* was still going on, Tahiti was having a great rash of visitors. The first to appear after the *Pandora*'s departure were Lieutenant William Robert Broughton in HMS *Chatham* and Captain George Vancouver in HMS

Discovery. Broughton and Vancouver were on their way from England to survey the north-west coast of America for the benefit of the fur trade. Broughton arrived at Matavai Bay on December 27, 1791, and Vancouver joined him three days later.

Vancouver, who had visited Tahiti on Cook's last two voyages, found conditions greatly changed. Most of his native friends of 1777 had died in the interval. Otoo, his father, brothers, and sisters were the only chiefs he still knew. Otoo, however, was now called Pomare (meaning 'cough in the night')—the name of Otoo having been passed on to his ten-year-old son. Young Otoo had been vested with the supreme authority, but Pomare was acting as regent until he became of age.

There were other changes, mainly for the worse. Pomare and his followers had become addicted to strong European spirits, and were very eager to adopt the manners and customs of their visitors. Most of the animals and plants which Cook had taken so much trouble to introduce to the island had been destroyed in the native wars. Even the women had changed.

'I cannot avoid acknowledging,' Vancouver wrote, 'how great was the disappointment I experienced in consequence of the early impression I had received of their superior personal endowments. The natives, themselves, freely admit the alteration . . . and seem to attribute much of the cause to the lamentable diseases introduced by European visitors to which many of their finest women, at an early period of life, have fallen sacrifices.'

Vancouver was also forced to admit that the Tahitians would be reduced to a 'deplorable condition' if they were ever cut off from European supplies.

> The knowledge that they have now acquired of the more useful implements [he said] has rendered these and other European commodities not only essentially necessary to their common comforts, but have made them regardless of their former tools, which are now growing fast out of use . . . and fast out of remembrance. Of this we had convincing proof in the few of their bone or stone tools and utensils that were seen amongst them. Those offered for sale were of rude workmanship and of an inferior kind—solely intended for our market to be purchased by way of curiosity. I am likewise

convinced that by a very small addition to their present
stock of European cloth, the culture of their cloth plant,
which now seems much neglected, will be entirely disre-
garded, and they will rely solely upon the precarious supply
which may be obtained from accidental visitors. Under
these painful considerations, it manifestly appears that Europeans are bound by all the laws of humanity regularly to
furnish those wants which they alone have created . . .

Vancouver and Broughton stayed in Tahiti until January 24,
1792, when they continued their voyage to the north-west coast of
America.

16. SHIPWRECK

THREE weeks after the departure of the *Discovery* and *Chatham*
two British whaling vessels put into the old Spanish anchorage at Vaitepiha Bay. They were the *Matilda* (Captain Matthew
Weatherhead) and the *Mary Ann* (Captain Munro). The two ships
were on their way to the whale fisheries off the coast of Peru after
bringing convicts to the Australian penal settlement at Port Jackson. They stayed at Vaitepiha Bay from February 14 to February
17, 1792, buying plenty of hogs and fruit.

A few days after they sailed, the masters agreed to part company and to meet again off the Peruvian coast in latitude 10° S.
But this rendezvous was not accomplished, for on the night of
February 25, the *Matilda* went aground on an uncharted reef and
quickly sank. The twenty-eight members of the crew, plus one
convict who had stowed away at Port Jackson, escaped in four
boats and reached the island of Mehetia on March 4. They continued to Tahiti on the following day and landed at various parts
of the island after being separated by a storm.

The natives' eagerness for European possessions soon became
apparent. Casting aside their usual hospitality, they turned on
the Englishmen and dispossessed them of all they had. The

greatest prizes fell in the hands of the Matavaians; the people of Pare became jealous; and war between the two districts was declared.

This war was interrupted on March 25 by the arrival of the *Jenny*, a three-masted schooner from Bristol, commanded by Captain James Baker. The *Jenny* stayed at Matavai Bay for six days. Baker agreed to provide passages for Weatherhead and four of his men to the north-west coast of America. Three other members of the *Matilda*'s crew left for Port Jackson in one of the whaleboats which they had fitted with matting sails. At the time of the *Jenny*'s departure, twenty-one Englishmen were still on the island. The war over their possessions broke out anew as soon as the *Jenny* was out of sight.

17. CAPTAIN BLIGH AGAIN

THE native war was still going on when two more English vessels—HMS *Providence* and HMS *Assistance*—anchored in Matavai Bay on April 10, 1792. The *Providence* was commanded by Captain William Bligh, and the *Assistance*, her armed tender, by Lieutenant Nathaniel Portlock. Bligh had been sent out to make a new attempt to transplant the breadfruit to the West Indies.

As soon as the two ships were moored, Bligh was visited by a number of his old native friends and some seamen from the *Matilda*. From them, he learned of the visits of Captain Edwards and Captain Vancouver and of the war between Pare and Matavai. He also received the following letter which Captain Weatherhead had left for the commander of any British warship which might touch at the island:

Parry, Otaheite,
March 29th, 1792.

Sir:

I beg you will rectify the wrongs I have received on this island by one Tabyroo . . . After the misfortune of losing the

76

Matilda, we were six days in the boat. We landed at Matavai and put ourselves under the protection of this man. I had with me one box containing all my papers, 407 dollars, 172 guineas, between 3 and 4 lbs. of English silver, and a bag containing a few necessary clothes. After being in the house six days, I was turned out without anything to shift for myself with only one shirt.

Your obed. servant,
Matthew Weatherhead.

Bligh was afraid that the native war would make it hard for him to collect the breadfruit. He did not go ashore for four days. But he then told the chiefs that he 'would have no more fighting' and landed to supervise the building of storage sheds for his plants.

The collection of the plants occupied almost three months. During that time, Bligh used all his influence to retrieve the articles stolen from Weatherhead and members of the *Matilda*'s crew, but without much success. The natives, who had acquired about fifty muskets and pistols from various ships, were no longer intimidated by his threats.

Bligh was greatly disappointed in the change that had come over the island. Three entries from his journal confirm the opinions expressed by Vancouver earlier in the year:

April 11, 1792.—Our friends here have benefited little from their intercourse with Europeans. Our countrymen have taught them such vile expressions as are in the mouth of every Otaheitan, and I declare that I would rather forfeit anything than to have been in the list of ships that have touched here since April, 1789.

April 16.—Little of the ancient customs of the Otaheitans remains. . . . It is difficult to get them to speak their own language without mixing a jargon of English with it, and they are so altered that I believe in future no Europeans will ever know what their ancient customs of receiving strangers were.

April 24.—The quantity of old clothes left among these people is considerable; they wear such clothes as truly disgust us. It is rare to see a person dressed in a neat piece of cloth

77

which formerly they had in such abundance and wore with such elegance. Their general habiliments are now a dirty shirt and an old coat and waistcoat. They are no longer clean Otaheitans, but in appearance a set of ragamuffins with whom it is necessary to observe great caution.

By July 13, Bligh had collected 2,126 breadfruit plants and about 500 others, and was ready to put to sea. He sailed on July 18, taking thirteen men from the *Matilda* in the *Providence* and two in the *Assistance*. The remaining six 'went bush' to avoid being taken off.

The voyage to the West Indies was without untoward incident. St. Vincent was reached on January 23, 1793, and a week was spent there landing a portion of the breadfruit plants. The rest were landed at Port Royal, Jamaica, a week or two later. Thus, after nearly six years, 'Breadfruit' Bligh accomplished his mission. It was a tribute to his finer qualities as a man and a seaman, but its results, unfortunately, were negligible. The Negro slaves, for whom the breadfruit was expected to provide cheap food, disliked the taste and refused to eat it.

18. END OF AN ERA

ONLY two other ships are known to have visited Tahiti before the arrival of the first permanent European settlers in 1797. The first was HMS *Daedalus*, the storeship of Captain Vancouver; and the second was Bligh's old ship, the *Providence*, which was on a new voyage under Captain William Robert Broughton.

The *Daedalus* arrived at Matavai Bay on February 15, 1793, en route to Port Jackson to obtain stores. Vancouver had sent her from Monterey six weeks earlier to pick up the *Matilda* men, whom he had heard of from Captain Weatherhead when the *Jenny* arrived at Nootka Sound in October, 1792. Lieutenant James Hanson, commanding the *Daedalus*, found, of course, that most of the *Matilda* seamen had been picked up by Captain Bligh. The six who had remained had either gone to other islands or had acquired such important positions among the natives that they could not be tempted to leave. Hanson's errand of mercy therefore came to naught, and after a stay of a fortnight (during which a Finnish seaman called Peter Hagersteine deserted), he continued to Port Jackson.

Broughton's visit in the *Providence*—from November 28 to December 11, 1795—was likewise of little significance. But there was an interesting sequel eighteen months later. After leaving Tahiti, Broughton sailed to the coast of Asia, where he conducted an extensive survey between latitudes 52° and 35° N. On completing this, he put into Canton for a refit and there bought Morrison's schooner, *Resolution*, which Captain Edwards had sold in Samarang in 1791. The *Resolution* had been employed in the meantime in the sea otter trade, and was reported to have made one of the fastest voyages ever known between China and Hawaii. That was not her final claim to fame. After Broughton had used her for several months as a tender, the little schooner became the means of saving the lives of 112 officers and men in the *Providence* when that vessel was wrecked off the coast of Formosa on May 16, 1797. The *Resolution* then served as Broughton's survey vessel for another twelve months before being sold again in Trincomalee. Her subsequent fate does not appear to have been recorded.*

* The story of the schooner's career after Captain Edwards sold her in Samarang is recorded in John Marshall's 'Royal Naval Biography' published in London in 1825. It was apparently given to Marshall by Peter Heywood, who, after narrowly escaping with his life from the 'Bounty' Court Martial, rose to the rank of post-captain in the Royal Navy and became one of its most notable surveyors. However, the known details of the mutineers' schooner do not tally with those recorded by Broughton for the vessel he purchased, and it could be that Marshall's attractive story is incorrect.

PART III

MISSIONARIES AND PROVISIONS

19. THE VOYAGE OF THE *DUFF*

IN 1797, the first Protestant missionaries to leave England for any foreign country arrived in Tahiti. They were members of the London Missionary Society—one of the religious organizations which sprang up in the wake of the evangelical revival of Whitefield and the Wesleys.

The London Missionary Society was founded on September 21, 1795. Its leading light was the Rev. Dr. Thomas Haweis, an enthusiastic reader of the voyages of Cook, Wallis, and Bligh. In a sermon in Surrey Chapel on September 24, 1795, Dr. Haweis suggested that the society should begin its work in some place where 'the difficulties were least'. He said that Tahiti or some other island in the South Seas seemed a suitable place as the climate was good, food was plentiful, there were no religious prejudices, and the government seemed 'monarchical, but of the mildest nature'. Dr. Haweis added that in Tahiti there was 'more to apprehend from being caressed and exalted, than from being insulted and oppressed'.

Dr. Haweis backed his views by giving £500 towards a South Seas mission project, which quickly gained support. Contributions flowed in rapidly and liberally; missionaries were signed on; and the society decided to buy and equip its own ship. Captain James Wilson, a retired sea-dog and survivor of some hair-raising adventures in India, offered to command the ship without pay. On his advice, the *Duff*—a vessel of 267 tons—was bought for £5,000 and fitted out for a similar sum.

By the time the *Duff* was ready for sea, thirty missionaries had been enrolled. Of these, four were ordained ministers and five were married. One of the married men, a 28-year-old minister, had a 64-year-old wife, and one had children. All of the party were trained in some handicraft or trade for it was believed that the natives would be more quickly converted if they saw the practical benefits of European civilization. Besides the missionaries, the *Duff* carried four officers and a crew of nineteen.

They were picked men, and most were church members. The first officer was William Wilson, the captain's nephew.

A solemn service, dedicating the missionaries to their new work, was held in Zion Chapel, London, on July 28, 1796. It was attended by several thousand people. On August 9, a farewell communion service was held in the Haberdashers' Hall, and the *Duff* sailed at 6 a.m. the following morning. Fluttering triumphantly from her masthead was the mission flag, depicting three doves argent on a purple field bearing olive branches in their bills. It was a fine morning, and the breeze was favourable. As the *Duff* glided down the Thames, those on board lifted their voices to heaven:

'Jesus, at Thy command,
We launch into the deep.'

At Woolwich, an immense crowd gathered on the bank to see the novel vessel sail by. During the night, she was hailed by a passing ship.

'What destination?'

'Otaheite.'

'What cargo?'

'Missionaries and provisions.'

On arriving at Spithead several days later, it was found that the *Duff* had missed the convoy she hoped to sail with—necessary because of the war with France—and six weeks were spent at anchor waiting for another. During this time, 'the godly behaviour of the crew was so different from that usually met with' that it 'excited no small measure of surprise and wonder at its novelty'. Meanwhile, the missionaries busied themselves in copying a manuscript vocabulary of the Tahitian language which *Bounty* midshipman Peter Heywood had compiled while waiting for his Court Martial and had given to a Portsmouth clergyman.

On September 24, 1796, the *Duff* sailed with a fleet of fifty-seven transports and Portugal traders. She parted company with the convoy six days later and sailed via the Cape Verde Islands to Rio de Janeiro. After an unsuccessful attempt to round the Horn in late November, Captain Wilson decided to make for Tahiti by the eastern route. This route—several degrees southward of Cape Town, Tasmania, and New Zealand—was 7,000 miles longer than the other, but the *Duff* made a quick passage. No land was seen until Tubuai was reached on February 21, 1797, by which time the *Duff* had sailed 13,820 miles without sighting land—a record that has probably never been equalled.

With Tahiti close at hand, the missionaries decided on their various destinations. Eighteen, including all the ministers and married men, chose Tahiti; two plumped for the Marquesas; and ten decided on Tonga. Those who elected to remain at Tahiti were:

Name	*Profession*	*Age*
James F. Cover	Ordained minister	34
John Cock	Carpenter	23
Samuel Clode	Whitesmith and gardener	35
John Gillham	Surgeon	22
Peter Hodges	Smith and brazier	29
Rowland Hassall	Indian weaver	27
Edward Main	Tailor, late Royal Artillery	24
Francis Oakes	Shoemaker	25
James Puckey	Carpenter	25
William Puckey	Carpenter	20
William Smith	Linen draper	21
William Henry	Carpenter and joiner	23
Thomas Lewis	Ordained minister, with knowledge of medicine	31
John Eyre	Ordained minister	28
John Jefferson	Ordained minister	36
Henry Bicknell	Carpenter, sawyer, and wheelwright	29
Henry Nott	Bricklayer	22
Benjamin Broomhall	Buckle and harness maker	20

Of the above, Cover, Hodges, Hassall, Henry and Eyre were married. Hassall had two children, and Eyre's wife was sixty-four.

The missionaries had their first glimpse of Tahiti on March 4, but did not reach Matavai Bay until the following morning—a Sunday. By the time the *Duff* had anchored, more than a hundred natives were dancing and capering on the decks 'like frantic persons', crying 'tayo, tayo' and a few sentences of broken English. They were unarmed, but Captain Wilson was apprehensive of mischief and ordered the great guns to be hoisted out of the hold to keep them in awe. But the natives did not seem to be intimidated for they cheerfully assisted in placing them in their carriages.

When this was done, the brethren held divine service on the quarter deck. Brother Cover officiated. The text chosen was from the First Epistle of St. John—'God is love.' The hymns were selected for their harmonious tunes—first, 'O'er the Gloomy Hills of Darkness'; then, 'Blow Ye Trumpet, Blow'; and finally, 'Praise God from whom All Blessings Flow'. The whole service lasted about an hour and quarter. During the sermon and prayers the natives were 'quiet and thoughtful', but when the singing struck up, they seemed 'charmed and filled with amazement'. If they talked or laughed, 'a nod of the head was sufficient to bring them to order', and, upon the whole, 'their unweariedness and quietness were astonishing'. The missionaries were delighted, and one noted that there was 'a peculiar solemnity and excellence in Mr. Cover's address that day'.

Two circumstances helped to make it easy for the missionaries to establish themselves on shore. At Point Venus there was a large house suitable for their needs, and two seamen were on hand to act as interpreters. The house at Point Venus was 108 ft. long, 48 ft. wide, and 18 ft. high, and had been built by the natives for Captain Bligh in expectation of his return. The two interpreters were the Scandinavian deserters—Andrew Cornelius Lind, of the *Matilda*, and Peter Hagersteine, of the *Daedalus*.

Captain Wilson and several missionaries inspected Bligh's house—the Fare Beretane, as it was called—on March 6. The young king Otoo, after learning the missionaries' purpose, said that they could take possession of the house and could occupy whatever land they required. The missionaries took formal possession on March 16. By this time, they had had ample leisure to look around. Most of them were not disappointed in what they saw. 'A second paradise planted in the watery waste,' wrote one. 'Only one thing seems wanting to render the happiness of the natives complete, viz., the glorious gospel of the blessed God, that fountain of purity, righteousness and felicity.' Another missionary said that some of the brethren seemed disappointed over the 'lack of beauty and elegance in the native women', but this was compensated by the 'kindness, good nature and generosity of the people'.

By March 26, the eighteen Tahiti missionaries were comfortably settled in the Fare Beretane, and the *Duff* sailed to land the others at their chosen stations. Those for Tonga were put ashore on April 10, and the two for the Marquesas—William Crook and John Harris—reached their destination on June 5. Here the first sign of weakness on the part of the missionaries appeared. Brother Harris, a 39-year-old cooper, had maintained all along that he would settle in the Marquesas even if it meant going there alone. But on his first night ashore, he was frightened out of his wits when some Marquesan women—curious about the whiteness of his skin—stripped him naked to see if his body was the same all over. Having satisfied themselves on this point, they made it clear that they would not be averse to sleeping with him. When Harris declined, they ran off with his clothing, and the poor fellow spent the rest of the night shivering with fright and wailing lugubriously on the beach. Next morning, he declared to Captain Wilson that he would not remain among the nasty Marquesans at any price, and Wilson agreed to take him back to Tahiti.

The *Duff* returned to her former anchorage on July 6. Nothing extraordinary had occurred during her absence, but the missionaries had begun to realize the immensity of their task in imposing bleak, puritanical ideas on the uninhibited, idolatrous islanders. The realization was apparently too much for Brother Gillham, the surgeon, for he applied to Captain Wilson to be taken back to England. His defection was a most serious loss, but the missionaries drew consolation from the fact that Brother Lewis knew something of the mysteries of medicine.

During the *Duff*'s second stay, Captain Wilson landed a quantity of iron and other articles for the missionaries' use. Meanwhile, William Wilson and Peter Hagersteine made a circuit of the island, the chief result of which was to prove that the population was much smaller than Captain Cook had estimated. Wilson and Hagersteine calculated it to be 16,000, whereas Cook had thought it was about 120,000.

On August 4, the *Duff* sailed for China. There she obtained a cargo of tea which was taken back to England and sold to the East India Company for £4,100. The London Missionary Society thus recouped most of the money spent in fitting out the *Duff* for her famous voyage.

20. 'COLD FEET' AT THE MISSION

THE eighteen brethren at Matavai watched the *Duff* fade from sight with tears in their eyes. The first fervour of their missionary enthusiasm had not yet died away, but the severance of their connexion with home made them feel a little uneasy. Brother Jefferson, who had been elected secretary of the pioneering band, summed up the general feeling in his journal.

> We are now situated in one of the most delightful countries in the world. Here the cares and anxieties which possess the poor man's breast with respect to the maintenance of his family require not a thought. But still we have our troubles and anxieties. . . . We have, it is true, received from the natives kind treatment greatly surpassing what we expected; but from our knowledge of human nature, we have cause to apprehend that much deceit and covetousness may be mingled with their actions . . . and are therefore taught the necessity of some degree of caution in our transactions with them. Probably, we are in no danger at present from an open attack as they stand in dread of our firearms. But what craft or stratagem they may use to injure us, we cannot tell, and therefore we keep a guard of two brethren through the whole night to prevent any sudden alarm.

Jefferson's journal on August 13 was even more pessimistic. 'The more I see of the customs, temper and conduct of these people,' he wrote, 'the more I am confirmed in the opinion that our success will not be speedy.' Jefferson found that the natives became more and more persistent in their pilfering habits, and less and less grateful for the things the missionaries did for them. The missionaries were appalled by the looseness of the natives' morals and their sanguinary religious rites, but what filled them with the greatest horror was the practice among members of the Areoi Society of smothering their children at birth.

For three days in early November, the missionaries held long discussions on their attitude towards this custom. But many of them were opposed to any bold and decided policy, and it was merely resolved to inform the chiefs of the 'dreadful consequences of murdering their offspring' and to promise to care for any of the children who might be saved.

A week or so later, Brother Oakes raised a very practical question. 'Was it improper for a missionary to marry a native woman?' This matter was considered at length on November 20 when one of the brethren asserted that 'to marry an idolatress would be unlawful in the eyes of God'. A second maintained that 'if a native woman is not taken in her present condition, there is no alternative but to remain single, and we would then be exposed to all the dreadful temptations that surround us'. The opinion of a third was that 'God did not change his mode of government for the accommodation of his creatures, and that whatever we are called to do, we should look to Him for strength to endure'.

The brethren were then called upon in alphabetical order to express their sentiments, and each acknowledged that 'to marry a heathen woman would be directly contrary to the word of God'. It was therefore resolved 'to abide in the Lord's strength' as they were.

Six weeks later, however, the mission band at Matavai received word that Brother Cock, a 23-year-old carpenter, had succumbed to the weakness of the flesh and was conducting a love affair with a young woman of Pare, where he had gone to live with Brother Jefferson. The missionaries bearded him on the matter on January 25 when he came to Matavai with Peter Hagersteine. The erring brother confessed that for some time he had been 'in great distress of soul through various temptations', and he requested that Brother Cover should have permission to marry him. His request was sternly refused. 'The church has already resolved that a marriage with a heathen would be a departure from the faith,' he was told. And for fear that he might be tempted to live in sin with the woman of his heart, Brother Cover was invited to return to live at Matavai.

On March 6, 1798, there was great excitement at the mission when the 60-ton vessel *Nautilus* put into port. The *Nautilus* was in great distress for want of provisions. She had originally been bound for the north-west coast of America on the fur trade, but adverse winds had driven her far out of her way, and she was now steering for the island of Mas Afuera in search of seals. Captain Bishop asked for help in getting provisions, and the missionaries agreed to do all they could provided no ammunition or muskets were given to the natives. Four days later, the *Nautilus* put to sea again with her holds well stocked, and the missionaries congratulated themselves that her visit had done them no harm. But on March 23, the *Nautilus* reappeared at Matavai Bay, and on boarding her the missionaries found that she had suffered severely in a gale, had altered course, and was now making for Port Jackson for repairs.

Meanwhile, young Otoo had become enraged at the missionaries for having prevented Captain Bishop from supplying him with arms. This became apparent when Brothers Jefferson, Main, Broomhall, and W. Puckey went to see him to request the return of two deserters from the *Nautilus*. Otoo received them with great coldness and said he could not assist them. So the missionaries decided to try their luck with his father, Pomare. They were on their way to his house when they were set upon by natives. The natives, who were obviously acting on Otoo's orders, stripped the missionaries naked and so maltreated them that they could 'only acknowledge the goodness of the Lord for saving their lives'.

News of this attack caused considerable alarm at the mission house. Some of the missionaries believed that an attack on their quarters was imminent, and extra guards were appointed to keep watch throughout the night. Next morning, most of the brethren agreed to a resolution moved by Brother Cover that 'the recent occurrence and present state of things' made it necessary for them to leave the island. This resolution was strongly supported by Captain Bishop, who agreed to provide passages for those who wanted to go.

The *Nautilus* sailed on March 31 carrying all but seven of the original band of eighteen. Those who remained were Brothers

Jefferson, Lewis, Bicknell, Harris, Broomhall, Nott, and Eyre. The moral fibre of some of these did not augur well for the future. Broomhall had decided to stay only after he had loaded his baggage in the *Nautilus*; Eyre had remained mainly on account of his 64-year-old wife who was prone to sea-sickness; and Harris had shown that courage was not his strong point during his brief spell in the Marquesas.

21. SCANDAL AT THE MISSION

THREE months after the departure of the *Nautilus*, Brother Lewis announced that he was leaving the station at Matavai and was going to live at Ahonu. The remaining brethren spent three days trying to dissuade him, but Brother Lewis's mind was made up, and he moved out on July 10, 1798. Three weeks later, he sent the following letter to the mission house:

Brethren and Sister:

After a long and great conflict of mind, I now inform you that it is my fixed determination to take to wife one of these natives and abide faithfully towards her until death, thinking it the most eligible step in the circumstances, all things considered. Dear brethren, although you may be otherwise minded, yet I pray you to remember this, that while in this tabernacle we see but in part and know but in part, many things might be said on this subject, but I forbear, submitting the whole to Him who disposeth of events to their final end. And may the Lord order our steps, both yours and mine, to his eternal glory and our felicity. I hope you will return an answer to this by the bearer.

I remain,
Yours affectionately,
In the bonds of the gospel,
Thomas Lewis.

August 1, 1798.

The brethren at the mission made no immediate answer, but held prayer meetings on two successive nights to decide what their reply should be. They were assembled in Brother Jefferson's apartment on the second night when Brother Lewis put in an appearance. After Brother Eyre had said prayers and read the seventh chapter of Joshua, he turned to the delinquent.

'Brother Lewis,' he said, 'the circumstances that gave rise to this church meeting are the many evil reports we all hear of your conduct and behaviour among the female natives of this island. As you sustain the sacred character of a minister of the gospel, a designated missionary to the ignorant, perishing heathen of Otaheite, and a member of our church—we hold it our duty as Christians to demand of you now a faithful declaration of the truth. Have you had carnal connexions with any one of the female natives of this island since the day of our first landing on it?'

'No,' said Brother Lewis, 'I have not.'

'Come now,' said Brother Jefferson, 'remember where you are and before whom. Do not forget that you are in the presence of a heart-searching God.'

'I am not insensible of that,' Brother Lewis said.

'Then have you had any carnal connexions with the female natives of this island?' Brother Eyre repeated.

'No.'

'Then are you willing that the woman with whom you are reported to have had connexions should be brought before me?'

'Yes.'

Brother Lewis was then asked to withdraw while his case was considered. Despite his protestations of innocence, the missionaries adjudged him guilty. Six of them said that the only punishment was excommunication, but Brother Bicknell maintained that suspension from church communion for a short time would be sufficient.

When Brother Lewis was acquainted with the majority decision, he immediately began to raise objections, but the missionaries refused to become involved in an argument. Two days later they sent him a formal letter of excommunication. He replied that they should not be 'too hasty'. Other letters followed in which he attempted to justify his conduct, but the brethren left them all unanswered. Nevertheless, Lewis continued to attend the Sunday services at Matavai even though Brother Jefferson noted with disapproval that he was 'living with a young woman of Ahonoó as his wife'.

Nearly eighteen monotonous months passed—broken only by the visits of two whalers and a Spanish prize. Then, on November 28, 1799, a native came from Ahonu to inform the missionaries that Lewis was dead. They found his body horribly bloated and bruised. He had been murdered, it seemed, after a quarrel with his 'wife's' relations.

The missionaries brought his body back to Matavai and gave him a Christain burial. They were still sorrowing over this affair on December 21 when the British ship, *Betsey*, with a Spanish brig as prize, hove in sight. Two days later, Brother Harris announced his intention of leaving the island in the *Betsey* 'to see how the brethren at Tonga had fared'. He sailed on January 1, 1800, and so the new century began with the mission force reduced to five.

Four days later, however, the little band was unexpectedly reinforced by the return of Brother Henry, one of the missionaries who had fled to Port Jackson in the *Nautilus*. He arrived in the whaler *Eliza* with his wife and daughter, and a number of domestic birds and animals. The missionaries were delighted to see him, but their pleasure was offset when they learned that the *Eliza*'s captain had given Pomare a carronade, two swivels, several muskets, and a great deal of ammunition. This threat to their well-being was increased by the fact that four dissolute sailors remained on shore when the *Eliza* sailed.

Nevertheless, the year 1800 passed without incident until the middle of June when Brother Broomhall announced that he had ceased to believe in the immortality of the soul and refused to submit any longer to the restraints of the Gospel. The brethren tried to reason with him for several weeks, but their words were of no avail and they were finally obliged to draw up their second letter of excommunication. Unlike Brother Lewis, however, Brother Broomhall did not seem to care, and went cheerfully to live with a woman from Raiatea.

Two days before the end of the year, the missionaries received

93

another blow to their shaky morale. The *Albion*, a British whaler from Port Jackson, brought news that the *Duff* had been captured by the French off the South American coast while bringing reinforcements to the Tahitian mission, and that the mission to Tonga had ended in disaster. At Tonga, one of the missionaries had been excommunicated, three had been murdered, and the rest had fled to Port Jackson in the *Betsey*. Meanwhile William Crook, the solitary missionary at the Marquesas, had also fled to the safety of New South Wales.

The prospects for Christianity in Tahiti seemed grim indeed.

22.   FIRST TRADERS

THE *Albion*, under Captain Ebor Bunker, was the first ship to visit Tahiti for the purpose of trade. It had occurred to Captain Philip Gidley King, Governor of the twelve-year-old colony of New South Wales, that the island might be a useful source of food for his frequently underfed people. He had read of Tahiti's abundance of pigs in the voyages of Captain Cook and was curious to know if there was any prospect of establishing a trade in salted pork.

King had supplied Bunker with six yards of red bunting and twelve pounds of Australian-made soap (probably the first Australian exports ever made to a foreign country) to be given as presents to Pomare. Bunker also had two hundred spike nails with which to acquire 'a compleat assortment of curiosities'. In a letter to Brother Jefferson, King requested the missionaries' assistance in obtaining the articles he wanted. In another letter to Pomare, he said that the soap and bunting were only 'a small token' of his future intentions, and he asked Pomare to write to him through the missionaries.

The governor's gifts brought a generous response. Pomare saw to it that the *Albion* was well supplied with hogs, fowls, and fruit, and when the vessel sailed on January 3, 1801, he sent the following letter to his unexpected benefactor:

May it please your Excellency:

Your letter and present I kindly accept. I love King George and his subjects and will, while I live, be a protector to those who put themselves under my care. But I must tell your Excellency, I at this time stand in fear of the commonalty, many of them being disaffected towards me, and their disaffection, I fear, is encouraged by some seamen who are on the island. And therefore I wish your Excellency to present me with a few firearms whereby my authority may be maintained and the peace of my kingdom preserved.

I request of your Excellency to accept of the articles I have sent by Captain Bunker as a token of my goodwill. I hope it will not be long before I have the pleasure of hearing from you again.

I remain,
Your Excellency's friend and humble servant,
Pomare X his mark.

Governor King was apparently impressed by the generally favourable tone of this letter and by Captain Bunker's report for he immediately sent Lieutenant William Scott to barter for hogs in HMS *Porpoise*. The *Porpoise* arrived at Matavai Bay on June 25, 1801, with some specially made robes for Otoo and Pomare. These gifts and a supply of arms and ammunition were handed over in an elaborate ceremony a few days later. The crew of the *Porpoise* then got down to the business for which they had come.

They were still occupied in this on July 10 when the *Royal Admiral* hove in sight. On board were eight new helpers for the mission—John Davies, James Elder, William Scott, Samuel Tessier, John Youl, Charles Wilson, William Waters, and James Hayward. The *Royal Admiral* also brought the first letters the missionaries had received from home for four years as well as a welcome supply of stores. She sailed three weeks later, taking with her 'three wretched runaway seamen' and Brother Broomhall, the excommunicated missionary. The *Porpoise* followed on August 14 with an ample supply of hogs.

The success of the *Porpoise*'s mission encouraged the New South Wales Government to send a second vessel to trade for hogs. This was the armed brig *Norfolk* which anchored at Matavai on

95

January 19, 1802, bringing William Shelley, formerly of Tonga, to reinforce the mission. Her captain had an authorization from Governor King to Brother Jefferson empowering him to act as magistrate and to round up any runaway seamen who proved troublesome. Three other vessels—the *Venus*, *Porpoise* (again), and *Margaret*—arrived from New South Wales before the end of the year on similar errands to the *Norfolk*. But all vessels came to disastrous ends and the Tahiti trade was temporarily abandoned. The *Norfolk* was wrecked in a gale at Matavai two months after her arrival. The *Venus**, after completing one trading mission, was apparently lost on the coast of New Zealand while coming to Tahiti on another. The *Porpoise*, after completing her second mission, was wrecked off the coast of Australia. And the *Margaret* was wrecked in the Palliser Group before any hogs had been obtained.

23. FLIGHT FROM THE MISSION

DURING the visits of the various trading vessels, the Tahitians were almost continuously at war. The cause of this was Otoo's possession of the native idol, Oro, which greatly incensed the chiefs of the other districts. The war continued until the beginning of September, 1802, when Otoo's enemies sued for peace. Their defeat was partly due to the generalship of PeterHagersteine, the Finnish seaman, and partly to the greater number of arms which Otoo had obtained from the trading vessels calling at Matavai.

While the war was going on, the missionaries were confined to the immediate vicinity of the mission house, where they had installed the guns of the shipwrecked *Norfolk* to protect themselves in case of attack. They were frequently in great want of food for the natives regularly plundered their gardens. But despite their setbacks and sufferings, they set out, as soon as the

---

* The *Venus* was commanded and owned by George Bass, discoverer of the strait between Australia and Tasmania now bearing his name.

war was over, to begin preaching tours of the island. They found little to encourage them in their work. Many of the natives told them flatly that they did not want to be taught by them. Others ridiculed every sentence they uttered, or brought dogs or cocks and set them fighting close to the spot where they were holding forth. Sometimes the Areois would begin their games near by, which would immediately distract such natives as had gathered to listen. At other times, the missionaries were told that as England did not produce breadfruit, coconuts, bananas, or arrow-root, it must be a poor country, and they had only come to Tahiti for its provisions.

Even more discouraging to the missionaries was the 'increasing wretchedness of the people and rapid depopulation of the island'. They said in their journals that war, human sacrifices, infanticide, quarrels, and diseases of European origin had carried 'alarm, suffering and death into almost every family' and threatened them with 'speedy and complete annihilation'. After making a complete circuit of the two peninsulas of the island, the missionaries found that the population was less than half of what it had been six years before. They said that despondency seemed to prey on the minds of the chiefs and people, and as they regarded their sufferings as the effects of the displeasure of their gods, human sacrifices were offered to them with increasing frequency.

Another setback to the missionaries at this time was the death of their most faithful ally, Pomare, Otoo's father. Pomare died on September 3, 1803, while paddling his canoe to the English vessel *Dart*, which had arrived from Port Jackson. His name then passed to Otoo, who became—to the missionaries, at least— King Pomare II.

Towards the end of June, 1804, the *Lady Harrington*, a brig of fourteen guns and fifty men, arrived from Port Jackson on a privateering voyage to the coast of South America. On board was a Mr. Caw, who had been sent out to assist the missionaries as shipwright. After a short stay, the *Lady Harrington* continued her voyage to South America. But she returned to the island on December 9 with a Spanish vessel as prize and stayed three weeks purchasing provisions for New South Wales. The missionaries were appalled at the nature of the trading that went on. The native men would not sell their hogs for anything but muskets, and frequently sold hogs worth £30 and £40 for muskets not worth 10s. The women, for their part, were loathe to exchange their 'favours' for anything but gunpowder, and their method of trading netted the island between 300 and 400 lb.

When the *Lady Harrington* sailed on December 29, she carried off Brother William Waters, who had 'exhibited painful symptoms of mental aberration' since his arrival in the *Royal Admiral* three and a half years before. She also took a long letter from Brother Jefferson to the directors of the Missionary Society.

> Civilisation appears to be making but small advances, but perhaps it is wrong to say it is making none. The chiefs are in general very dissolute; and the common people lovers of ease; and both are so much attached to their way of doing things . . . that they do not plainly see the value of improvement. . . . The Gospel has not yet met with a favourable reception among them; neither dare we say that there is any very pleasing prospect that it soon will. Since the death of Pomare, Otoo has maintained his authority without opposition. For the past seven months, he has been residing in Eimeo (Moorea) . . . and he has, by gifts and force, got the greater part of the muskets that were in the hands of the *ratteras* (petty chiefs) there into his own possession. It is rumoured that he expects to do the same in Tahiti when he returns. But it is also said that those who have them are determined not to give them up to him except with loss of life. If the king is resolved on that matter, war, we think, will undoubtedly follow. . . .

The war which the missionaries feared did not eventuate immediately, and during the next two years—1805 and 1806—they were left in peace to work on a Tahitian dictionary. Only five vessels called at the island during that time, three of which added to the natives' supply of muskets and ammunition. The *Hawkesbury*, a small colonial vessel, which reached Matavai on November 25, 1806, brought the missionaries their first letters and stores for over five years. For some time previously, they had had to go about barefooted and to do without such comforts as tea and sugar. The society at home had not forgotten them, but the Napoleonic wars had played havoc with shipping and many of their letters and stores had been lost at sea or had accumulated in New South Wales.

On May 3, 1807, the missionaries sent a copy of a Tahitian catechism and a spelling book to be printed in England by the *Lady Harrington*, which called on her way from Port Jackson. Their chief hope at this time was in a school which they had opened a short time before. But just when it seemed that they might perform some useful work, a new evil overtook the land. The natives succeeded in constructing stills with which they produced a strong liquor from the ti-root. According to the missionaries, drunkenness became so prevalent that it 'threatened to sweep from the face of the earth the few natives that war, infanticide, idolatry and disease had spared'.

Captain Bligh, who had become Governor of New South Wales, did not endear himself to the missionaries when he sent Pomare a musket and some rum, powder, and ball in the *Elizabeth*, which arrived at Matavai on May 12, 1807. The same vessel brought a Mr. Gregory Warner to reinforce the mission. But when she sailed on May 23, she carried off Brother John Youl, who had apparently decided that missionary work was not for him.

On the day the *Elizabeth* sailed, a new native war broke out. Pomare had just learned that one of his enemies in Atehuru had made a fish hook from the bone of a chief of Raiatea who had been killed in the previous war. This sacrilege so incensed him that he descended on Atehuru with a large force determined on vengeance. A large number of Atehuruans were slain and many refugees fled to the mission house. The missionaries said that Pomare seemed 'bent on the entire annihilation' of his enemies. He had the bodies of the slain collected on the sea-beach, and he 'seemed to derive a savage gratification from gazing on them—ordering their bodies to be washed so that he might recognize them more readily'.

The war continued until Pomare had nearly exterminated his enemies in Tahiti-nui and had deprived those of the smaller peninsula of their muskets. The land of the vanquished was then distributed among his friends and favourites.

During the war, the work of the missionaries was again brought more or less to a standstill. The missionaries also received a

99

severe setback when Brother Jefferson, their secretary, died of consumption on September 25, 1807. The mission force was further reduced early in the following year when Brothers Elder and Bicknell left for New South Wales to try to find themselves wives. At this time, about forty natives were attending the mission school at Matavai, but many of them seemed to think they were conferring a favour on the missionaries for which they ought to be paid.

On October 25, 1808, the *Perseverance* anchored at Matavai, having on board Brother Elder and his newly found wife. Mrs. Elder must have been an alluring woman. The missionary record says that the captain of the *Perseverance* shot himself because of his infatuation for her on the night of her arrival.

Eleven days later, while Pomare was blind drunk on the *Perseverance*, news was brought that his enemies at Matavai were assembled in arms. It was learned a little later that they were being joined by natives from the eastern part of the island. As Pomare had little hope of defeating this combined force, he recommended the missionaries to leave the island. The missionaries immediately transferred their wives and children to the *Perseverance*, but they made a final effort to avoid abandoning their station. Two of the brethren tried to get the insurgent chiefs to settle their differences with Pomare by conference. The chiefs, however, refused to meet him except in battle. In these circumstances, all but four of the missionaries decided to sail in the *Perseverance* for Huahine. They quitted Tahiti on November 10. Those who remained were Brothers Hayward, Nott, Scott, and Wilson.

On the night after the *Perseverance* sailed, the remaining four were forced to abandon the mission house and take refuge in Pomare's camp. They remained there until December 22 when Pomare's forces were defeated. They then fled to the neighbouring island of Moorea, where they were soon joined by Pomare. Brothers Hayward, Scott, and Wilson sailed for Huaheine early in the new year to join the other missionaries. Brother Nott was thus left to carry on alone.

After the defeat of Pomare, the insurgent natives plundered the districts of Pare and Matavai. The houses of the missionaries were ransacked and burnt. Their books were either committed to the flames or torn up for cartridge papers. Every implement of iron was converted into an instrument of war. The printing types were melted into musket balls, and most of the missionaries' cattle were destroyed.

A small schooner, the *Venus*, which arrived at Matavai during the plunder, was captured by the natives. They held the captain and crew on board with the intention of sacrificing them to the god, Oro. But before they could carry out their plan, the brig *Hibernia* arrived on the scene and succeeded in rescuing both the vessel and crew. The *Hibernia* and *Venus* then proceeded to Huaheine, where they arrived on October 17, 1809. The story which the missionaries learned from these vessels was the final blow to their shattered hopes of introducing Christianity in Tahiti.

> There is nothing to encourage our continuance in these islands [Brother Davies wrote in his journal]. Our prospect seems to be more and more gloomy. The state of Tahiti is more unfavourable than it has been since the commencement of the war. There is but small probability that Pomare will recover his authority. . . . The common people will be in arms everywhere, and we may expect nothing but anarchy and confusion, and Europeans, as favourers of the chiefs, will be looked upon with an evil eye. We can hardly expect safety anywhere while we have any property left, and even our persons will be in great danger. But leaving the present state of the islands out of the question, we have no inducement whatever for the continuance of the mission. Our time is apparently spent in vain, answering no good purpose either to ourselves or those about us. No one appears desirous of instruction and we must confess that we have no heart to make further use of means . . .

In these circumstances, the missionaries decided to make for Port Jackson. The captain of the *Hibernia*, who was proceeding to China, agreed to take them as far as Fiji for an exorbitant sum and they sailed from Huahine on October 26. But their trials and tribulations were not yet at an end. On the night of November 11, the *Hibernia* struck a reef off an island in the Fijis and all on board awaited the dawn 'with uncommon anxiety of mind'. Despite the pounding of the surf, the vessel did not break up, and when daylight came the missionaries were able to land on a sandy island, about half a mile around. There they fried in a fierce sun for about eight weeks, living on coconuts, fish, and salted pork, and in constant dread of the cannibalistic Fijians.

The *Hibernia* was finally repaired with the help of a carpenter from an American vessel which was collecting sandalwood at an island near by. She sailed to Port Jackson for further repairs on January 9, 1810, and reached there five weeks later. The missionaries immediately wrote to the governor of the colony describing their misfortunes of the preceding twelve years and 'humbly soliciting the privilege of becoming settlers'. The governor gave them what help he could.

'To all human appearance, the Tahitian mission was now at an end,' the missionary record says. 'The attempt to communicate the knowledge of Christianity to an idolatrous and savage nation had been perseveringly and faithfully made for nearly thirteen years and had failed.'

PART IV

INTERLUDE AT PITCAIRN

24. CHRISTIAN'S HIDE-OUT DISCOVERED

In March, 1810—the month following the arrival of the missionaries at Port Jackson—a notice appeared in the English *Quarterly Review* referring to an extraordinary discovery in the South Pacific. The notice said that a Captain Mayhew Folger, master of the American whaler *Topaz*, had discovered the hide-out of Fletcher Christian and his fellow mutineers. The mutineers (there were nine of them) had not been heard of since leaving Tahiti in the *Bounty* on September 24, 1789, with twelve Tahitian and Tubuaian women and six men. The facts of Captain Folger's discovery were these:

In the early days of February, 1808, he had been sailing eastwards across the Pacific in search of seals. At half past one on February 6, he sighted a high, rocky island which seemed to be miles from the position marked on the charts. Yet as there were no other islands in the vicinity, he presumed it was the same island that Captain Carteret had discovered in the *Swallow* after separating from the *Dolphin* in 1767. Carteret had named it Pitcairn Island in honour of the young officer who had first sighted it. Although no landing was made, he had recorded that it appeared to be uninhabited.

To Captain Folger, Pitcairn Island seemed a likely place for seals and he steered the *Topaz* towards it. By 2 a.m. on February 7, he had come within two leagues of it. He then lay offshore until daylight when he put off with two boats to see what he could find.

On approaching the shore, Folger was surprised to see smoke ascending; and on going still closer, he saw a canoe being paddled towards him by three young men. Folger's surprise turned to astonishment when the young men called to him in English, asking who he was. Folger replied that he was an American from Boston, but the young men did not seem to understand this.

'You are an American?' one said. 'You come from America? Where is America? Is it in Ireland?'

Folger did not know what to make of these extraordinary

young men who spoke English but had never heard of America. So he tried a few questions on them.

'Who are you?' he inquired.

'We are Englishmen,' they said.

'Where were you born?'

'On that island which you see.'

'How can you be Englishmen if you were born on that island?'

'We are Englishmen because our father was an Englishman.'

'Who is your father?'

'Aleck.'

'Who is Aleck?'

'Don't you know Aleck?'

'How should I know Aleck?'

'Then, do you know one Captain Bligh in England?'

At the mention of Captain Bligh, the details of the *Bounty* affair flashed into Folger's mind. He made further inquiries and learned that he had stumbled on the refuge of the nine mutineers. The person whom the young men called Aleck was Alexander Smith, the only mutineer still alive on the island.

Eager to learn more, Folger accepted the young men's invitation to go ashore. He was met on the beach by Smith and about thirty other islanders and escorted up a steep slope to Smith's house. There Smith told him an extraordinary story, which he wrote up in his logbook—as well as he could remember it—when he returned on board.

> Smith informed me that after putting Captain Bligh in the long boat and sending her adrift, their commander—Christian—proceeded to Otaheite. There all the mutineers chose to stop except Christian, himself, and seven others. They all took wives at Otaheite and six men as servants and proceeded to Pitcairn Island, where they landed all their goods and chattels, ran the ship, *Bounty*, on shore, and broke her up. This took place, as near as he could recollect, in 1790. Soon after this, one of their party went mad and drowned himself, and another died of fever. After they had remained about four years on the island, their men servants rose upon and killed six of them, leaving only Smith alive—and he, desperately wounded, with a pistol ball in the neck.

However, he and the widows of the deceased arose and put all the servants to death, which left him the only surviving man on the island with eight or nine women and several small children. He immediately went to work tilling the ground so that it now produces plenty for them all, and he lives very comfortably as Commander in Chief of Pitcairn's Island. All the children of the deceased mutineers speak tolerable English. Some of them are grown to the size of men and women, and to do them justice, I think them a very human and hospitable people. Whatever may have been the errors or crimes of Smith, the mutineer, in times back, he is at present, in my opinion, a worthy man and may be useful to navigators who traverse this immense ocean. Such is the history of Christian and his ancestors (sic). Be it remembered that this Island is scantly supplied with fresh water so that it is impossible for a ship to get a supply. . . .

Captain Folger stayed on Pitcairn for five or six hours. As a parting gift, Smith gave him the *Bounty*'s azimuth compass and a Kendall chronometer, which had been used by Captain Cook on the *Resolution*'s last voyage. Folger then sailed eastward to the Spanish island of Mas Afuera and on to Juan Fernandez (Robinson Crusoe's island), where the compass and chronometer were confiscated by the Spanish governor.

In Valparaiso several months later, Folger reported his discovery of the mutineers' hide-out to Lieutenant William Fitzmaurice, of the Royal Navy, who was serving on the Chilean station. Fitzmaurice made an extract of the entry in Folger's logbook, which he sent in a despatch to the commander of the British naval station in Brazil. The despatch was dated October 10, 1808, and contained some additional information from Folger's second mate.

'The second mate of the *Topaz*,' Fitzmaurice wrote, 'asserts that Christian, the ringleader, became insane shortly after their arrival on the island, and threw himself off the rocks into the sea. Another died of fever before the massacre of the remaining six took place.'

The British Admiralty received Fitzmaurice's despatch, through the commander of the Brazilian station, on May 14, 1809. But its contents were not widely publicised until the notice appeared in the *Quarterly Review* ten months later. About the same time an extraordinary incident occurred in England which later threw doubt on the discrepant reports of Folger and his second mate that Christian had died in Pitcairn. The incident involved the former *Bounty* midshipman, Peter Heywood who, after being pardoned in the *Bounty* Court Martial, had rejoined the Royal Navy and had risen to the rank of captain. The incident was made public in 1831—the year after Heywood died—when Sir John Barrow, the Admiralty Secretary, anonymously published the first full-length account of the *Bounty* mutiny.

> About the years 1808 and 1809 [Barrow wrote] a very general opinion was prevalent in the neighbourhood of the lakes of Cumberland and Westmorland that Christian was in that part of the country, and made frequent private visits to an aunt living there. Being the near relative of Mr. Christian Curwen, long member of Parliament for Carlisle, and himself a native, he was well known in the neighbourhood. This, however, might be passed over as mere gossip, had not another circumstance happened at the same time for the truth of which the Editor (Barrow) does not hesitate to avouch.
>
> In Fore-Street, Plymouth Dock, Captain Heywood found himself walking behind a man whose shape had so much the appearance of Christian's that he involuntarily quickened his pace. Both were walking very fast, and the rapid steps behind him having aroused the stranger's attention, he suddenly turned his face, looked at Heywood, and immediately ran off. But the face was as much like Christian's as the back, and Heywood, exceedingly excited, ran also. Both ran as fast as they were able, but the stranger had the advantage, and upon making several short turns, disappeared.

Barrow added that Heywood's first thought was to make further inquiries, but when he realized the pain and trouble that Christian's discovery would cause, he decided to let the matter drop.

Nothing further was heard of Christian or Pitcairn until 1814 when the Admiralty received a letter written in Valparaiso by Sir Thomas Staines, commander of HMS *Briton*. The *Briton*, in company with HMS *Tagus*, had been chasing a marauding American frigate in the South Pacific.

Staines said that on the morning of September 17, 1814, he had fallen in with an island 'where none was laid down in the charts'. To his great astonishment, he found it inhabited by forty English-speaking islanders who proved to be 'the descendents of the deluded crew of the *Bounty*'. 'A venerable old man named John Adams'—for some reason he had changed his name from Alexander Smith—was looked up to as the father of the community. Staines said that the oldest child of the mutineers was Thursday October Christian, who was about twenty-five years old. The elder Christian had 'fallen a sacrifice to the jealousy of an Otaheitan man within three or four years after the mutineers' arrival on the island'. The six Tahitian men had been 'swept away by desperate contentions between them and the Englishmen', and five of the twelve Tahitian and Tubuaian women had died at different periods. Adams and seven women were thus the only survivors of the original community. 'During the whole time they have been on the island,' Staines continued, 'only one ship has ever communicated with them, which took place about six years since, and this was the American ship, *Topaz*, of Boston, Mayhew Folger, master.'

The account of Pitcairn given by Staines was later supplemented by another officer of HMS *Briton*—Lieutenant John Shillibeer, of the Royal Marines, who published *A Narrative of the Briton's Voyage to Pitcairn* in 1817. In Shillibeer's book, there was another reference to the puzzling rumours about Christian's escape. 'For many years,' Shillibeer wrote, 'the ultimate fate of Christian was uncertain. The prevailing opinion was that after he had left and destroyed the *Bounty*, he returned to the coast of South America and entered the Spanish service. It has even been asserted that he had been recognized in that situation, and after the account given by Mayhew Folger, there were many who retained the same opinion. But the matter is at present too clearly demonstrated to admit of a doubt, and those idle tales must now meet the fate they then merited.'

Shillibeer then described the arrival of the *Briton* and *Tagus* at

Pitcairn, where a number of canoes came out to meet them. The first person to come aboard the *Briton* was a young man called McCoy, who inquired whether anyone knew William Bligh. He was immediately asked whether he knew Christian.

'Oh yes,' he said, 'his son is in the boat there coming up. His father is dead now—he was shot by a black fellow while at work in his yam plantation.'

'What became of the man who killed him?'

'Oh, that blackfellow was shot afterwards by an Englishman.'

'Have you ever heard how many years it is since Christian was shot?'

'I understand it was about two years after his arrival at the island.'

'What became of his wife?'

'She died soon after Christian's son was born, and I have heard that Christian took forcibly the wife of one of the black-fellows, which was the chief cause of his being shot.'

Shillibeer's account of the date of Christian's death was thus a year or two different from the one given by Staines, and both versions were contradicted by Captain Pipon, commander of the *Tagus*. Pipon, in a long letter to Sir John Barrow, said that Christian 'was shot by a black man whilst digging in his field. This happened about eleven months after they (the mutineers) were settled on the island, but the exact dates I could not learn.'

Further information about Pitcairn appeared in the *Narrative of Voyages and Travels* of Captain Amasa Delano, a close seafaring friend of Mayhew Folger. Delano's book was published in Boston in 1817. It included two chapters on the *Bounty* affair and a number of details about Pitcairn that had not previously been published. Delano was particularly sore about the discrepant accounts of Christian's death and was anxious to get things right.

'I have lived a considerable time with Capt. Folger,' Delano wrote, 'and he very often conversed with me upon this subject (of the Pitcairn Islanders). Smith (alias Adams) said—and upon this point Capt. Folger was very explicit in his inquiry at the time as well as in his account of it to me—that they lived under Christian's government several years after they landed; that during the whole period they enjoyed tolerable harmony; that Christian became sick and died a *natural death*; and that it was after this that the

Otaheitan men joined in a conspiracy and killed the English husbands of the Otaheitan women . . .'

Thus, within nine years of the rediscovery of Pitcairn, three different stories had been recorded about Christian's death—(1) that he had become insane and jumped into the sea, (2) that he had been murdered by the native men, and (3) that he had died a natural death. The accounts of the date of his death varied from eleven months after his arrival on the island to three or four years after. There were also three accounts of his being seen elsewhere—(1) in the English Lake District, (2) in Plymouth, and (3) in South America.

What did all these contradictory stories mean? Did they mean that Christian had really escaped and that Adams was trying to shield him? Or were they the result of confusion and inaccuracy on the part of the people who wrote them down?

It was not until 1825, when Captain F. W. Beechey visited Pitcairn in HMS *Blossom*, that the mystery of Christian's fate was elucidated and a clear picture obtained of what had happened on the island in the early years. Beechey stayed on the island for several weeks and took down a circumstantial account of the mutineers' history which John Adams signed.

Adams told Beechey that about a month after the mutineers settled on Pitcairn, the wife of John Williams (one of the able-seamen) was killed while searching for birds' eggs. After about two years, Williams became dissatisfied with his wifeless condition and threatened to leave the island unless he was given the wife of one of the native men. This demand outraged the natives and eventually led to orgies of slaughter in which five Englishmen, including Christian, and the six native men were killed. The last massacre took place on October 2, 1793. The mutineers then left alive were Edward Young (a midshipman), William McCoy, Matthew Quintal, and Smith, alias John Adams (seamen). There were also ten women and several children.

About two months after the massacre, Young began a manuscript journal, which he continued until about 1799. The journal was still in existence at the time of Beechey's visit, and one entry proved conclusively that Christian had died on the island. The entry was dated March 12, 1794, and described how Young had seen one of the Tahitian women, whom the mutineers called

Jenny, holding the skull of a dead mutineer. 'I desired it might be buried,' Young wrote, 'but the women who were with Jenny gave me for answer that it should not. . . . Accordingly, when I saw McCoy, Smith and Mat. Quintal, I acquainted them with it, and said I thought that if the girls did not agree to give up the heads of the *five* white men in a peaceable manner, they ought to be taken by force and buried.'

In April, 1796—Beechey's account continued—McCoy succeeded in producing an intoxicating liquor from the ti-root, and some time after Young's journal terminated, he threw himself off a cliff in a fit of delirium. About 1799, Quintal's wife was also killed while searching for birds' eggs, and Quintal became so crazy that he threatened to kill both Adams and Young. Adams and Young therefore felt justified in killing him before he could kill them, and did so with an axe. Young died of asthma in 1800, leaving Adams the only man alive on the island. Adams then became a community husband to the nine remaining women and set about educating the mutineers' nineteen children.

At the time of Captain Beechey's visit, the population of Pitcairn was over sixty. Adams died four years later at the age of sixty-five.

PART V

ONWARD, CHRISTIAN SOLDIERS

25. THE MISSIONARIES RETURN

Towards the end of 1810, the missionaries who had fled from Tahiti in 1808 held a meeting at Port Jackson at which most of them expressed their willingness to return.

The first to take the plunge was Brother Bicknell, who arrived at Moorea with his wife and nephew in July, 1811. He was soon followed by five others—Brothers Henry, Wilson, Davies, Scott, and Hayward. Henry was accompanied by his wife and family; and Davies, Scott, and Hayward by newly married wives—three 'godly young women' who had been sent out to Port Jackson by the London Missionary Society to become their partners in life. The food at Moorea, however, soon put an end to the marital bliss of Henry, Davies, and Hayward. Mrs. Henry died on July 28, 1812; Mrs. Davies on September 4; and Mrs. Hayward on October 4. Meanwhile, Brother Nott, who had remained on Moorea with Pomare since the troublous days of 1808, had gone to Port Jackson to marry a Miss Turner, another envoy of the London Missionary Society. He returned with her to Moorea on October 5.

Despite the tragedies of their private lives, the year 1812 was an encouraging one for the missionaries. Soon after their arrival, Pomare greatly scandalized his attendants by ordering a turtle— a creature previously held sacred to the gods—to be cooked for his own use without offering any part of it to the Polynesian deities. This bold act was followed by a request to the missionaries for Christian baptism—Pomare apparently believing that he might win back his kingdom if backed by the white men's god. In any case, he left for Tahiti soon after to make a new attempt to restore his authority.

While he was gone, the missionaries continued their evangelistic efforts, but progress was slow. Brother Bicknell showed more interest in building a boat and engaging in trade than in his missionary work; Brother Henry left for Port Jackson to look for a new wife; and the others quarrelled among themselves. Brother

Henry's family, which included Nancy Connor, daughter of one of the *Matilda* deserters, were also a menace. Bicknell wrote to a friend:

Nancy (Connor) is a drunkard, a whore, a blasphemer, a deist and a liar; and Sarah has been drunk and is a horrid blasphemer as if she had been used to it for 50 years. She wishes the Bibbel in the fire and all of us in Hell and her father, too; herself also, and Jesus Christ. (She) has cursed the king and the king of Huaheine to his face in such a way as we thought ourselves much exposed to their resentment: we entreated their forgiveness, so it was winked at for the present. She also told a great many natives that we deceived them, that Jehovah was not the true God, but that Oro and Tane was the true gods and much more. It is said that she hath done more harm than ever her father did good in this mission. She also played the whore in her father's house. Samuel is a bad boy; he has no employ; he gets drunk, etc. I hope the young people will be better now their father is gone ...

On September 8, 1813, Pomare was still at Tahiti where, according to the missionaries, he was 'exposed to many and strong temptations, but particularly that of drinking'. Nevertheless, 'his example in publicly renouncing the idol gods and declaring his full conviction of the truth, superiority and excellency of our religion had a powerful effect on the minds of many both at Tahiti and on Moorea'. Brothers Scott and Hayward went over to Tahiti to see how the land lay and found things far more favourable than they expected. Prayer meetings were being conducted at Pare by two natives who had previously lived near the mission house on Moorea. At one such meeting, Scott and Hayward obtained the names of thirty-one natives who wished to receive further religious instruction.

In a letter dated April 23, 1814, the missionaries said: 'Our people whose names are written down are, in general, constant in their attendance on the means of instruction and exact in their observance of the Sabbath. They often retire for secret prayer, and, where a number dwell together, have family prayer in their houses. They are very particular in asking for a blessing on their food, for which they have been much derided. They have also frequent prayer meetings among themselves, and are known among the islanders by the name of "pure atea", or praying people. In a word, they are greatly altered in their moral conduct to what they were some months ago. . . .'

After an absence of nearly two years, Pomare returned to Moorea with a large number of followers, who regularly attended the missionaries' meetings for worship and instruction. Meanwhile, Brothers Henry and Tessier had returned from Port Jackson, where the government chaplain was superintending the printing of a Tahitian catechism, a sketch of the life of Christ, and a summary of Old Testament history. About September, 1814, Brother Nott and one or two other missionaries visited some of the leeward islands of the Society Group for the instruction of the natives. 'Everywhere the desire for instruction is general,' Nott wrote on his return, 'but we are inadequate to the present demands, and the work which we have in hand forbids us to separate.'

By the end of 1814, 2,300 natives were attending the missionaries' prayer meetings, and the number of praying people had increased to 204. The missionaries, however, were unable to begin wholesale baptisms because of the attitude of Pomare. 'The case of Pomare grieves and perplexes us,' they wrote on January 14, 1815. 'He wishes to be baptized previous to the baptizing of any of his people, but we are far—very far—from being satisfied that he is a proper subject. He has an extensive knowledge of the doctrines of the Gospel, but is a slave to drinking. We have repeatedly warned him and spoken very plainly and faithfully to him, but with very little success. Thus are we, and a number of our poor people who may be fit subjects, kept in a disagreeable delay and suspense. . . .'

The missionaries, however, continued to receive encouragement in their work. One night, about the middle of February, 1815, the chief priest of Papetoai, the district of Moorea where they resided, announced that he had embraced the new religion and was going to burn his idol gods. On the following afternoon, the priest and his followers split a quantity of wood and piled it high on the beach near the great *marae*. A large crowd assembled to watch the conflagration. Many of the people expected some terrible calamity to follow, but when nothing happened, the chief priest's example was copied in many other parts of the island and in Tahiti.

Another event of considerable importance to the missionaries occurred on March 28, when Pomare held a feast for a number of chiefs who had recently arrived from the leeward islands. At this feast, a chief called Farefau got up and addressed the Christian God as the giver of all good things and asked his blessing on the food. The assembly, according to the missionaries, was 'thunder-struck', and as the food was no longer suitable for heathen cere-monies, the feast proceeded without them.

Then came the crowning event of the year—the total over-throw of idolatry on Tahiti. This event followed a complicated series of battles between the worshippers of the old gods and the praying people, which resulted in large numbers of the praying people fleeing to Moorea. There they joined the ranks of Pomare, who soon had a following of several thousand. After the refugees had been on Moorea for some months, they were invited to return to Tahiti—according to old Polynesian custom—to take repos-session of their lands.

Pomare set out at the head of his large party towards the end of the year, but on his arrival he was met on the beach by a hostile army of idolaters, who at first opposed his landing. Peace, how-ever, was eventually made, and many of the praying people were able to return to their lands without opposition. Nevertheless, fears and jealousies still existed on both sides. This state of affairs continued until Sunday, November 15, when the heathen party made a sudden and furious assault on Pomare and his people while they were assembled for prayers at Punaauia. Pomare & Co., however, had been warned by the missionaries of the possi-bility of such an attack and had attended the prayer meeting under arms. Although they were temporarily thrown into some confusion, they soon organized to repel their assailants. A bloody encounter ensued and several natives were killed on both sides. It ended in a complete victory for Pomare's party after the leader of the heathen party was slain.

Pomare then gave orders that the vanquished should not be pursued; that their women and children should be well treated; that their property should not be plundered; and that the bodies of those who fell in the battle should be decently buried. These orders, the missionaries said, 'had a happy effect on the minds of the idolaters. They unanimously declared that they would trust their gods no longer; that they had deceived them and sought their ruin; and that henceforward, they would cast them entirely away and embrace the new religion.'

On the evening after the battle, the professors of Christianity 'assembled together to worship and praise Jehovah for the happy turn which their affairs had taken'. In this, they were joined by many of their recent enemies. By universal consent, Pomare was then restored to his former position of supreme chief of the island, after which he nominated chiefs for the various districts.

In this manner, Tahiti became a Christian island. The way was now open for the missionaries to return.

26. HALLELUJAH! HALLELUJAH!

THE period from 1816 to 1826 was a time of intense activity on the part of the missionaries.

Brothers Hayward and Nott returned to Tahiti soon after the victory of Pomare's army and preached to large congregations all over the island. A school, run by Brother Davies on Moorea, attracted nearly seven hundred natives who soon learned to read and write in their own language. Copies of religious books arrived from New South Wales and were widely distributed. Churches were built in every district of the two islands, the Sabbath was strictly observed, and prayer meetings were held every Wednesday night. There were mass conversions on the neighbouring islands of Huahine, Bora Bora, Raiatea, and Tahaa. And Pomare sent the missionaries his heathen idols so they could send them to England.

The rapid spread of Christianity was almost an embarrassment to the small mission band, and their letters home were full of appeals for more workers and more elementary books. At the time of Pomare's victory, only seven of the brethren remained— Brother Scott having died in February, 1815. During the next two years, however, the strength of the mission was brought up to sixteen. William Crook, who had fled to New South Wales after making a lone attempt to christianize the Marquesas, arrived at Moorea on May 8, 1816, having acquired a knowledge of printing in Sydney. Eight other workers—Messrs. William Ellis, J. M. Orsmond, Robert Bourne, Robert Darling, George Platt, John Williams, Charles Barff, and Lancelot Threlkeld—arrived from England with their wives and families in 1817. The standard of education of these new missionaries was generally higher than that of those who had come out in the *Duff*. Ellis, Orsmond, and Williams were men of a particularly high calibre. (Ellis later wrote a book called *Polynesian Researches* which is one of the most useful sources of information on old Polynesian customs; Orsmond collected a great deal of material on early Tahitian history which has since been published by Hawaii's Bishop Museum; and Williams, who wrote a book called *Missionary Enterprises in the South Seas* and was eventually killed by natives at Erromanga, was the most energetic and intrepid missionary in the early history of the Pacific.)

Ellis, who had been carefully instructed as a printer, brought with him a printing press and all the necessary equipment for printing small books. The press was landed at Afareaitu in Moorea on March 26, 1817. Pomare took a keen interest in this press, and pulled the first sheet of any book ever printed in the South Seas on June 30. The book was a spelling primer of which 1,200 copies were run off. An edition of 2,300 copies of the Tahitian catechism was then printed, after which work began on a Tahitian version of the Gospel of St. Luke, as translated by Henry Nott. An edition of 3,000 copies of this was produced in the early part of 1818. Numerous other religious and educational books were printed during the next few years.

Wilson and Tessier returned to Tahiti in 1817 and reopened the mission station at Matavai. Crook and Bicknell opened stations at Papeete and Papara in 1818, and several others were opened a year or two later. In May, 1818, a meeting of two thousand natives decided to form a Tahitian auxiliary of the Missionary Society to aid the parent society in England to send missionaries to other islands. About the same time, the missionaries decided to make the natives pay for their religious books in 'bamboos' of coconut oil. Preparations were also made for sending three of the brethren—Ellis, Williams, and Orsmond—to the leeward islands.

In December, 1817, the missionaries at Moorea launched a brig called the *Haweis* which they had begun building with the help of the natives several years before. The *Haweis* sailed for the leeward islands early in the following June. She was used for the rest of the year to take the missionaries to their new stations and to obtain a cargo of native produce for the colony of New South Wales.

In 1818, a Mr. Gyles, who had been sent out by the Missionary Society, arrived from England to start a sugar plantation and set up a factory for refining the product. The plantation was established at Oponohu on Moorea, but the natives could not be induced to work on it regularly and the scheme fell through. Mr. Gyles departed for New South Wales in 1819. His refining machinery was later shifted to Tahiti by Mr. G. Bicknell, the nephew of the missionary, who succeeded in producing enough sugar for the missionaries' tables.

By the beginning of 1819, the missionaries had obtained considerable sway over the natives and were exerting great influence over Pomare. On May 12 of that year, they won their greatest victory by getting Pomare to promulgate Tahiti's first code of civil laws. The code consisted of fourteen regulations which sought to remove the arbitrary power of the chiefs, increase the power of the missionaries, and stamp out some of the old customs which the missionaries regarded as obnoxious. The penalty of death was prescribed for murder (including child murder); thefts were to be punished by making the thief return a stolen article fourfold; and there were various penalties for the maltreatment of pigs. Persons receiving stolen articles were penalized in the same way as thieves; exile was prescribed for persons inciting war, fights, or sedition; polygamy was prohibited; and marriages were henceforth to be performed by missionaries or native judges. Article 7 of the code exhorted the natives 'not to be obstinate in breaking the Sabbath or in counselling others to do so'. Those who did were to be detailed by the judges to do work for their chiefs.

Six days after the promulgation of the Tahitian Code, Pomare was baptized. From that time onwards, the work of the missionaries was mainly confined to extending and consolidating their power. But although they succeeded in imposing the outward form of Christianity on the natives, they did not effect any change in their hearts and minds. The natives were still as free and easy in sex matters as ever, and the women were easy victims for the foreign seamen who called at the island in increasing numbers. The seamen added to the missionaries' difficulties by selling the natives liquor. Drunkenness became common. One of the worst offenders on this score was Pomare himself, who died in the end of a combination of alcoholism, elephantiasis, and dropsy.

The missionaries also had their own private difficulties. The directors at home refused to recognize that the missionaries required settled and regular salaries, and the result was that they had to 'disgrace their cloth' and 'become a set of trading priests'. The children of the missionaries were also a serious problem. Growing up among the Tahitian children, they learned more about sex and immorality than their parents thought good for them. A brave attempt to remedy this was made in 1824 when the missionaries established a school for them at Moorea with the high-sounding title of 'The South Seas Academy'. The school was far removed from the ports and the chief centres of native life, but it was doomed to failure. The first master, J. M. Orsmond, had no aptitude for schoolteaching, and Alexander Simpson, who followed him in 1831, had even less.

Another missionary enterprise which was doomed to failure was the attempt to establish a cotton plantation and a factory for the spinning and weaving of cloth. The attempt was made by two artisans, Messrs. Blossom and Armitage, who arrived in Tahiti in September, 1821, with all the necessary seeds and machinery. The artisans had been sent out by the London Missionary Society, which had not consulted the resident missionaries about the possible success of their project. The project fell through within two years for the same reason as the sugar plantation had done.

Meanwhile, the missionaries had supplanted the original Tahitian Code with a more stringent one which aimed at reducing the immorality around them. Some of the effects of this code were described by the Russian navigator, Captain Otto von Kotzebue, who visited the island in 1824.

By order of the missionaries [he said] the flute which once awakened innocent pleasures is heard no more. No music but that of psalms is suffered in Tahiti. Dancing, mock-fights and dramatic representations are no longer permitted. Every pleasure is punished as a sin among a people whom Nature destined to the most cheerful enjoyment.

Although the vice of theft has certainly greatly diminished, the Tahitians cannot always refrain from endeavouring to appropriate the articles they prize so highly. Every theft, however, is punished without distinction of persons, and the criminal, on conviction, is generally sentenced to work on the highway. A road has been made round the island on which those who have committed transgressions are condemned to labour. But it is probable that neglect of prayer or any trifling offence against the missionaries would entail this punishment upon them. It appears certain, at all events, that thefts do not take place oftener than among civilized nations.

With the chastity of the Tahitian women, the case is similar and it does not appear to me that the breaches of this virtue are more frequent on the whole than in Europe. It was with the utmost caution and secrecy, and in the most fearful anxiety lest their errors should be betrayed to the missionaries, that the females complied with the desires of our sailors.

To pray and obey are the only commands laid upon an oppressed people, who submissively bow to the yoke and even suffer themselves to be driven to prayers by the cudgel. A police officer is especially appointed to enforce the prescribed attendance upon the church and prayer meetings. I saw him in the exercise of his functions armed with a bamboo cane, driving his herd to the spiritual pasture. He seemed himself, to be conscious of the burlesque attaching to his office—at least, he behaved very absurdly in it and many a stroke fell rather in jest than in earnest. The drollery of the driver did not, however, enliven the dejected countenance of his flock.

It is true that the religion of the missionaries has, with a great deal of evil, effected some good. It has abolished heathen superstitions and an irrational worship, but it has introduced new errors in their stead. It has restrained the vices of theft and incontinence, but it has given birth to bigotry, hypocrisy and a hatred and contempt for all other modes of faith. . . . It has put an end to avowed human sacrifices, but many more human beings have been actually sacrificed to it than ever were to their heathen gods.

Captain F. W. Beechey, commander of HMS *Blossom*, who visited Tahiti in 1826, shared the opinions of Captain von Kotzebue in many respects. 'Whoever framed the laws,' he said, 'would have more effectually attained his object had the amusements been restricted within proper limits rather than entirely suppressed. . . . Without amusements and excessively indolent, the natives now seek enjoyment in idleness and sensuality, and too much pains cannot be bestowed to rouse them from their apathy, and to induce them to emerge from their general state of indifference to those occupations which are most essential to their welfare. . . . Had (the missionaries) taught them such parts of the Christian religion as were intelligible to their simple understandings and were conducive to their moral improvement and domestic comfort, these zealous and really praiseworthy men would have made greater advances towards the attainment of their object.'

27. OF POLITICS AND OTHER MATTERS

ONE of the first pupils at the missionaries' South Seas Academy on Moorea was young Pomare III, who succeeded to the kingship when his father died on December 7, 1821. Pomare III, who was only one year old when he became King, was crowned by the missionaries in an elaborate, British-style ceremony in 1824. The missionaries hoped that under their tuition

Captain Samuel Wallis, of HMS *Dolphin,* formally meets the chiefess Purea, whom the Englishmen knew as Queen Oberea. From an engraving in Hawkesworth's *Voyages.*

Captain Cook.

Bougainville.

HMS *Pandora* goes down on the Great Barrier Reef on the morning of August 29, 1791. The drawing was made from a sketch by Midshipman Peter Heywood, of the *Bounty*, who was one of the last prisoners to escape from "Pandora's Box". The *Pandora's* four boats can be seen astern of the ship.

Omai, after a painting by
Sir Joshua Reynolds.

Captain Bligh, from a
portrait by J. A.
Russell.

Cession of land at Matavai to the first missionaries. The chief, Hitihiti,
kneeling at the left. Otoo (Pomare II) and his wife, Idia, are borne o
men's shoulders. On the right are Mrs. Rowland Hassall and her tw
children, and William and James Wilson of the *Duff,* with missionari
standing behind them. The Swedish deserter, Peter Hagersteine, who acte
as interpreter, is the fair-headed man in the centre of the picture. The scer
was painted by Robert Smirke from a sketch by William Wilson.

Pagan idols being destroyed and a church being built at Tahiti after th
Tahitians' conversion to Christianity. An engraving in *Missionary Sketche*
July, 1819.

and guidance, he would grow up to be 'a wise, God-fearing man and a good ruler'. In the meantime, they were seriously alarmed by the growing numbers of riff-raff whaling seamen who were coming to Tahiti, playing havoc with the natives' morals and disregarding the island's laws. They were also afraid that a foreign power might decide to annex Tahiti as a repair base for its whaling vessels. For these reasons, the missionaries wrote a petition to King George IV in the young King's name asking for British protection and for permission to use the British flag.

The young King's petition, which was dated October 5, 1825, was taken to England by the missionary Henry Nott, who was going home for his first leave in nearly thirty years. About ten months after Nott sailed, Tahiti was visited by an American warship, the *Peacock*, which came to the island for the very purpose the missionaries had feared. At least, its purpose was to obtain a preliminary foothold in Tahiti. American whaling and trading interests had become alarmed at the growth of British interests in the islands and had induced the US Government to despatch the *Peacock* to impress native rulers with American might, and, where possible, enter into agreements with them. The *Peacock*'s commander, Captain ap Catesby Jones, obtained an agreement with six-year-old Pomare III through the interference and persuasion of J. M. Orsmond, who was then master at the South Seas Academy. Under the agreement, Pomare promised to protect US ships and citizens and allow them to trade freely.

According to Thomas Elley, who had just been appointed British Vice-Consul in Tahiti, the negotiations for the agreement were conducted in the 'utmost secrecy'. He told the Foreign Office that the principal chiefs of the island were greatly alarmed over the agreement and were afraid it would give offence to the British Government. 'They have requested me,' he said, 'to assure His Majesty's ministers that they were wholly unacquainted with the transaction, that they disapprove of the measures adopted by the missionary, Orsmond, and highly censure his conduct.'

Pomare's agreement with the US caused little concern at the Foreign Office, but it excited considerable alarm in New South Wales. The *Sydney Gazette*, in a leading article, said that the 'American wish to obtain bases in the Pacific was not unconnected with the intention of attacking the Australian settlements'. The US was also accused of encroaching on the 'innumerable islands that bespeck that ocean, of which Australia is destined to hold material sway'. The *Gazette* recommended that action should be taken to maintain British predominance against American and French threats.

The British Government thought otherwise. When Nott presented Pomare's request to the Foreign Secretary (Mr. George Canning), he received a very lukewarm reply. 'His Majesty commands me to acquaint you,' Canning said, 'that consistently with the usages established among the nations of Europe, it would be improper to grant the permission you solicit to use the British flag. However . . . he will be happy to afford to yourself and to your dominions all such protection as His Majesty can grant to a friendly Power at so remote a distance from his kingdoms. . . .'

Meanwhile, young Pomare had died in an influenza epidemic and the sovereignty of Tahiti had passed to his fourteen-year-old sister Aimata, who took the title of Queen Pomare IV. The new Queen was just at the age when Polynesian girls 'go wild' and devote themselves to songs, dances, amusements, and sport. Abandoning the government to the chiefs, she spent her days and nights having fun with boys and girls of her own age. Her example threatened to destroy the work of the missionaries, and it set the island in a ferment.

Elley, the British Vice-Consul, gave an account of the situation to the Foreign Office on February 8, 1827. 'I am necessitated to be constantly armed,' he said, 'to protect my person from acts of violence, and if a vessel of war does not speedily arrive to assist and support me, I shall be compelled to quit my station as I am in constant danger of being murdered by the lawless savages. The crews of whalers and other vessels touching here, as well as the disaffected Europeans who reside on this island, endeavour to take advantage of its disturbed state. . . .'

Seven weeks later, Elley reported on the situation in even stronger terms:

The true character of the Otaheitans, which has been for some years masked beneath the garb of religion, is now developing itself in strong colours [he said]. When Pomare

II, with all the zeal of a new convert, compelled his subjects with spear and firebrand to abjure their religion, the missionaries believed they had made real converts of men who were thus suddenly driven from the deepest shades of bigoted heathenism. But the illusion is now vanishing. Two-thirds of the population of this island are lawless unprincipled ruffians who are openly and determinedly opposed to the missionary cause, and the other portion chiefly consists of bigoted, fanatical hypocrites, devoid of both religion and morality.

The evils which arise from the want of an efficient person at the head of the government are incalculable. The laws are broken and trampled upon; the most daring outrages are committed at midday; and neither person nor property can be, at any time, considered safe or secure from acts of violence. . . . The lawless vagabonds are daily increasing in strength and insolence. They openly declare their intentions of overturning the government and murdering the Europeans. . . . Their attempts have been hitherto rendered abortive by the active vigilance of a few principal chiefs. The missionaries are at all times prompt in rendering me their assistance, but they possess little influence with the natives and have not the power of being essentially serviceable. . . .'

Elley added that he was quitting Tahiti for Huaheine until a British warship arrived and restored order.

During this period of lawlessness, a sect called Mamaia was formed by the natives. Its object was to abolish the laws promulgated by Pomare II and to revive some of the old savage practices under a cloak of religion, part Christian, part heathen. Members of the sect were given to much prayer to the Unseen and were grossly immoral. The young Queen came under their influence for a while, and for the time being, the missionaries were helpless. They became so discouraged in their work that they seriously considered abandoning Tahiti and continuing their labours elsewhere. Two of their number were sent to the Marquesas and Austral Islands in March, 1829, to investigate possible new fields. They returned two months later and advised the others to stay where they were.

The riotous behaviour of the natives continued throughout 1829 and the following two years. It was at this unfortunate period of Tahitian history that two British naval vessels arrived bringing the eighty-seven descendants of the *Bounty* mutineers from Pitcairn. Before old John Adams died in 1829, he had told Captain Beechey that he was afraid the Pitcairners might have to be moved for lack of water. Beechey had reported the matter to the Admiralty which sent a sloop and a transport vessel to take the Pitcairners to Tahiti. The two vessels arrived in February, 1831. Their passengers were given land on which to make new homes, but the disordered state of Tahiti made them ill at ease, and they soon yearned for their own island. They were also assailed by a variety of illnesses and twelve of them died. Among the twelve was Thursday October Christian, Fletcher Christian's eldest son. By September, 1831, they were so homesick and heartsick that a number of foreign residents, led by George Pritchard, the resident missionary at Papeete, subscribed to a fund which enabled them to be sent home.

From that time onwards, George Pritchard played a leading role in Tahitian affairs. As Papeete had become the seat of the Tahitian Government and the most frequented port of the island, his station was easily the most important Of the twelve missionaries then residing in Tahiti and Moorea, Pritchard was the best equipped to occupy it. He had had a good general education; was generous; and had acquired—after seven years in Tahiti—an excellent knowledge of the native language. He was a strong-willed man; a little narrow-minded, perhaps; but a zealous and tireless worker in the cause of Christianity. His all-round ability and strength of character placed him head and shoulders above the other missionaries.

It was largely through Pritchard's efforts that the Mamaia sect was abolished and the Queen was induced to give up her dissolute ways and take an interest in the government. As Pritchard gradually brought the Queen to heel, all the missionaries tried hard to enforce the laws against the sale of liquor and so prevent the rampant drunkenness. Temperance societies were formed in the two islands, and the missionaries got the natives to join them.

On April 7, 1834, Nott recorded that the Queen, her husband, and all the royal family had signed the pledge. Towards the end of the same year, two laws of special importance were passed. One made attendance at church compulsory, and the other prohibited the importation of spirits. The object of the first law was not only to improve church attendance but to prevent bad characters from loitering about and robbing the houses of those who were at worship.

Under a more settled and sober state of things, Tahiti developed a prosperous trade. The great whaling era of the Pacific was in full swing. The numerous English and American whaling vessels calling at the island created a big demand for supplies which the natives profited by. Many of the native men also earned money as shipwrights, blacksmiths, carpenters, and joiners when the ships were in need of repairs. Most of the trade of the island, however, was in the hands of the missionaries and the many foreigners who had settled there. The chief items of export were pearl shell, sugar, coconut oil, and arrow-root, and the chief imports hardware and cloth. Schooners and sloops were employed in collecting and distributing articles of trade between Tahiti and all the neighbouring islands, and their voyages sometimes extended to South America and New South Wales. A visitor in 1834 said that Tahiti was second only to Oahu, Hawaii, in commercial importance among the islands of the Pacific.

One of the foreign traders who settled in Tahiti around this time was Jacques Antoine Moerenhout, a Belgian, who was destined to play an important role in Tahitian history. Moerenhout had migrated to Chile in 1826 to become secretary to a Santiago merchant who was also Consul for the Netherlands. After making two visits to Tahiti and the surrounding islands between 1828 and 1831 in search of island produce for his employer, Moerenhout settled in Tahiti as an independent trader. There he wrote a book called *Voyage aux Îles du Grand Océan* which he took to Paris in 1835 to see through the press. On his return to Tahiti, he travelled via the United States where he was appointed American Consul in the Society Islands.

The missionaries—particularly Pritchard—and a number of other British residents were seriously alarmed to hear of the appointment when Moerenhout returned to Tahiti in January,

1836. Thinking that it might herald a new American move to obtain a foothold on the island, Pritchard got the Queen and four principal chiefs to write a letter to the British Foreign Office asking that he be appointed Consul for Great Britain. A similar petition was signed by twenty-four British residents. Pritchard also wrote to the Foreign Office himself pointing out that since the departure of Thomas Elley he had frequently undertaken the duties of Consul. His claims to the appointment were later supported by Captain Robert Fitzroy, who had visited Tahiti in HMS *Beagle* in November, 1835. Fitzroy, when asked by the Foreign Office, said that Pritchard was 'decidedly the best qualified to act as Consul of all the Britishers on the island'. 'Of his integrity and thoroughly estimable character, I have good reason to think highly,' he said.

Another member of the *Beagle* who spoke well of Mr. Pritchard was Charles Darwin, the biologist, who later won fame for his revolutionary theory on the origin of species. Some of Darwin's comments on other matters were equally favourable. 'I was pleased with nothing so much as the inhabitants,' he said. 'There is a mildness in the expression of their countenance which at once banishes the idea of a savage, and an intelligence which shows they are advancing in civilization. Their dress is as yet incongruous—no settled costume having taken the place of the ancient one. But even in its present state, it is far from being so ridiculous as it has been described by travellers of a few years standing. . . . Most of the men are tattooed, and the ornaments follow the curvature of the body so gracefully that they have a very pleasing and elegant effect.'

Darwin said he was disappointed in the personal appearance of the women, but he thought their custom of wearing white or scarlet flowers at the back of the head or through a small hole in the ear was pretty. He spoke favourably of the law prohibiting the sale of liquor.

When one reflects on the effect of intemperance of the aborigines of the two Americas I think it will be acknowledged that every well-wisher of Tahiti owes no common debt of gratitude to the missionaries. On the whole, it appears to me that the morality and religion of the inhabitants is highly creditable. There are many who attack even more acrimoniously than Kotzebue the missionaries, their system, and the effect produced by it. Such reasoners, however, never compare the present state with that of the island only twenty years ago; nor even with that of Europe at this day; but they compare it with the high standard of Gospel perfection. They expect the missionaries to effect that which the Apostles themselves failed to do. They forget or will not remember that human sacrifices, the power of an idolatrous priesthood, a system of profligacy unparalleled in the world, infanticide . . . and bloody wars, where the conquerors spared neither women nor children . . . have all been abolished and that dishonesty, intemperance and licentiousness have been greatly reduced by the introduction of Christianity.

Part VI

THE FRENCH PROTECTORATE

28. AN IRISH SPY

THE Protestant missionaries had been established in Tahiti for almost forty years when a small band of Catholic missionaries landed on the island of Mangareva, nine hundred miles away. Their arrival in the Pacific was the beginning of a series of events which brought England and France to the brink of war; contributed to the downfall of the French monarchy; and led to the seizure by France of almost all islands in the eastern South Pacific.

The Catholic missionaries belonged to the Society of Picpus. This society was founded in France in 1814 with the object of 're-animating the Catholic faith at home and propagating it among the infidels'. A decree of propaganda, confirmed by Pope Leo in June, 1833, entrusted it with the task of catholicizing all the islands of the Pacific from Hawaii to the Antarctic Circle, and from Easter Island to the non-existent archipelago of Roggewein. After the decree, M. Etienne Rochouse was named Vicar Apostolic of Eastern Oceania with the title of Bishop of Nilopolis. M. Chrysostome Liansu was made Prefect Apostolic. Three others were named as assistants. They were Fathers François d'Assise Caret and Louis Jacques Laval, and an Irish catechist, Colomban Murphy. These three, together with Liansu, set out from France early in 1834 to begin their mission. When the Bishop of Nilopolis joined them at Mangareva in May, 1835, Colomban Murphy was sent to Tahiti to investigate the prospects of disseminating the Catholic faith.

Murphy, disguised as a carpenter, arrived in the schooner *Peruvian* on May 21. He wore a thick, black beard, smoked a 'cutty' pipe, and told the story that he was travelling to Hawaii in search of work. But the missionaries soon learned what his real intention was, and—jealous of the powerful and profitable positions they had obtained for themselves as well as out of narrow-minded bigotry—they refused, at first, to let him land. The Queen, on Pritchard's advice, sent a messenger to the captain of the

Peruvian to inform him of the law that no passengers could be landed without the permission of herself and the principal chiefs. Murphy protested at this and threatened to write to the British Government. But he was not allowed to come ashore until June 28 when the brig *Harmony* arrived in port on her way to his pretended destination of Hawaii. He remained in Tahiti until the end of July when the *Harmony* sailed.

Meanwhile, Pritchard had written to the British Foreign Office giving an account of Murphy's arrival and trying to justify the missionaries' attitude towards emissaries of another faith. 'It appears to us unreasonable, ungentlemanly and un-Christian,' he said, 'for a body of Roman Catholics to come to these shores and enter into other men's labours. If these gentlemen are anxious to do good amongst the heathen, why not look out for new fields of labour? There are many islands in these seas where they can give full scope to their philanthropic exertions without interfering with the labours of others. If these gentlemen were allowed to reside on this island, numerous evils would immediately follow. There are, at present, a number of natives who are anxious to throw off all restraint. These would unite with the Roman Catholics and form a party who would bid defiance to the civil authorities and involve the island in war and bloodshed. . . .'

Pritchard's words were more prophetic than he knew, and it was not long before the island was visited by the 'numerous evils' that he predicted. Murphy had informed the Bishop of Nilopolis that several chiefs had told him that the Catholic missionaries would be welcome on their island. . . .

29. MEDDLESOME PRIESTS

O N November 6, 1836, the Bishop of Nilopolis sent Fathers Caret and Laval to Tahiti to establish a Catholic mission. They sailed in the schooner *Eliza*, owned by a member of their own faith, Captain William Hamilton. A brig, which had refused to give them a passage, left Mangareva for Tahiti on the same day.

The brig reached her destination several days before the *Eliza* and gave warning of the impending arrival of the priests. Pritchard got the Queen to call a meeting of chiefs in Papeete at which they were told that the priests were not to be allowed to come ashore. Pritchard also wrote to the British Foreign Office asking whether the Queen could be compelled by any government to receive any foreigners she did not want. The Queen wrote a similar letter—probably at Pritchard's dictation.

On November 20, the *Eliza*, which had been delayed by contrary winds after visiting Anaa, put into Tautira on the northeastern side of Tahiti-iti—the port most distant from Papeete. The two priests made haste to get ashore in the canoe of a Swede who lived in the neighbourhood. It was well for them that they did for they had 'scarcely given the kiss of peace to the benighted island' when a chief went aboard to tell the captain that no passengers could be landed without permission. Finding that the priests had already landed, he sought them out on shore and ordered them to return on board. When the priests refused, the chief did not insist.

After spending the night in the house of the Swede, the priests set out to walk the sixty-odd miles to Papeete in company with three natives who had come with them. According to their own account, they were greeted by large numbers of natives at every village, many of whom were bitterly critical of the Protestant missionaries. Paraita, the chief judge of the island, told them to see the Queen and inform her that he would be glad to have them settle in Tahiti.

The priests reached Papeete on the night of November 22. They immediately called on M. Moerenhout, the American Consul, and presented a letter of introduction from their bishop. Moerenhout, who was a Catholic, put them up in a house next to the consulate. They had scarcely moved in when a messenger came from the Queen to inform them that they could not remain and that the *Eliza*, which had arrived in the meantime from Tautira, would not be allowed to land their baggage. Moerenhout replied: 'These gentlemen wish to see the Queen. I have no other answer to give.'

During the next few days, the priests were visited by a number of chiefs. According to Father Caret, the chiefs were 'delighted' to see them and said they were sure they would be allowed to stay unless the Protestant missionaries compelled the Queen to send them away. One of the chiefs, Hitoti, even brought a trunk for them from the *Eliza*.

The priests had an interview with the Queen on November 25. It is impossible to know exactly what took place at this interview as Pritchard and the priests gave entirely different accounts of it. Caret said that the Queen accepted a shawl and four ounces of gold which were offered to her as presents. Pritchard said that the presents were refused. All accounts indicate, however, that the Queen asked the priests to leave, that the priests refused, and that the interview ended inconclusively.

A public meeting on November 27 to discuss the position of the priests was equally inconclusive. One of the native judges said that the laws of the island prevented the priests from remaining in Tahiti without permission. The priests replied that the law was of such recent date that even the American Consul was unaware of it. Moerenhout confirmed this and said that the prohibition against the priests was 'against the law of nations' and 'an insult to America'. The priests asked to be allowed to stay until a warship arrived to decide their case. But the meeting broke up without a decision being reached.

Next day, however, the priests received a letter from the Queen ordering them to leave the island in the *Eliza*. The priests again refused to go. They then learned that preparations were in hand to place them aboard the *Eliza* by force. At this, they drew up a declaration protesting against the 'threatened violence' and holding the Tahitian Government responsible to France for any 'losses and inconveniences' they suffered. The declaration was handed to Moerenhout and a copy sent to the Queen.

Five or six natives arrived at the priests' house on December 11 and again requested them to leave. When they reiterated their refusal to do so, the natives threatened to break the door down. But they went away without carrying out their threat. Next morning, a French carpenter warned them that 'the police of Mr. Pritchard' were coming to enter their house through the roof in order to take them away by force. Soon after, the priests noticed an officer in military uniform and several native assistants approaching the house followed by 'a large crowd of idle spectators'.

'Aware that the last moment was at hand', the priests barricaded the door, closed the windows, and 'retired to the most hidden part of the house' to say the seven penitential psalms. They were praying on their knees when there was a loud knock on the door. The priests ignored it, and 'continued to implore mercy and resignation from Heaven'. Presently, 'an opening was effected through the roof' and the 'pretended agents of the Queen' descended. The priests were given a last chance to go peacefully. They were then seized and carried ignominiously to a canoe which was waiting to take them out to the *Eliza*. Caret said that Moerenhout met them on the way with tears in his eyes.

'Gentlemen,' the Consul said, 'I cannot prevent this outrageous treatment for I have no armed forces at my command; but it shall one day be known that I am Consul for the United States.'

One of the priests replied in a melodramatic apostrophe to the natives.

'Behold!' he said, 'the man who has always protected us against persecutors—persecutors whose mission obliges them to preach charity. We are fully satisfied that you are not the authors of our sufferings.'

The two priests were then placed in the canoe and paddled out to the *Eliza*. The *Eliza* sailed the same day.

Four days later, Captain Lord Edward Russell arrived in HMS *Actaeon* and a public meeting was held to discuss the priests' expulsion. The meeting was attended by a large number of natives, several missionaries, including Pritchard, and M. Moerenhout. Moerenhout produced a declaration from several chiefs stating that the priests had been expelled on Pritchard's orders. Pritchard hotly denied this, called Moerenhout some unpleasant names, and obliged him to leave the meeting. Russell tried to restore order by saying that the Caret-Laval affair was closed, and that the Queen should write to the President of the United States if Moerenhout gave further trouble. But the matter did not rest there.

On December 22, Moerenhout wrote a highly coloured account of the priests' expulsion to the French Consul-General in Chile in which he described it as 'a cruel and savage act worthy of the king of the vandals'. He inferred that Pritchard was entirely responsible. Moerenhout sent the priests' declaration of protest in a second letter on December 27. The Consul-General duly transmitted the two letters to the French Government.

When Pritchard learned of Moerenhout's activities, he wrote to the US Secretary of State asking for an impartial investigation into the whole affair and suggesting that a more suitable person be appointed as Consul. Queen Pomare supported Pritchard in a letter to the US President. Both letters were dated December 31. Thus ended the year 1836, and thus—in a remote corner of the world—began a conflict which was to throw England and France into turmoil.

30. GUNBOAT DIPLOMACY

FOR the next eighteen months or so, affairs in Tahiti were generally quiet. The French priests at Mangareva made only one more attempt to establish themselves on the island. This occurred at the end of January, 1837, when Father Caret, with another priest called Maigret, arrived in Papeete in an American vessel and requested the Queen's permission to land. When the request was refused, the ship's captain attempted to land the priests in a boat, but the natives waded into the sea and prevented the boat from reaching the shore.

The only other important political event of the year 1837 was the appointment of Pritchard as British Consul. The Foreign Office told Pritchard that he would have to resign from the London Missionary Society. Pritchard did this, but he continued for a time to preach in Papeete as an independent pastor.

Meanwhile, the French Government had received the two letters from Moerenhout on the Caret-Laval affair, and had decided that the 'scandalous treatment' of the two priests could not go unpunished. In a letter dated June 10, 1837, M. Rosamel, the French Minister of Marine, ordered Captain Abel Du Petit-Thouars to proceed to Tahiti in his frigate *Venus* to demand 'a full reparation' from the Queen for 'the insult done to France in the person of our compatriots'. The letter suggested that Du Petit-

The victor, the vanquished, and the pawn in the struggle for Tahiti in the mid-nineteenth century. RIGHT: Rear-Admiral Du Petit-Thouars, of France. ABOVE: George Pritchard, the British Consul. BELOW: Queen Pomare.

Tahiti's capital, Papeete, is a perennially popular port for cruising yachtsmen from all over the world, and it is rare for fewer than a dozen yachts to be tied stern to quay right in the centre of town.

The development of Tahiti's tourist industry in recent years has provided plenty of scope for the Tahitians' love of dancing, music and merry-making. The hollow wooden drums in the picture at left are called *toeres*. The photo opposite is by courtesy of Air New Zealand.

Since Papeete became a key centre for France's nuclear testing project at Mururoa Atoll in recent years, its harbour facilities have been greatly extended by reclaiming about 35 acres of coral reef from the sea at a cost of about $A6 million. Motu Uta, the little harbour islet, where the French flag was first raised in 1842, has been almost obliterated in the process. A few of Motu Uta's trees can be seen near the ship at right in the lower photograph. In the top picture (courtesy of Qantas), Matavai Bay, where the early explorers anchored, can be seen at the far left with Point Venus behind it.

Thouars should confer with Moerenhout to determine the kind of satisfaction that should be demanded. Du Petit-Thouars, who was making a survey of Pacific whale fisheries for the French Government, received the Minister's instructions in Valparaiso in June, 1838. He sailed for Tahiti almost immediately and anchored in Papeete on August 29.

Du Petit-Thouars called on Moerenhout soon after he arrived. Moerenhout was not in a happy mood. He had just received his notice of dismissal as American Consul. His wife was desperately ill, and he himself was recovering from some severe injuries. He and his wife had been attacked by two foreign ruffians who broke into their house on the night of June 9.

It is not known what advice Moerenhout gave to the French commander, but he obviously suggested that Du Petit-Thouars should not be lenient in demanding reparation for the 'outrages' against the Catholic priests. In an ultimatum sent to the Queen at ten o'clock next morning, Du Petit-Thouars threatened to declare war unless the following demands were met within twenty-four hours:

(1) That the Queen write a letter to the King of France in French and Tahitian apologizing for the 'insults' against French citizens.

(2) That an indemnity of 2,000 Spanish dollars be paid for the losses suffered by Caret and Laval.

(3) That the French flag be hoisted on the island of Motu-utu in Papeete harbour and saluted with twenty-one guns.

The ultimatum added that the French King and Government had been 'justly irritated' by the 'cruel treatment' towards French citizens, and that French vessels calling at the Society Islands would not cease hostilities until reparation was made.

Queen Pomare sent an immediate acknowledgement to this ultimatum, but she later informed Du Petit-Thouars, through Pritchard, that she could not comply with two of the conditions. She said she could not pay the fine of 2,000 Spanish dollars because the Tahitian treasury did not contain so much money, and that she could not salute the French flag on Motu-utu because she had neither the flag nor the powder. Du Petit-Thouars, however, was not to be put off by excuses, and the three conditions of the ultimatum were finally met. Queen Pomare wrote the letter of apology; Pritchard and two other English residents put up the 2,000 Spanish dollars; and Du Petit-Thouars himself provided the flag and powder for the salute.

Peace having thus been restored, the French commander wrote to the Queen requesting an audience. This was granted at 10 a.m. on September 4 in the principal church—four hundred natives and a number of missionaries being present. Du Petit-Thouars presented Moerenhout to the Queen and asked her to accept him as the first Consul for France. The Queen replied that she would rather have someone else, but climbed down under further threats. The French Commander then proposed that a treaty of perpetual peace be drawn up between Tahiti and France, and this was done in the Queen's palace later in the day. The treaty gave Frenchmen 'of every profession' the right to 'go and come freely, to establish themselves, and to trade in all the islands composing the Government of Tahiti'. It also proposed that they should be 'received and protected as the most favoured foreigners'. Du Petit-Thouars pointed out, however, that 'it was competent to Her Majesty to enact a law forbidding the teaching of Roman Catholic doctrines in her dominions'.

Having made this magnanimous gesture, the French commander's work was complete. But before he sailed for Sydney on September 17, two other French ships—the corvettes *Astrolabe* and *Zelee*, under Captain Dumont d'Urville—put into port. The timing of their arrival was unpremeditated, and their purpose was merely to check instruments and obtain provisions. But their appearance served to impress on the terrified Tahitians that France was not a nation to be trifled with.

Fortunately for Tahitian morale, the terrible 'Wee-wees' had barely departed when a reassuring British warship—HMS *Fly*—hove in sight. The commander, Captain Russell Elliott, was soon acquainted with the activities of the French, and he advised that the law suggested by Du Petit-Thouars forbidding the teaching of Roman Catholic doctrines should be enacted without delay. The law was passed on November 8, 1838, at a special meeting of the Tahitian Legislative Assembly. On the same day, Queen Pomare and four of the principal chiefs wrote to Queen Victoria asking for British protection. 'Lend us your powerful hand,' they wrote. 'Take us under your protection; let your flag cover us and your lion defend us. Determine the form through which we could shelter ourselves lawfully under your wings. Cause our children to bless you and to cherish your Christian feelings as we do. May the great Jehovah preserve you and recompense you for all you do in our behalf.'

The Queen's letter was carried to England by Captain Elliott, but it was nearly a year before the Foreign Secretary, Lord Palmerston, replied on Queen Victoria's behalf. Meanwhile, Tahiti was visited by another terrible 'Wee-wee' in the shape of Captain Cyril Pierre Théodore La Place, commander of the frigate *Artémise*. La Place, with instructions from the French Government received in Sydney, arrived off Tahiti on April 24, 1839. His mission was to 'show the flag' and obtain further concessions for France.

Had it not been for the assistance of the natives, La Place's mission would have ended in disaster. On the night of April 24, his vessel went aground on a coral bank on the north-east coast and was soon in great distress. But she was saved from sinking by 120 friendly natives who came off from the island to work at the pumps and, with the help of an English pilot, she reached Papeete on the following day. Queen Pomare fled to the opposite end of the island as soon as the vessel appeared.

During the next six weeks, the *Artémise* was careened for repair, and La Place obtained permission from the chiefs to cut down whatever trees he needed to make planks. The French sailors were billeted ashore in native houses, where they indulged in the greatest riot of debauchery since the visit of the *Bounty*. La Place held frequent conferences with Moerenhout, from whom he was pleased to learn that Pritchard, the British Consul, was in England on leave. Moerenhout said that with Pritchard out of the way, it would be easy for France to make Tahiti a protectorate. But the French captain decided against this for fear of 'provoking the people of Tasmania and New South Wales', who had been greatly incensed by the actions of Du Petit-Thouars. La Place thought it would be quite sufficient for the time being to obtain a revocation of the law forbidding the teaching of the Catholic faith. To gain his ends, he was prepared to declare war, although the thought of this troubled him a little in view of the help the Tahitians had given him.

La Place, of course, did not reveal the reason for his visit until the *Artémise* was refloated. He then sent a message to the Queen requesting an audience 'to make an important communication'. The Queen replied that she was too sick to see anyone, but she sent an old chief to represent her at a meeting with La Place in the Protestant church at Papeete. The meeting took place on June 20 and was attended by Moerenhout, several missionaries, and the principal chiefs. La Place proposed that a new clause be inserted in the treaty between Queen Pomare and Du Petit-Thouars to permit 'the free exercise of the Catholic religion . . . in the island of Tahiti and any other possessions of Queen Pomare'. This clause, he said, would show that the Tahitians wished 'to give France a testimony of their desire to entertain relations of friendship and alliance and to assure Frenchmen . . . of the means of fulfilling their religious duties'.

The clause was supported by Tati, one of the most eloquent chiefs, and accepted by most of the others. But it could not be put into effect until the signature of the Queen was obtained. This, however, was obtained the same afternoon when the Queen —curious to know what was going on—arrived in Papeete. La Place went to see her at the palace and told her that unless she agreed to the clause, he would land 250 armed men to set fire to the church, palace, houses of the chiefs, and finally the whole town. The Queen submitted to the Frenchman's proposal after vainly protesting that the law which the clause revoked had been passed at the suggestion of Du Petit-Thouars. La Place then demanded, with further threats, that a portion of land be provided in Papeete as a site for a Roman Catholic church, and that similar sites be set aside in all villages where Protestant churches had been erected. The Queen agreed.

Having thus gone a good deal further than Du Petit-Thouars, La Place weighed anchor on June 22 and sailed for Hawaii. 'The victory was decidedly ours,' he wrote in his narrative of the *Artémise*'s voyage. It was. But it was not yet complete.

31. THE PLOT THICKENS

For two years after the departure of the *Artémise*, Tahiti was not troubled by menacing French naval captains. But Queen Pomare's difficulties continued.

In January, 1840, Pritchard returned from his leave of absence in England bringing a disappointing reply from Lord Palmerston to Pomare's appeal for protection. The Foreign Secretary said that Queen Victoria expressed 'deep concern at the difficulties under which Queen Pomare appeared to labour . . . but it would be impossible for her to fulfil, with proper punctuality, any defensive obligations towards the Government and inhabitants of Tahiti'. For that reason, Queen Victoria was unable to make Tahiti a protectorate of Great Britain, although she was always ready 'to attend to any representations' that Queen Pomare might wish to make. Palmerston added that Queen Victoria would also be glad 'to give the protection of her good offices to Queen Pomare in any differences which might arise' with any foreign power.

As soon as Pritchard learned of the visit of the *Artémise*, he wrote to Palmerston suggesting that the time had already come for Queen Victoria to intervene with her 'good offices'. 'The natives have no wish to give up their islands to any foreign power,' he wrote on February 18, 1840, 'but if this must be the case, they would a thousand times rather they fell into the hands of the English than the French. It is now more than two years since we have been favoured with a British ship of war from New South Wales. It appears highly desirable that we should have two ships annually—one from the South American station and one from the East Indies. The French and Americans have many more ships of war touching at these islands than we have, and they are of a far larger class.'

Palmerston's reaction to this letter was to request the Admiralty to send warships to Tahiti 'on every convenient occasion'.

Meanwhile, affairs in Tahiti were so quiet that Pritchard,

who was in poor health, felt that he could risk another period of leave in England. He sailed on February 2, 1841, leaving the consulate in the charge of Charles B. Wilson, the bibulous son of one of the early missionaries. He took with him another letter to Queen Victoria asking for assistance, signed this time by Buareia, secretary to Pomare.

About six months after Pritchard's departure, Moerenhout, the French Consul, took advantage of the absence of Queen Pomare in Raiatea to trick four of the principal chiefs into signing a document asking for French protection. The document was written in faulty Tahitian by Moerenhout himself and referred, among other things, to a 'deceitful plot' which the chiefs required French assistance to overthrow. The four signatories were Paraita, the regent, and the chiefs, Tati, Hitoti, and Paete. Paraita, however, disavowed the document on August 20, 1841, in a letter to the British Vice-Consul in Samoa. 'We did not know what was written, neither did we know well its contents,' he said. 'We signed our names to the letter as it were in the dark. Have the letter considered null and void. It was written by Moerenhout.' The document was also disavowed by Queen Pomare when she returned to Tahiti on September 9. In a letter to Queen Victoria, the President of the United States, and the King of France, she said: 'During my absence from my own country, a few of my people—entirely without my authority—wrote to the King of the French soliciting his assistance. I disavow any knowledge of that document.'

News of Moerenhout's intrigues reached Pritchard, in England, on March 10, 1842, on which day he wrote an urgent letter to Lord Aberdeen (who had replaced Palmerston as Foreign Secretary) requesting an interview. The interview was granted on March 19. But in reply to Pritchard's fervent pleas for British assistance in Tahiti, Lord Aberdeen merely said that he would see what could be done. Pritchard, however, later extracted £100 from the Foreign Office to buy furniture and a second-hand phaeton for Queen Pomare, which he was to present to her as 'evidence of the British Government's continuing interest in the prosperity of her dominions'. He left England with these gifts on August 11.

Meanwhile, Moerenhout's document had reached Paris, where

the French Government found it ideally suited to its needs. The Government had been looking around for some time for a base in the Pacific for its warships, whalers, and merchant vessels. The British Government had forestalled it in occupying New Zealand and the Hawaiian Islands, so it had been decided to send out an expedition under Rear-Admiral (formerly Captain) Du Petit-Thouars to take possession of the Marquesas. Moerenhout's document was an excellent pretext for obtaining a foothold in strategically situated Tahiti as well.

32. MORE GUNBOAT DIPLOMACY

On August 27, 1842, Rear-Admiral Du Petit-Thouars—having taken possession of the Marquesas—arrived at Papeete in his flagship, *La Reine Blanche*, to establish the French protectorate. Queen Pomare was absent at the time. She was in Moorea awaiting the birth of a child. Paraita was acting as regent.

Du Petit-Thouars called on Moerenhout to determine the best means of accomplishing his mission. Moerenhout, as usual, was helpful. He suggested that the admiral should complain to the Queen and principal chiefs about the numerous 'insults' committed against French citizens. A document containing an imposing list of 'insults' was compiled on September 8. It said that:

(1) Du Petit-Thouars had not met with the reception he was entitled to expect from a power allied by treaty to the French Government.

(2) There was not a single Frenchman* in Tahiti who did not have cause to complain of the 'iniquitous or rigorous conduct of the Queen's government towards him'.

(3) The houses of several Frenchmen had been 'violated during their absence' and left 'open and pillaged'.

(4) Seizures of property had been 'unjustly ordered and executed in the most brutal manner'.

* There were only six Frenchmen on the island at the time.

(5) Several Frenchmen had been 'beaten by police officers'.

(6) Others had been 'thrown into prison without previous trial, treated as criminals, and executed as villains without being able to obtain a hearing, etc'.

(7) Treaties had been 'violated and put aside in the most outrageous manner for France'.

(8) The murderer of a Frenchman, whom the Queen had promised to exile, was still living in Tahiti.

After listing these insults, Du Petit-Thouars said that the Queen was 'ill-advisedly submitting to an influence fatal to her true interests', but would 'learn for a second time that the good faith and loyalty of a power such as France' was 'not with impunity to be trifled with'. He added that as France could 'not expect justice from the Tahitian Government' and could 'no longer trust the word of the Queen and principal chiefs', it was necessary to demand 'a substantial security' to protect French rights. This 'security' was the payment of 10,000 Spanish dollars within twenty-four hours. In default, Tahiti would be occupied until satisfaction was given. Du Petit-Thouars concluded his document on a magnanimous note. He said that as it would pain him to adopt 'such severe measures', he would be pleased to consider within twenty-four hours any counter-proposal from the Queen and principal chiefs which would 'satisfy the just resentment' of his country and 'lead to a sincere reconciliation between the two peoples'.

Du Petit-Thouars did not get his document translated into Tahitian, and as the principal chiefs—Paraita, Tati, Utomi, and Hitoti—could not read French, he merely invited them aboard his frigate to discuss it. The discussion began on the evening of September 8 and extended well into the night. It was transferred in the early hours of the morning to Moerenhout's house. When day dawned, the following document had been prepared and signed, after threats, by the four chiefs:

Tahiti, September 9, 1842.

To Admiral Du Petit-Thouars:

As in the present state of affairs we can no longer govern so as to preserve a good understanding with foreign Governments without exposing ourselves to the loss of our islands, our authority and our liberty, we, the undersigned, the Queen and the principal chiefs of Tahiti, address the present letter to you to solicit the King of the French to take us under his protection upon the following conditions:

1. The sovereignty of the Queen and her authority, and the authority of the chiefs over their people, shall be guaranteed to them.

2. All laws and regulations shall be issued in the Queen's name and signed by her.

3. The possession of lands belonging to the Queen and to the people shall be secured to them, and shall remain in their possession; all disputes relative to the right to property or lands shall be under the special jurisdiction of the tribunals of the country.

4. Everyone shall be free in the exercise of his form of worship or religion.

5. The churches at present established shall continue to exist and the English missionaries shall continue in their labours without molestation; the same shall apply to every other form of worship, no one shall be molested or constrained in his belief.

Under these conditions, the Queen and the principal chiefs solicit the protection of the King of the French, resigning into his hands, or to the care of the French Government, or to the person appointed by him and approved by Queen Pomare, the direction of all relations with foreign governments, as well as everything relative to foreign residents, port regulations, &c. &c., and to take such further measures as he may judge necessary for the preservation of peace and good understanding.

Although the document indicated that the Queen had agreed to the French protectorate, the Queen was actually in ignorance of it until it was taken to her at Moorea by a native messenger called Tairapa. Tairapa said: 'Pomare, write your name under this document. If you do not, you must pay a fine of 10,000 dollars.' The Queen, however, did not affix her signature to it until she had called for Alexander Simpson, one of the resident English missionaries at Moorea. She then said: 'I sign this document through fear to prevent greater evil—the effusion of blood—and because I feel assured that if the French commence hostilities upon my land, my people will become desperate and spare no foreigners residing in my dominions.'

When the document, with the Queen's signature thus forcibly obtained, was taken back to Papeete, Du Petit-Thouars wrote a formal letter provisionally accepting 'the proposal to place the government of Queen Pomare under the protection of His Majesty Louis Philippe, King of the French'. He added that the 'decision' take by the Queen and chiefs removed 'every symptom of dissatisfaction' which the 'harsh measures' towards French citizens had caused.

Du Petit-Thouars's next move was to set up a provisional government of three to regulate the affairs of foreigners. Moerenhout was named Commissioner Royal, and two lieutenants of *La Reine Blanche* were appointed to the posts of military governor and captain of the port of Papeete. The duties of the provisional government were proclaimed in a long document jointly signed by Paraita and the French admiral. This proclamation elicited three letters from British residents which later proved useful. On September 12, Charles Wilson, the acting British Consul, wrote to Du Petit-Thouars that he was 'happy' to see the difficulties between Tahiti and France end without conflict. A similar letter containing the signatures of twenty-nine British residents was sent aboard *La Reine Blanche* about the same time. On September 21, the thirteen resident English missionaries on Tahiti and Moorea signed their names to the following:

'We, the undersigned, ministers of the Protestant mission on the islands of Tahiti and Moorea, in committee assembled, having a knowledge of the late changes which have taken place in reference to the Tahitian Government, beg to assure his Excellency that, as ministers of the gospel of peace, we shall consider it our imperative duty to exhort the people of these islands to a peaceable and uniform obedience to the "powers that be", considering that by such means their own interests will be best provided, but more especially as such obedience is required by the "laws of God", which we have hitherto made it our special business to inculcate.'

Only one other matter occupied the attention of Du Petit-

Thouars before he sailed at the end of the month. This was to add the French colours to the old Tahitian flag in the upper part next to the staff. Tahiti was then left in the hands of the provisional government supported by a small band of French troops.

33. A YANK IN THE CALABOOSE

THREE days before the departure of *La Reine Blanche*, a small Australian whaler, the *Lucy Ann*, put into Papeete. On board was a young American sailor, Herman Melville, who later became famous as the author of the great whaling classic, *Moby Dick*. Melville had been picked up at the Marquesas after spending several months among the cannibals of Taipi valley. He had earlier deserted from another whaler.

In Tahiti, Melville had the dubious distinction of being imprisoned with his fellow-seamen of the *Lucy Ann* in the stocks of the calaboose, or Calabooza Beretane, as it was called. The imprisonment of the seamen followed a mutiny in the *Lucy Ann* over a plan to put the captain ashore and leave the vessel at sea in the command of the drunken mate.

Melville described his experiences in the Calabooza Beretane and his later wanderings in Tahiti and Moorea in a half-factual, half-fictional novel called *Omoo*. This novel was one of his most successful books. It gave a delightful picture of many aspects of Tahiti, particularly the confusion that reigned among the natives over the proceedings of the French. There were detailed descriptions of *La Reine Blanche*; of Colomban Murphy, the Irish catechist, who had arrived on the island to take up Catholic missionary work; of Charles Wilson, the bibulous acting British Consul; and of careworn Queen Pomare. *Omoo* made Tahiti known again to a wide public after a long, lean literary period of nothing but missionary tracts.

Melville had few good things to say about the Protestant missionaries, and he indicated that they had changed the native ways but little.

'Ah, Ideea, mickonaree oee?' he said one day to a young native girl. This was the same as saying: 'By the by, Miss Ideea, do you belong to the Church?'

'Yes, me mickonaree,' the girl replied. Then, laying her hand upon her mouth and with a strong emphasis on the adverb, she said: 'Mickonaree ena'—'Church member here.' In the same way, and with similar exclamations, she touched her eyes and hands. This done, her whole air changed in an instant; and she gave Melville to understand, by unmistakable gestures, that in certain other respects she was not exactly a 'mickonaree'. In short, Melville said, Ideea was:

> A sad good Christian at the heart—
> A very heathen in the carnal part.

Melville gave an equally amusing description of a missionary's sermon in the Papara church:

'Good friends,' the missionary said, 'I glad to see you; and I very well like to have some talk with you today. Good friends, very bad time in Tahiti; it makes me weep. Pomare is gone—the island no more yours, but the Wee-Wee's. Wicked priests here, too; and wicked idols in women's clothes and brass chains.

'Good friends, no you speak, or look at them—but I know you won't—they belong to a set of robbers—the wicked Wee-Wees. Soon these bad men be made to go very quick. Beretanee ships of thunder come, and away they go. But no more 'bout this now. I speak more by by.

'Good friends, many whale-ships here now; and many bad men come in 'em. No good sailors living—that you know very well. They come here, 'cause so bad they no keep 'em home.

'My good little girls, no run after sailors—no go where they go; they harm you. Where they come from no good people talk to 'em—just like dogs. Here, they talk to Pomare, and drink ava with great Poofai.

'Good friends, this very small island, but very wicked and very poor; these two go together. Why Beretanee so great?

Because that island good island, and send mickonaree to poor kanaka. In Beretanee, every man rich; plenty things to buy; and plenty things to sell. Houses bigger than Pomare's, and more grand. Everybody, too, ride about in coaches, and wear fine tapa every day. (Several luxurious appliances of civilization were here enumerated and described.)

'Good friends, little to eat left at my house. Schooner from Sydney no bring bag of flour; and kanaka no bring pig and fruit enough. Mickonaree do great deal for kanaka; kanaka do little for mickonaree. So, good friends, weave plenty of coconut baskets, fill 'em, and bring 'em tomorrow . . .'

Such was Melville's unflattering description of the missionary's sermon. Soon after hearing it, he crossed over to Moorea, where he lived for over a year. While he was there, the 'Beretanee ships of thunder', which the missionary had so confidently predicted, arrived on the scene. . . .

34. BERETANEE SHIPS OF THUNDER

THE first British warship to anchor in Papeete after the departure of *La Reine Blanche* was HMS *Favourite* under Captain Sulivan. Sulivan had been sent to Tahiti by the Governor of New South Wales to investigate reports that the island had been made a French protectorate. He arrived in early December, 1842; found everything quiet; and sailed again on December 13 without perturbing the provisional government.

The next British visitor gave the provisional government a nasty headache. This was Captain Sir Thomas Thompson, commander of HMS *Talbot*, who was sent to Tahiti by the commanding admiral of the British naval station in Valparaiso on a similar mission to that of Sulivan. Thompson arrived off Papeete on January 13, 1843, to find the new Tahitian flag with the French colours in the upper quarter flying on shore. When the *Talbot* entered the harbour next day, Thompson did not salute the new flag, and when he was visited by the French military governor and the captain of the port, he merely acknowledged them as officers of *La Reine Blanche*. The three members of the provisional government were furious.

They became even more furious five days later when Queen Pomare arrived from Moorea in the royal barge flying the original Tahitian flag. Thompson added insult to injury by hoisting the same flag on the *Talbot* and firing a salute of twenty-one guns. He fired a second royal salute when the Queen came aboard his ship later on. The provisional government immediately sent a despatch to Thompson presumably protesting against his insulting conduct, but Thompson returned this unopened with a message saying that he could only receive despatches through the Queen. The provisional government replied with a letter to Queen Pomare protesting against her insulting conduct and enclosing two letters addressed to Thompson. The first letter requested Thompson to inform the government of his reason for coming to Tahiti; and the second protested against his insulting salutes and held him responsible for 'all the sad consequences which might result from a step so openly hostile to the French'. Thompson and the Queen left all letters unanswered.

On February 8, the Queen enraged the government still further by holding a public meeting at Papeete at which she protested against the proceedings of the French and asked Thompson for British assistance. This outburst caused warlike preparations to be made on board the French frigate *Boussole*, which was lying in harbour close to the *Talbot*. Thompson made similar preparations in his own vessel. The natives became alarmed and fled inland. But there was no outbreak of hostilities for Thompson had orders to return to Valparaiso as soon as possible.

He sailed on February 15, carrying with him another request from Pomare for British assistance and a letter from the chiefs, Tati and Utomi, stating that Moerenhout had obtained their signatures to the original document requesting French protection by promising them 1,000 dollars on the arrival of Du Petit-Thouars.

Meanwhile, George Pritchard, the British Consul, had arrived in Sydney on his return from sick leave in England. Horrified to learn that the French had assumed a protectorate over his beloved island, he immediately wrote to the British Foreign Secretary warning him that the French appeared to have designs on all the islands of Polynesia and again requesting him to send warships to Pomare's aid. Pritchard also obtained the assistance of the Governor of New South Wales in getting HMS *Vindictive*, which was then returning to England from China, to call at Tahiti and take him home.

The *Vindictive*, under Commodore John Toup Nicolas, left Sydney for Tahiti on January 22, 1843. She arrived at Papeete on February 25—ten days after Thompson's departure. On the following day, Commodore Nicolas wrote to the Admiralty that he had already been successful in mediating for Queen Pomare with the commander of the *Boussole* to enable her to hoist her own flag over her own house and in her own boat. In another letter two days later, he said: 'The more I learn respecting the extraordinary measures pursued by Admiral Du Petit-Thouars here, the more satisfied do I feel that even his own government cannot confirm the usurpation which he has established.'

From that time onwards, Commodore Nicolas was an indefatigable champion in the cause of Pomare. On March 5, when the Queen complained to him that Moerenhout had been rude to her, he wrote a firm but polite letter to the Commissioner Royal advising him 'to take immediate measures to ensure towards Her Majesty a close observance of those rules of courtesy and etiquette which are uniformly shown towards every sovereign'.

On March 12, Nicolas wrote to the provisional government informing them that he could not recognize the protectorate treaty. He said that according to international law and the principles of justice, the treaty was 'null and void *ab initio*' for two reasons. The Queen had signed it through fear and threats; and she had not been given the chance of refuting the charges of Du Petit-Thouars of violating a former treaty. The document containing the charges had, in fact, never been shown to her nor to any of the principal chiefs. 'It is my sincere belief,' Nicolas added, 'that the information conveyed to Rear-Admiral Du Petit-Thouars upon which the charges made in the declaration are founded and upon which he immediately acted was mainly incorrect, or I feel convinced that an officer of the Rear-Admiral's high character would not have taken such severe measures against Queen Pomare and her government as those of which Her Majesty so loudly complains. It will now be for our respective governments to decide on this important question, and until that decision arrives, I trust that the subjects of each will maintain peace and tranquillity on this island in every form.'

Nicolas became more and more indignant about the manner in which the protectorate had been established. With the help of George Pritchard he obtained numerous declarations from the Queen, the chiefs, and the missionaries which proved that the French had used unfair means. He sent these documents to the Admiralty on March 14 in a schooner especially chartered for the purpose. In a letter to the Admiralty, he said he was doing this because he had 'discovered a circumstance' that would be 'of vast importance in any negotiations that may arise between the Governments of England and France'. 'I could desire especially,' he continued, 'to call their Lordships' attention to the fact that this declaration of the French admiral . . . containing the foundation of the pretended cause of all their late hostile measures against Queen Pomare and her dominions was never seen by the Queen nor by any of her chiefs until I discovered it amongst the consul's papers and got it translated . . . It had been sent to our consul by the French admiral in the French language, but it had never before been translated into the Tahitian language. Consequently, even if the Queen and her chiefs had seen it, it would have been wholly unintelligible to them. But Her Majesty most solemnly declares that she did not even know that such a document was in existence. If she had done so, she could at once have refuted it. The Queen said: "All I ever heard was that I must pay ten thousand dollars within twenty-four hours or sign the paper that was sent to me, or the admiral would fire upon my people from his ship."'

Nicolas said he felt sure that the 'unprecedented' and 'dishonest' proceedings of the French would incur the indignation of the Admiralty and the British Government. He considered it his duty to remain at Tahiti and protect the Queen until he heard from the commanding admiral in Valparaiso, provided his provisons would hold out.

I understand [Nicolas continued] that the French admiral purposes bringing all his forces here as soon as he receives his reply from France. Consequently, I have addressed letters to the captains of any of Her Majesty's ships that may arrive in New South Wales previous to the 1st June earnestly advising them, if their orders will possibly admit of it, to come on without a moment's delay to Tahiti. I have likewise as earnestly recommended them to keep their ships constantly prepared for action in case any events may arise here that may cause the ships of war of France, which they may chance to fall in with, to act at once with hostilities towards our flag.

I consider it right further to observe that whilst the French in all their documents connected with the usurpation of Queen Pomare's authority have artfully sought to make it appear that the Queen and chiefs had voluntarily solicited their aid, and that Queen Pomare and her subjects had themselves addressed those several letters and papers to the French admiral, yet it is an irrefutable fact that the whole of the documents were written and framed either by the French admiral, through his secretary, or by the French Consul, who has been the chief instrument in all these proceedings. Not one of these letters and papers was ever written or dictated by the Queen or her chiefs. Thus, throughout these proceedings, the French seem to have been replying to the letters and papers of their own framing, after forcibly obtaining the signatures to them that they desired. The declaration of Rear-Admiral Du Petit-Thouars was a mere pretext for the measures he had determined on adopting. It is now very manifest that it was framed to be sent through the several consuls to the courts of Europe only as a blind and was never intended to be shown to the chiefs of Tahiti.

Commodore Nicolas stayed in Tahiti for five months after sending this letter to the Admiralty—the first two months on his own initiative, and then on the instructions of his superior officer in

Valparaiso. He sailed for Valparaiso on August 6, 1843, but was replaced on September 30 by Captain J. J. Tucker in HMS *Dublin*. Tucker had orders to watch over British interests and protect those of the Queen.

Meanwhile, the proceedings of Du Petit-Thouars were causing considerable trouble in England.

35. BRITAIN SHOWS HER HAND

Because of the slowness of communications in the days of sail, it was six months before news of the French protectorate reached England. The British Government was still in ignorance of the activities of Commodore Toup Nicolas and Captain Sir Thomas Thompson when the Marquis of Lansdowne rose in the House of Lords on March 27, 1843, to request information on the protectorate from the Foreign Secretary (Lord Aberdeen). Lord Aberdeen's reply was the first public expression of the British Government's policy towards Tahiti.

'I am not aware,' he said, 'of the precise terms in which the French Government has put forward its complaints against the ruling authorities of the Society Islands which appear to have led to the convention. I am not able to give any explanation of those transactions, nor do I feel called upon to express any opinion. But I am not one of those who looks with jealous apprehension on the establishment of the French in those islands. I am not of the opinion that the commerce or political activities of England will be at all interfered with by the establishment. On the contrary, I think there is reason to look to it with satisfaction and to anticipate advantageous results from it. Nevertheless, it is just and right that those parties who have been the means of civilizing the inhabitants of those islands ought to receive due attention from Her Majesty's Government.'

Although Lord Aberdeen's statement was received with numerous approving 'hear, hears' in the House of Lords, the various missionary societies in England found it far from satisfactory. The societies felt that the establishment of the French protectorate was a menace to the Protestant faith throughout Polynesia as well as a blow to England's reputation. During the next two months, meetings of protest were held all over the country; deputations called on the British Cabinet and the French Ambassador; and memorials signed by thousands of people poured into the Foreign Office. The views of the missionary societies were supported by eleven influential members of the House of Lords and House of Commons. They suggested to Lord Aberdeen that the protectorate of France should be substituted by a joint protectorate of England, France, and the United States.

Lord Aberdeen, however, refused to change his tune. All he was prepared to do was to obtain assurances from the French Government that the Protestant missionaries in Tahiti would be given full protection and would be allowed to carry on their work. These assurances were unhesitatingly given by M. Guizot, the French Minister of Foreign Affairs, both in the French Parliament and to the British Ambassador in Paris. Meanwhile, the French Parliament went ahead and voted the sum of 5,987,000 francs to defray the expenses of French establishments in the Pacific for the year 1844.

On June 14, 1843, Lord Aberdeen wrote to Pritchard, the British Consul in Tahiti, informing him that both Houses of Parliament had acquiesced in the French protectorate, and that he should shape his 'conduct and language in exact conformity with the tenor and spirit of Government policy'.

On July 11, the Foreign Office wrote to the Secretary of the Admiralty giving instructions on how British naval officers should act in relation to Tahiti. The letter (with copy to Pritchard) read, in part, as follows:

> Although HM Government has not acknowledged the right of France to assume and exercise a protectorship over the Society Islands, they nevertheless do not intend to call that right in question.
>
> It certainly would appear from various reports received by HM Government . . . respecting the transaction which ended in the surrender by the Queen of Tahiti of a portion of her

sovereign power . . . that that cession was brought about partly by corrupt intrigue and partly by intimidation. But the surrender was, notwithstanding, voluntarily made and completed in due form by Queen Pomare under whatever impulsion she may have acted. It therefore appears to HM Government that, independent of other considerations, there is no sufficient ground on the case of informality for disputing the validity of that cession, however favourably HM's Government may be, and are, disposed towards Queen Pomare, and however great is their regret at seeing her reduced to subjection by a foreign power. . . .

HM Government desire, therefore, that no difficulty should be made by any of HM naval commanders who may visit the Society Islands with regard to the point of saluting the flag which has been introduced by the French admiral, and that no dispute should be entered into as to the right of the French to exercise authority in conjunction with the sovereign in those islands. HM Consul in Tahiti will have orders to watch closely the proceedings of the French authorities with regard to the Protestant missionaries and to the liberty of religious worship enjoyed by English subjects established in the Society Islands. He will be asked to report to HM Government on any deviation which may be made from the line of conduct which the French Government have solemnly pledged themselves to pursue towards British subjects in this respect.

The letter added that the Admiralty should send more British warships to Tahiti to keep a watch on the proceedings of the French, and that the Government intended to send an officer of higher rank than ordinary Consul to Hawaii to superintend all British consular agents in the Pacific. This officer would have the power to decide British policy in all disputes.

A third letter setting out British policy on Tahiti was written by Lord Aberdeen to Pritchard on September 25. The letter severely criticized Pritchard for the action he had taken on returning with Commodore Nicolas, and said that such action 'might endanger the harmony of the relations between Great Britain and France'.

You appear to have altogether misinterpreted the passages in the letters of Mr. Canning and Lord Palmerston [the letter of Lord Aberdeen continued]. From the whole tenor of those letters, it is obvious that His Majesty's Governments of that day were not prepared to interpose actively in support of the sovereign of the Society Islands, although they willingly proffered her such protection and good offices as—without active interference—they could properly afford. But it is not to be supposed that, at the very moment they were declining to take the Society Islands under the protection of the British Crown, HM Government could have intended to interpose their good offices in behalf of the sovereign in such a manner as to incur the almost certainty of a collision with a foreign Power.

HM Government do not approve the late proceedings of the French authorities at Tahiti. On the contrary, they consider those proceedings to have been unjust and oppressive; and they sincerely deplore the pain and humiliation inflicted by them on Queen Pomare. Moreover, they are willing to do everything in their power to alleviate her distresses. But, unfortunately, the letter in which French protection was solicited was signed on the Queen's own free will, and HM Government do not, therefore, intend to raise any question as to the exercise of authority nor to the legitimacy of the new flags. . . . Nevertheless, the Government will maintain the rights of the British Protestant missionaries . . . and will intercede on all convenient occasions with the Government of France in behalf of the Queen of Tahiti in order to obtain protection for her against the harsh treatment which she seems to have experienced. . . .

But she would, perhaps, do wisely to submit to the evil circumstances which her own fears and the intrigues of some of her corrupt chiefs have brought upon her. Resistance to those who have assumed the rights of protectors over her would aggravate the miseries of her position and provoke even worse treatment than she has already received.

The letter added that Pritchard should inform the Queen that she could expect no active help from the British Government, and that Pritchard should be tolerant in his actions towards the French authorities.

With the despatch of this letter, Lord Aberdeen temporarily ceased to be interested in the troublesome affairs of Queen Pomare. He had told his officers how to act. It was up to them to follow his instructions. Unfortunately, however, none of his letters had reached Tahiti when Rear-Admiral Du Petit-Thouars arrived at Papeete for the third time.

36. THE REAR-ADMIRAL TAKES OVER

REAR-Admiral Du Petit-Thouars anchored at Papeete in his fifty-gun flagship, *La Reine Blanche*, on November 1, 1843. A second French naval vessel, the *Embuscade*, was already in harbour, and two others, the frigates *Uranie* and *Danae*, arrived on November 4. The only British warship on hand was Captain Tucker's fifty-gun frigate *Dublin*.

Du Petit-Thouars's first act was to inform the Queen and the British Consul that as the French King had ratified the protectorate treaty of September 9, 1842, the treaty was 'definite and irrevocable'. This, he said, meant that the administration of the affairs of Europeans and all affairs connected with foreign governments became the exclusive business of the Protectorate Government in conjunction with Queen Pomare. Foreigners could no longer interfere in the politics or interior administration of the island. The Rear-Admiral's letter to Pritchard then referred to the 'unanimous adhesion to the Protectorate' of the English residents of Papeete, the former acting British Consul, and the Protestant missionaries, as testified by their letters to him on his previous visit. The letter added that the liberty of the missionaries' creed, of their persons, and of their properties would be 'religiously respected' by the Protectorate Government.

Pritchard's reply to the Rear-Admiral's letter was uncompromising:

In reference to the letter I had the honour of receiving from you yesterday, permit me to observe that Queen Pomare has assured me again and again that Her Majesty never willingly demanded the French protection. When the document presented by Mr. Moerenhout to the four chiefs (was taken to her), she spent the whole night weeping, and at the last moment signed it to prevent hostilities commencing.

Perhaps you are not aware that, instead of all the great chiefs demanding French protection, there is but a small minority, and they have been considered by Her Majesty and the people generally as Traitors.

The King of the French and his government—under the impression that Queen Pomare and the chiefs really wished French protection—may have ratified the treaty, but you are aware, sir, that I, as British Consul, cannot acknowledge that treaty till I am authorized by my government to do so.

You intimate that it is with the liveliest satisfaction that you have seen the unanimous adhesion of the English residents. I beg to assure you that it is a mistake to suppose that there is anything approaching unanimous adhesion to the protectorate. Several of the most respectable of the British residents have been and still are decidedly opposed to it. With respect to the letter of congratulation from the acting British Consul, its value may be testified by the well-known fact that he was almost always intoxicated and would willingly have signed anything to please those who would furnish him with wine or spirits. He has written a letter to the British Government apologizing for having so far committed himself as to write the letter which he addressed to you.

Is it not possible that you have mistaken the purport of the letter addressed to you by the English missionaries? They simply assured you that as ministers they should not interfere with politics, but preach the gospel and teach the natives 'to be subject to the powers that be'.

The Rear-Admiral did not reply to Pritchard's letter, and for the rest of his stay addressed his communications solely to the Queen. He first requested her to strike her flag, as the flying of it, he said, was an 'insult' to the French Government.

The Queen (acting on Pritchard's advice) replied that she would not strike it as there was no mention of flags in the protectorate treaty. On the same day—November 4—she addressed a petition to the King of France begging him to cancel the treaty because she had signed it through fear.

The Queen's attitude on the question of her flag gave Du Petit-Thouars a pretext for getting 'tough' again. On November 5, he wrote to her, saying:

> Since in your letter of yesterday's date you still refuse to strike your flag, and by that you continue to insult France and the King . . . it is with regret that I declare to you that . . . if, at the expiration of two hours after the receipt of this letter, your flag is not struck . . . I will no longer recognize you as Queen and Sovereign of the . . . Society Islands, and I shall take definitive possession in the name of the King of France. By this act, all the lands of Queen Pomare and those of her family who will not submit within twenty-four hours to the King's government shall be confiscated for the good of the state.

Queen Pomare refused to be intimidated by this letter and her flag continued to fly over her palace. At 7.45 a.m. on November 6, Du Petit-Thouars called on her and laboured hard to convince her that it was against his inclination to use harsh measures, but that he had been sent by the King of France and must fulfil his mission.

'Is that all you have to say?' Queen Pomare asked.

'Yes.'

'Then I have a little more to say to you. Whatever you wish me to do, I beg you will send it to me in writing that I may consider its character well.'

'We will write no more,' Du Petit-Thouars said. 'If the flag is not taken down by twelve o'clock, we will send an armed force on shore and haul it down, and take full possession of the Government of Tahiti and the Society Islands.'

The Queen continued immovable. It was clear to her now that the French were determined to take her islands and were only seeking for a pretext.

As soon as the Rear-Admiral had gone, Pritchard advised

her to issue a proclamation commanding her people to keep perfectly calm, to make no opposition to the French soldiers, and to bear things patiently even if they were maltreated. The proclamation was posted up in various parts of Papeete as the French troops prepared to come ashore. It exhorted the natives 'to rely upon the justice and clemency of the King of France and the other sovereigns of Europe'.

About five hundred French troops began to land at twelve o'clock—first, the artillery, then the marines, and finally, the marine infantry. Marching to music, they headed towards the Queen's palace. When they had surrounded the flagstaff in the courtyard, a Tahitian chief, who had been appointed to protest against the proceedings in the name of the Queen, attempted to interpose. But the French interrupted him with a roll of drums, after which one of the officers made a short speech. 'In the name of King Louis Philippe I, our august master,' he said, 'we plant the French flag over this land and would rather die than abandon it. As for you, the people of the country, we have come to protect you and bring you civilization and peace.'

The Queen's flag was then hauled down by one of the sailors and the French flag hoisted in its place. This act was saluted by three cries of 'Long Live the King'. The band played the *Marseillaise*, and the French warships in harbour fired a salvo of twenty-one guns. A proclamation was issued soon after informing the people that Pomare was no longer queen; that Louis Philippe was king; and that Captain Armand Bruat was his representative.

During the next few hours, Pritchard and Captain Tucker, of the *Dublin*, wrote letters of protest to Du Petit-Thouars. Pomare, in the meantime, had fled to the safety of the British Consulate. Pritchard's letter said:

Having been officially informed by Queen Pomare that you have taken from Her Majesty the sovereignty of these isles, I have the honour to acquaint you that my functions as Consul must now cease. I have accordingly struck my flag, not having been accredited by the British Government as Consul to a French colony.

I do now in the name of my Government and on behalf of

the British residents most solemnly protest against your proceedings in this taking possession of the dominions of an independent sovereign, who, for nearly half a century, has enjoyed the friendly protection of Great Britain, from which she has received repeated assurances 'that Her Majesty (Queen Victoria) will at all times be ready to attend to any representations that Queen Pomare may wish to make . . . and will always be glad to give the protection of her good offices to Queen Pomare in any difficulties which may arise between Queen Pomare and any other power'.

You, sir, cannot be in ignorance of the fact that these islands are indebted solely to Great Britain for their civilized and religious advantages.

I now hold you responsible to the British Government for the losses and damages which may arise to British subjects or British property by your proceedings.

Pritchard wrote two long letters to the British Foreign Secretary during the next few days informing him of the 'outrageous' and 'unparalleled' proceedings of the French and of his action in striking his flag. 'I most sincerely hope,' he said in one of them, 'that the British Government will not allow these aggressions to be made by the French without using some means to restore the sovereignty of these islands to an injured and helpless woman.' In the second letter, he warned of the dangers that might result from the French occupation.

'Should the French keep possession of these islands,' he said, 'they will soon so establish themselves in these seas as to enable them greatly to injure our commerce in this part of the world. And in the event of a new war between the two nations, they would greatly distress our colonies of New South Wales, Van Diemen's Land (Tasmania), and New Zealand.'

Pritchard's letters also included copies of documents which Pomare had written at his house. There was a short letter appointing him to act as her agent; another petition to the King of France protesting against the 'harsh measures' of Du Petit-Thouars and asking him for 'compassion and justice'; and another of her endless and pitiful requests to Queen Victoria for assistance. 'This is my little word to you,' she said in her letter to the Queen. 'Let not the cord with which we both are bound together be broken, but compassionate me in my troubles.'

Meanwhile, Captain Bruat had taken up residence in the Queen's palace as Governor of the Society Islands, with Lieutenant Foucher d'Aubigny acting as his assistant. Du Petit-Thouars had sailed in *La Reine Blanche*, leaving about five hundred artificers and troops to erect forts and instal guns.

The Queen continued to live at Pritchard's house, where she was frequently visited by condoling natives from various districts. But she did not feel safe. There were persistent rumours that the French soldiers would come to the house and take her away by force. Pritchard, also, was apprehensive. He told the Foreign Office on November 23 that the French had spies around his house from day to day, and that he had it on good authority that they were determined, if possible, to send him off the island.

So things went on until January 8, 1844, when HMS *Basilisk*, a small ketch, arrived from Hawaii with the news that the British Government had decided to recognize the protectorate. The *Basilisk* also brought orders to Captain Tucker telling him to sail for Hawaii in the *Dublin*. Tucker immediately wrote to Bruat: 'I have the honour to inform you that I have directions from my Commander-in-chief to acknowledge the French Protectorate Government, and were it now in existence, I should hasten to acknowledge the same. Sufficient time not having elapsed for the reappointment of Mr. Pritchard as consul . . . to these islands as a French possession . . . I feel it my duty, until further instructed by my commander-in-chief, to appoint George Pritchard as the most eligible person to take care of the British interests . . .'

The first sentence of Tucker's letter was regarded by Bruat as a blatant insult, and he got his own back by refusing to accept Pritchard as Consul on the ground that his conduct 'had been very hostile to the French Government'. When Tucker politely asked him to reconsider his decision, he replied that Pritchard was unacceptable as his opposition to the protectorate was 'well known'. Having been thus rebuffed, Tucker instructed the commander of the *Basilisk* to remain in Tahiti to protect British interests and to assist Pomare 'in the way of advice'. Tucker also wrote to Pomare advising her to do everything to preserve the peace, and to rely on the 'known magnanimity' of the French King and the 'intercession' of Queen Victoria for the restoration of her kingdom. 'I can assure Your Majesty,' he said, 'that at the time Admiral Thomas sent me orders to rejoin him at the Sandwich Islands, he had no knowledge of the capture of these islands by Admiral Du Petit-Thouars.'

The preparations for departure in Tucker's well-armed frigate caused considerable excitement among the natives and great delight to the French. 'What do you think of British help now?' the French soldiers tauntingly asked the natives. 'Where is Commodore Nicolas in the *Vindictive*? Has he abandoned you? And where is Admiral Thomas, whom you've been expecting for so long? Instead of coming, hasn't he sent for his ship to go away?'

To allay the doubts which these questions aroused in the natives' minds, Pomare had another proclamation nailed up in Papeete. It was issued on January 31—the day the *Dublin* was ready to sail. It said:

> Health and peace to you all. I make known to you that our ship of war is about to leave. It has been sent for by the admiral to return to Oahu. There is a small ship of war to protect us. Another is coming. Do not listen to the men who will pain you by reporting that we shall not be assisted. Britain will not cast us off. Let our conduct be good and wait till the letters arrive.
>
> This is my word to you. Do not on any account cause evil to grow. By no means ill-treat the Frenchmen. Have great patience. Take me for a pattern and follow me, and let all of us pray earnestly to God that he may deliver us from our trials as he formerly delivered Hezekiah.
>
> Peace be with you all.
>
> > Pomare.

The Queen's proclamation gave great offence to the French authorities, and new rumours began to fly about that she would be arrested. Feeling that it would be unsafe to remain on shore, the Queen fled with her family and secretary to HMS *Basilisk*. She had scarcely got on board when nine or ten soldiers with bayonets fixed arrived at Pritchard's house. A couple of sentinels were placed at the front door, while the others went into a house occupied by the Queen's domestics. There they arrested one of the maids, whom they believed to be the Queen, and took her to prison. This woman was not released until Moerenhout revealed that the soldiers had made a mistake.

As soon as Bruat learned that the Queen had gone aboard the *Basilisk*, he wrote to her saying that her 'act of defiance' in issuing her proclamation had caused her to renounce the support of the French, and that she was prohibited from landing in the Society Islands without his permission. From this time onwards, Bruat was increasingly high-handed in his dealings with the natives and also with the British residents. Three chiefs at Papeete were arrested and imprisoned in the *Embuscade*. Three others from a neighbouring district were placed in irons in a prison on shore. Four more chiefs, who were living near the isthmus of Taravao, were outlawed as 'rebels' on February 17 for not listening to Bruat's 'words of peace'. These chiefs were given eight days to 'make their submissions', and fines were threatened to be imposed on any districts which harboured them. A schooner, and later the *Embuscade* with a large number of troops, went to Taravao to arrest the 'rebels', but the natives retreated to the mountains. The French prepared for a long siege by taking possession of a large house belonging to Queen Pomare and converting it into a barracks. They also began to build a fort.

About the same time, two British sea-captains were arrested for saying that they thought a chief was justified in protecting his property. They were liberated after several days on condition that they went aboard their respective vessels and did not land again without permission.

On February 19, the natives were greatly excited by the arrival of a large British naval vessel, HMS *Cormorant*. The natives felt that, with this vessel to support them, the time had come for them to take up arms against the French. Fighting broke out in Hitiaa, Arue, Faaa, and Taravao at the end of the month. Bruat became desperate, and on March 2 he left for Taravao at the head of a large force to try to regain control. Lieutenant d'Aubigny, who was left as acting-governor in Papeete, proclaimed martial law until Bruat returned.

At four p.m. next day, Pritchard was arrested as he was about to step into a boat to go aboard the *Cormorant*. He was led through the town by a group of soldiers and taken to a blockhouse on the side of a hill. Inside the blockhouse, he was forced through a trap-door into a dungeon, where he was kept without food or water until eight or nine o'clock next morning. The trap-door was then opened and a note signed by d'Aubigny handed down to him. The note said that a French sentinel had been attacked on the night of March 2, and that he had been arrested in reprisal as 'the only daily mover and instigator of the disturbances of the natives'.

Owing to the dampness of the dungeon, Pritchard became ill with a violent attack of dysentery. After he had begged for medical assistance, a doctor was brought to the blockhouse to see him. But the doctor was not allowed into the dungeon, nor was Pritchard allowed out of it. The doctor was only permitted to examine the patient's tongue and feel his pulse as he stood in his weakened condition on a ladder. As a result of this examination, the doctor wrote to d'Aubigny that Pritchard would die unless he was removed from the dungeon promptly. This letter produced no results; nor did the protests of Captain Gordon of the *Cormorant*. It was not until Bruat returned from Taravao six days later that Pritchard was released. He was then removed in the dead of night to the French frigate *La Meurthe*, and placed in a special compartment screened off from the rest of the ship.

After a sharp correspondence between Gordon and Bruat, Bruat agreed to put Pritchard aboard the *Cormorant* if Gordon would give a pledge to clear out of Tahiti and not land Pritchard on any of the Society Islands. Gordon gave the pledge. On March 13, the *Cormorant* steamed out of port followed by *La Meurthe*, which transferred its prisoner on the open sea. The *Cormorant* then steered for Valparaiso, where Pritchard found his old friend, Commodore Toup Nicolas, willing to give him a passage home in HMS *Vindictive*.

37. ENGLAND IS SCANDALIZED

ABOUT three weeks before Pritchard's deportation, news arrived in England and France that Du Petit-Thouars had not merely established a protectorate in Tahiti but had actually taken full possession in the name of the French King.

In England, the Rear-Admiral's action soon became a lively topic. 'It is a disgrace and a danger to England,' one man told Lord Aberdeen. 'Tahiti will be a greater difficulty to the British cabinet than Ireland,' a foreign diplomat said. British newspapers denounced the action in angry editorials, and even the politicians were troubled. When the Prime Minister (Sir Robert Peel) was questioned in the House of Commons on February 22, 1844, he replied evasively and with an emotion he found difficult to conceal. 'All I can say on the subject,' he said, 'is that I deeply regret what has taken place. At the same time, I have no reason to believe that the course pursued had the previous sanction of, or was in consequence of, any instructions from the French Government.'

For a few days, a rupture of the *entente cordiale* between the British and French Governments seemed possible. But the French Government was determined to be conciliatory, and on February 25, it eased the tension in diplomatic circles by disavowing the action of its rear-admiral. M. Guizot, the French Foreign Minister, announced that the authorities in Tahiti would be instructed to re-establish the protectorate and reinstate the Queen as sovereign. This statement was sufficient to allay the doubts and fears of the British Cabinet, and when Sir Robert Peel was asked about the matter of February 27, he said he had 'a strong and confident impression that it would not be necessary for England to interpose'. In Paris, however, Guizot's statement provoked bitter criticism from the many opponents to his shaky government. One member of the Chamber of Deputies contended that the Government had yielded to British pressure, and that as the French flag had been planted in Tahiti, it could 'not be struck without dishonour'. He said that Du Petit-Thouars had obviously been instructed in the line of action he was to take. Guizot hotly denied the charge that his Government had bent the knee to a foreign power. 'The resolution of the cabinet was spontaneous,' he said, 'and was adopted before entering into any communication with the British Government.' He went on to say that Du Petit-Thouars had committed 'an egregious error' in raising the question of the flag, and had acted 'neither with prudence nor wisdom' throughout the affair. 'The admiral,' Guizot added, 'had a right to demand the execution of the treaty which Pomare had signed, either voluntarily or through fear, but he was not justified in taking forcible possession of her dominions. Under these circumstances the Government conceived that the admiral had exceeded his powers.'

Guizot's statement brought the discussions on Tahiti in the French and English Parliaments temporarily to an end. But the French and British Cabinets were still worried. Reports arriving from Tahiti indicated that Pritchard was acting in a way that could cause them further embarrassment. M. Guizot suggested that the best way to avoid this was to transfer the Consul elsewhere. Lord Aberdeen meekly agreed. A letter 'exonerating' Pritchard from his consular duties in Tahiti and transferring him to Samoa was despatched on April 10, 1844. It said that the Government was 'far from wishing to express any disapprobation' of his conduct, but it thought that it would be better for his own comfort and for the 'good understanding' between England and France that he should be replaced.

This letter was still on its way to Tahiti when Pritchard arrived in England on July 26 in HMS *Vindictive*. Reports in the Press of his arrest and deportation immediately turned England into uproar. The whole nation was scandalized. It was bad enough that the French had occupied Tahiti and dispossessed the Queen, but to arrest and deport the inviolate person of a British Consul, that, it was thought, was going too far. The matter was heatedly discussed in pubs, clubs, drawing-rooms, and the editorial columns of the Press. The *Illustrated London News*, the only illustrated paper of the day, came out with an article on the affair with a picture of Pritchard in his Consul's uniform and drawings of his house in Papeete and the blockhouse in which he had been imprisoned. Newspapers on both sides of the Channel began to talk of war, and relations between the two countries became severely strained.

When Sir Robert Peel was questioned in the House of Commons on July 31, 1844, he said he would 'not hesitate to say that an outrage had been committed', and that he presumed the French Government would 'at once make that reparation' which England had 'a right to require'. Lord Aberdeen was even more indignant in the House of Lords on the following day. 'It is undoubtedly true,' he told a questioner, 'that a gross outrage has been committeed against the person of a British subject— indeed, so flagrant an outrage that if I had not received an authentic account of the transaction, it would appear to me to be incredible. But I wish to observe that this proceeding has taken place not only without the possible knowledge or instruction of the French Government, but under a state of things which has been disavowed by them. I have no doubt that they will regard it with as much concern as we do. I am afraid, however, that the late transaction will prove a godsend to the enemies of peace between the two countries, and that it will be turned to good account in furthering their views.'

Lord Aberdeen was right. With each passing day, the clamour for war became more insistent—a course which was supported by the Duke of Wellington, hero of Waterloo. The French newspapers went to great lengths to calumniate Pritchard. They represented him as the head of a set of rebels and the instigator of insurrection against the French authorities in Papeete. One went so far as to say that about twelve years before his deportation, Pritchard had spent several months in France with a woman who was not his wife, that he had run away without paying his bills, and that he had left his children at school unprovided for.

The inflammatory articles continued throughout the month of August, and the governments of England and France became seriously alarmed. Neither wanted war, but both could see the difficulty of averting it. M. Guizot was careful to avoid adding fuel to the flames when questioned in the French Parliament. 'In this affair,' he said, 'there are questions of fact and questions of right to be cleared up between the two governments. The tribunes of these chambers must not be made like the public newspapers, which every morning state whatever they may know of the affairs that may be pending between governments. Convinced as I am that serious difficulties would arise if we discussed the matter now, I absolutely refuse to do so. When all the questions of fact and right have been cleared up between the two governments, then I shall be ready.'

This carefully worded declaration was followed by a series of delicate negotiations between Guizot and Lord Aberdeen. Lord Aberdeen hinted that the recall of d'Aubigny or Bruat, or both, would be a suitable apology for the 'gross outrage'. But Guizot refused to recall anyone on the grounds that Pritchard was no longer Consul at the time of his deportation, and that the governors had the right to remove any resident who tried to disturb the established order of things. Guizot, however, finally compromised by apologizing to the British Government for the 'circumstances which preceded the removal of Mr. Pritchard from the island of Tahiti', and by offering to pay him an 'equitable indemnity' for his losses and sufferings. The amount of the indemnity was to be determined by the commanders of the French and English naval stations in the Pacific.

Guizot's apology and proffered indemnity were accepted by the British Government as an honourable settlement. When the British Parliament was prorogued on September 5, 1844, the Lords Commissioners were able to announce that the danger of 'interrupting the good understanding and friendly relations' with France had been 'happily averted'. The French Government, however, had not yet heard the end of the troublesome Pritchard affair.

38. REPERCUSSIONS IN FRANCE

As soon as it was learned in France that the Cabinet had agreed to an indemnity, the anti-government newspapers accused Guizot of 'cowardly complacency' and loudly proclaimed that he was shamefully humiliating his country before England. *Le National*, one of the most rabid of these papers, actually discussed the chances and practicability of a French invasion of England. The paper also asked school children to subscribe to a sword of honour for Du Petit-Thouars.

Many members of both Houses of Parliament were so indignant about the indemnity that they declared in advance that they would never vote in favour of it. This sort of talk frightened King Louis Philippe into writing to Guizot offering to pay Pritchard 25,000 francs out of his own purse on the pretext that it would take the French and British naval commanders in the Pacific a long time to decide on a suitable amount. The King was afraid that a debate on the subject in the French Parliament would wreck the *entente cordiale* with Great Britain. 'I find it very convenient,' he said, 'that it should be the King alone who supports an expense that his government and he regard as equitable, honourable and proper, to facilitate the continuance of our good relations with England. I would add that I would be delighted, as king, to assure that advantage to France without exposing it to the inconveniences . . . which might follow the demand for legislative action over such a bagatelle.'

Guizot rejected the King's offer, and insisted that a debate be held. The result was disastrous for the monarchy and himself. The debate began on January 13, 1845. It revolved around the following paragraph in the Address-in-Reply:

'Incidents which at the first moment appeared calculated to disturb the friendly relations existing between France and England had sensibly moved the two countries and occupied the attention of your government. We are satisfied to learn that a mutual feeling of goodwill and equity has maintained that happy accord between the two states which is indispensable to their prosperity, and the guarantee of the repose of the world.'

The first speaker was Count Mole, who criticized Guizot for his 'excessive anxiety' to maintain the alliance with England, and condemned the government for the 'imprudence' of its occupation of Tahiti. He said that the Government should have known that the occupation would not be viewed with indifference by the British Cabinet.

M. Thiers said that the Guizot ministry had 'blindly compromised' the interests of their country over Tahiti. 'The occupation of a few miserable islands in Oceania,' he said, 'is neither

necessary to the trade of France nor to her naval power. It makes
one shudder to think on what a slender thread the peace of the
world hung. If the French and British naval forces in Tahiti had
been equal, blood would perhaps have been shed in the Bay of
Papeete, and in Europe, the pacifiers would not have been able
to stop its torrents. The "ministry of peace" has brought France
nearer to war than any previous one.' (Cries of 'oh, oh.') M.
Thiers became more and more animated as he passed on to other
matters of French foreign policy. This created such an uproar
that the sitting was temporarily suspended. When it was resumed, M. Guizot rose to answer his critics.

The Government [he said] never had any idea of possessing
itself of Tahiti and putting France and England in contact on
that point. All it sought was a desirable port in those seas.
The admiral sent on that expedition considered it his duty to
assume the protectorate of Tahiti, of which no mention had
been made in his instructions. Two reasons determined us
not to refuse what the admiral had done. The first reason
was that the protectorate of the island of Tahiti was of some
importance to our establishment in the Marquesas; and the
other was that we did not wish to see the French flag with-
drawn immediately after its appearance. This provisional
protectorate—a protectorate not yet sanctioned by the government—continued for fourteen months. It had, it is true,
met with difficulties and embarrassments, but there had not
been anything like tumult or sedition. The disturbances
began when Admiral Du Petit-Thouars thought it his duty
to convert the protectorate into a sovereignty. Thus, during
the fourteen months of the protectorate, Mr. Pritchard, who
was in Tahiti, was unable to excite any insurrection. It was
after the assumption of sovereignty that he was able to
do so.

I now come to the last incident, that of Mr. Pritchard. You
will remember the strong sensation created in England on the
receipt of the news of his arrest. This emotion appeared to
proceed from two causes—first, the quality of agent of the
English Government with which he was invested; and, next,
his religious character. The conduct adopted by us in this

matter was (1) to prove that Mr. Pritchard was not an official agent, but simply a foreigner living under the protection of a law common to all, and (2) to prove that the most perfect religious liberty was preserved in Oceania. This done, we remained quiet in order to allow the angry feeling which had been aroused in England to subside. When the proper moment arrived . . . we fully maintained . . . that although there was enough in the circumstances of the case to warrant the authorities undertaking every measure for their safety, yet it was unnecessary to keep Mr. Pritchard in solitary confinement for eight days and prevent his seeing his wife and children. We have admitted that there were certain points connected with this affair for which it was honourable in us to express our regret and our disapproval, and we also thought there might be reasons why a pecuniary indemnity should be granted. (Murmurs from members of the opposition.) The Chamber sees that I do not avoid any point connected with this question. (Cries of approbation.)

Guizot added that the payment of the indemnity to Du Petit-Thouars over the Catholic priests served as a precedent for the French Government to grant an indemnity to Pritchard.

When a vote on the disputed paragraph of the Address-in-Reply was proposed, M. Leon de Malleville moved the following amendment:

'We are happy to learn that the accord so necessary to the repose of the world has been maintained between the two states, but we regret that, in granting a reparation which was not due, the rules of justice and reciprocity—which France shall always respect—were not sufficiently taken into account.'

M. de Malleville then launched a bitter attack against the Government. 'The indemnity awarded to Pritchard,' he said, 'is unanimously disapproved by the country.' (Cries of 'no, no' from the ministerial benches.) 'Pritchard was no missionary. He was a mere traitor; an intriguer; the mayor of the palace of Queen Pomare.'

M. Peyramont briefly defended the Government. Then M. Odillon Barrot hotly attacked it. 'There is no equity and no reciprocity in granting an indemnity to the instigator of a war of savages against civilization,' he said, 'particularly under the threats which have been proffered from the British tribune.'

M. Guizot denied that any threats had been made by the British Cabinet, but he admitted that France had not wanted absolute sovereignty in Tahiti because of the complications it would cause between England and France. Regarding Pritchard, he said that two facts had been overlooked. One was that Pritchard had been recalled from Tahiti to go elsewhere on the remonstrances of France, and that Britain had 'given satisfaction' in recalling him. The second fact was that Pritchard had demanded an inquiry into his behaviour to see if he had been exciting trouble, and it was possible that if such an inquiry were held nothing would be proved against him. 'The Government,' Guizot continued, 'was therefore placed between the alternative of a compromise or a rupture. The compromise, of which the Chamber knows the conditions, appeared to us to be equitable and proper.'

The president of the Chamber then put the question of M. de Malleville's amendment to the vote. The result of the first count was proclaimed doubtful by the secretaries. It was defeated on the second vote, but the majority was so small that many deputies maintained that the amendment had been carried. The Chamber then adjourned with deputies hotly discussing the matter.

Next day, January 27, the discussion on the original paragraph in the Address-in-Reply was resumed. After some lively exchanges the president rose and was about to put the question to the vote when a list of twenty members demanding a secret ballot was put in his hand. The president's announcement about this caused a great uproar amongst members of the opposition which was still going on when the ballot began. The result was 213 in favour of the paragraph and 205 against. It was greeted by vociferous cheering from members of the opposition, and stunned silence from the Government. The majority was so small that Marshal Soult, the nominal head of the Guizot Government, went immediately to King Louis Philippe to tender the resignation of himself and colleagues. But the King declined to accept the resignation and exhorted the Government to carry on. Guizot agreed, and the law on the indemnity was eventually voted through.

The French public, however, was excited into fury by those

deputies who voted for the law, and thus in favour of France's 'humiliation'. *Le National* and other anti-government newspapers printed a list of them and condemned them with the unflattering name of 'Pritchardistes'. 'Our aim is no mystery,' one of the newspapers said. 'It is a list of proscription that we erect in view of the coming elections.'

The Pritchard affair was kept alive in French parliamentary circles for the next three years. Partly as a result, the Guizot Government became increasingly unpopular, and the Government and monarchy were finally overthrown in the famous revolution of February 24, 1848. Thus, for the second time in less than sixty years, the tiny island of Tahiti played an important part in the shaping of French and world history.

39. POMARE STRUGGLES ON

PRITCHARD's departure from Tahiti did not bring an end to the struggles of Pomare. The Queen and her people continued to live and fight in the hope that British warships would come to their aid. On June 13, 1844, the Queen addressed another pitiful letter to Queen Victoria from HMS *Basilisk*, where she was still virtually a prisoner:

> The supplication of Pomare to Victoria:
> My elder sister and Queen, behold, I am yours. Stretch forth your powerful arm and save me. Overshadow me that I may respire for my breath is spent in this struggle. I am near my confinement and am much discomforted by the smallness of this vessel. I now fasten again the rope which has connected us. Do you not cut it. You are powerful to save.
> Your younger sister in captivity:
> > Pomare.

Skirmishes between the natives and the French troops continued to take place, in which the natives frequently got the upper hand. On June 30, Thomas McKean, an English missionary, was accidentally killed by a native bullet while standing on his veranda. This was too much for the rest of the missionaries. On July 2, they held a meeting at Papeete at which all but two decided to clear out to other parts.

July 12 was a day of great rejoicing for Queen Pomare. Lord George Paulet, captain of HMS *Carysfort*, anchored off Papeete and came into harbour in his boat with news that the French Government did not recognize the seizure of Tahiti and merely wished to preserve the protectorate. Bruat, however, had not received official advice of this and refused to change the established order of things. But after several interviews with Lord George, he agreed to allow Queen Pomare to sail for the leeward islands of the group and there remain unmolested until definite instructions arrived from France. On being acquainted of this, the Queen sent letters to the various chiefs beseeching them to remain in peace until affairs were decided on.

Two days later, HMS *Basilisk* steamed out of harbour and transferred the Queen to the *Carysfort*, which carried her to Raiatea. On her arrival, she wrote another letter of appeal to Queen Victoria:

Raiatea, July 27, 1844.

Most gracious Queen:

Do not, do not indeed leave me. Do you raise me again from captivity. Be you the protector that I may never, no never, be reduced again to captivity. I have no government. Philippe is king. Pomare.

Two months later, she wrote again:

Encampment at Vaiaau, Raiatea,
September 27, 1844.

O great Queen of Britain:

My elder sister,

I am wandering in this place and that place, on mountains and in valleys with fear. This is my word to you: do not regard with strictness my errors and ignorance. Shelter me with your great compassion that I may not faint in the day of heat. Pomare.

This was Pomare's last letter to her great sister Queen. There had been no response to any of the others, and there was to be no response to this. Pomare realized at last that Palmerston's offers of Queen Victoria's 'protection' and 'good offices' were merely idle words. Britain had left her in the lurch. She would have to fight on alone.

The realization of this seems to have made her even more determined to win back her kingdom. On October 12, she despatched the following stiff letter to Bruat:

> I have been informed that the King of the French and his wise counsellors have disapproved of the proceedings of Admiral Du Petit-Thouars in seizing my government, my house, and my lands because my personal flag did not please him. The great King of the French and his wise counsellors have also said that Admiral Du Petit-Thouars acted without being commanded and with injustice and without wisdom, and that they have commanded you to restore my government and my lands. I thought, and wise men thought also, that you would regard the commands of your master, the King, and restore quickly to me my flag, my house, and my lands. But you have not done so. You are still obstinate in building barracks and erecting forts upon my land and upon my people's land, and you interfere with my people in appointing judges and other officers which you have no right to do. I write this word to you that you may know that I throw all the evils of these things upon you, and to make known to you that until you restore to me my flag, my lands, and my property, and rehoist the proper flag agreeably to the command of your King, I can place no confidence in what you say or even listen to you.
>
> And now may you be kept and saved by the true God.
>
> Pomare.

It was not until the first days of 1845 that action was taken to restore the Queen to her sovereignty. By that time, Admiral Hamelin (Du Petit-Thouars's successor) had arrived in Papeete with instructions from his Government to re-establish the protectorate. On being informed that the Queen was in Raiatea, he sailed thither to induce her to return to Tahiti. The Queen, however, fled to the mountains as soon as the Admiral's vessel was sighted, and refused to have any correspondence with him unless the French surrendered her lands to her unconditionally. Hamelin returned to Papeete on January 8; announced that Pomare had been deposed for ever; and appointed Paraita to the sovereignty. The French flag was then hauled down, and Tahiti returned to the status of a French protectorate.

The natives, however, did not cease to hope that Britain would assist them, and fighting with the French broke out anew. The fighting was particularly stubborn. Bruat had his hands full, and his soldiers were almost run off their feet. On August 11, the natives were excited by the arrival of Admiral Sir George Seymour in HMS *Collingwood*. Seymour, however, had merely come to acknowledge the protectorate on behalf of Great Britain and to come to an agreement with the French admiral on Pritchard's indemnity. The natives were astonished. They could not believe that Britain had deserted them. At a meeting in the missionary chapel at Papenoo, the chiefs told Seymour that they would always remain 'the attached allies of England'. 'We pledged ourselves as the allies of England while the *Talbot* was here,' they said, 'and nothing can shake our resolution. We will bide by the decision of our Queen. If she submits, we will submit: if she resists, we will defend her.' Seymour tried to dissuade them from following their resolution, and advised them to submit quietly to the French protectorate. But the natives would not, and more stubborn fighting broke out as soon as the *Collingwood* sailed. It continued for the rest of 1845 and throughout the following year.

The end of the useless struggle came in February, 1847, when Queen Pomare finally harkened to the advice of a strong-minded Tahitian woman, the chiefess Arii Taimai, and agreed to submit to the French protectorate. A French warship was sent to Raiatea to fetch her. It brought her to Papeete on February 9 flying the protectorate flag. The forts around the harbour broke out into a royal salute; the French soldiers lined up on shore for her inspection; and her old enemy, Bruat, handed her the keys of a palace which had been brought ready-made from France in 1844 for her benefit. So ended another chapter in Tahitian history.

40. A DISSOLUTE BACKWATER

For fifteen years after the return of Pomare, Tahiti was a dissolute backwater with little commercial activity and no religious freedom.

The French governors were mainly naval officers who cared nothing about developing the agricultural possibilities of the island, and merely regarded it as a military outpost and naval station. The prosperous trade that had been developed under the missionaries fell away to practically nothing. The value of exports (mainly oranges and pearl shell) seldom exceeded £20,000 a year, while the cost to France of maintaining a 400-man garrison ranged annually from £24,000 to £28,000. This adverse trade balance made provisions at Papeete exorbitantly expensive, and the whalers and other vessels which had once frequented the port in such large numbers took their business elsewhere.

Under Governor Lavaud (the successor to Bruat), the guarantee of religious freedom promised by Guizot was forgotten. The few remaining missionaries were virtually prohibited from following their calling. The native chapels were converted into national property (thus uniting church and state), and some of the missionary dwellings were appropriated by the Government. A law passed in March, 1851, prohibited a missionary from preaching outside his own district without a written invitation. Another law made it almost impossible for the London Missionary Society to send out reinforcements. And a third prevented the missionaries from printing religious or educational material unless authorized by the Government. By 1853, only three foreign ministers were allowed to preside in the native churches, and these had seceded from the London Missionary Society and made themselves subservient to the French Government. The only other teachers were natives whose educational and religious attainments were not high.

Under this state of things, it was not surprising that the natives relapsed into their bad old ways. 'A moral blight has been making steady progress throughout the land,' a visitor said in 1853. 'Dissipation walks unblushingly in the face of day. It has lately been discovered that those natives who, through all the turmoil of foreign warfare and its attendant evils, had been looked upon as the bulwarks of the church, have occasionally yielded to the allurements of dissipation, and it is to be feared that Queen Pomare herself is becoming remiss in the performance of her religious duties.' Another visitor said that the Queen led 'a rollicking, sportive life surrounded by troupes of frolicsome attendants' and spent much money 'decking her dark-eyed favourites with trinkets'.

Dr. Karl Scherzer, who visited Tahiti in the Austrian frigate *Novara* in February, 1859, said that there was no public school in Papeete and most of the Protestant schools were closed. The rising generation was therefore growing up in utter ignorance.

> While in the interior [Dr. Scherzer continued] Sunday is observed with much strictness, there is great indifference to its observance in the seaport. Nowhere does one witnesss more shamelessness than at what is known as the Pre Catalan, a lawn-like meadow, which extends directly in front of the governor's palace, and is, in fact, one of its dependencies. Here, in the presence of the French gendarmes and soldiers and under the very eyes of the protectorate authorities . . . dances of the most dissolute kind are executed by half-drunk Tahitian girls. One must have seen the 'upa-upa' (hula-hula) danced by these lascivious Tahitians . . . to apprehend the mingled shame and indignation with which it fills any but a French by-stander. The musicians sitting on the ground strike a little kettle-drum with the flat of the hand and beat time as well with their feet. Suddenly a dancer of either sex springs into the enclosure and goes through a number of extraordinarily animated movements, which are the louder laughed at and applauded in proportion to their indecency. After this he or she mingles once more with the crowd, excited and breathless. . . .

The dissolute behaviour of the natives and the lethargy that brooded over them after the establishment of the French protectorate had an alarming effect on vital statistics. A census taken at the beginning of 1848 gave the number of natives as 8,082. Ten years later the number had dropped to 5,988. These figures compared with a population of 16,000 on the arrival of the *Duff* in 1797.

The only positive result of the first fifteen years of peaceful French rule was the extension of the protectorate over the Tuamotu Archipelago and some of the islands of the Society Group, the erection of bridges, and the improvement and extension of roads in Tahiti. It was not until the 1860's that Tahiti began to go ahead.

41. THE ROMANCE OF ATIMAONO

THE outbreak of the American Civil War on April 12, 1861, was the beginning of a romantic (if somewhat unsavoury) episode in Tahitian history—the founding of a cotton plantation of unprecedented proportions in the district of Atimaono.

Due to the blockade of the cotton ports of the southern United States, the world was suddenly faced with an acute shortage of raw cotton. This had a cataclysmic effect on the great milling industry of Lancashire, where two million people were thrown out of work by the beginning of 1862. The price of cotton rose abruptly from below 7d. a pound in the early months of 1861 to more than 2s. 6d. a pound in 1864. This was naturally a great stimulus to the growing of cotton in other parts of the world, and agents were sent out from England to find suitable sites for new plantations. On September 14, 1862, an Irish adventurer called William Stewart arrived in Tahiti.

William Stewart was a big man with a long black beard, black hair, and piercing dark eyes. He is said to have been born in the north of Ireland in 1825 and to have spent his youth as a cavalry officer with the British Army in India. He was subsequently in the wine business in Spain and Portugal, and later again in a similar business in Sydney, Australia, where his brother, James, was a customs officer. The two brothers stayed in Australia until 1858 when they got into trouble with the authorities over a conspiracy to avoid the payment of duties on a shipment of wine, spirits, and tobacco. Finding Sydney too hot for them, they escaped in separate schooners to Lord Howe Island, after which nothing is known of their history for about four years. It is probable, however, that William Stewart eventually gravitated to Tahiti, where he could not have failed to glimpse the tremendous possibilities of mending his fortunes in agriculture. It is likewise probable that he returned to England with the idea of raising capital for an agricultural project.

At any rate, when Stewart arrived in Tahiti in September, 1862, he was acting as agent for the Polynesian Plantation Company, which had been formed with a capital of £35,000, to buy land for the cultivation of cotton. The company's principal backer was a Portuguese financier of London and Paris called Augusto Soares. Soares was Stewart's brother-in-law.

Stewart's easy manner, glib tongue, and enthusiasm over the future of cotton-growing in Tahiti soon won the ear of the island's Governor, M. Gaultier de la Richerie. Articles on the culture of cotton began to appear in *Le Messager de Tahiti*, the Government newspaper, and de la Richerie promised to provide Stewart with 12,000 acres of native land for the establishment of a plantation. The purchase price was to be £2,000. The land, which had been chosen by Stewart himself, was to be free of taxation for twenty years, and all the machinery and other articles of prime necessity for the plantation were to be exempt from customs duty for a similar period.

Having obtained these concessions, Stewart returned to England, where he was able to interest other capitalists in the plantation project. A new company called the Tahiti Cotton and Coffee Plantation Co. Ltd. was incorporated in London on June 4, 1863, with a capital of £100,000. This company acquired all the rights and interests of the Polynesian Plantation Company so that its capital was actually £135,000.

Meanwhile, Government agents had been sent to the projected plantation site in the districts of Atimaono, Mataiea, and Papara to get the native landowners to agree to sell the 12,000 acres

186

which de la Richerie had guaranteed. The agents, however, met with unexpected difficulties, for many of the natives refused to give up their birthrights even though their land was largely unused. Their refusal caused the Governor to threaten them with expropriation, which so aroused the ire of a number of Papeete residents that a letter of complaint was sent to the French Government in Paris.

When Stewart returned to Tahiti in January, 1864, he found that the Governor had been forbidden to carry out the threatened expropriations and that he was therefore unable to make the sale of the promised land. Nevertheless, the Governor promised to use his influence to make the natives sell their land to Stewart. News of this soon leaked out through the Government interpreter and caused further resentment among people in Papeete. Mr. George Miller, the British Consul, who had watched over native interests since the departure of Mr. Pritchard, was particularly annoyed. He bearded the Governor on the matter at a party at the British Consulate; the Governor heatedly denied any suggestion of interference and left the party in a huff. A few days later, a letter from the Government secretary to the native councils of Atimaono-Papara and Mataiea was published in the Government newspaper stating that the natives were 'completely free' to sell their lands or not. 'Thus if anyone says to you,' the letter continued, 'that the Governor has given you the order to sell your land, you can reply to him that it is a lie.' Despite this public protestation, de la Richerie's successor admitted that Government pressure was used to make the natives sell. But Stewart also used his own methods to win the natives' favour. Having established himself on a property of 900 acres at Teahupo, the lease of which he had had transferred to him in 1862, he paid considerable attentions to a handsome chiefess and gave a number of parties to which the native landowners were invited. This combination of Government pressure, amorous insinuation, and good fellowship soon brought results. From March 12 onwards, the Government newspaper was flooded with notices stating that this or that native had consented to lease or sell. Stewart's success made the British Consul and others increasingly hostile, and this hostility was frequently manifested as the years passed. Miller actually took Stewart to court on one occasion over an 'insulting' letter which Stewart wrote him. Stewart retaliated by trying to get the British Foreign Office to dismiss the Consul from his post.

Although Stewart soon acquired an extensive property, he could not induce the natives to work on it. The Governor, however, again proved a useful ally. On March 30, 1864, a law was promulgated which authorized Stewart to import 1,000 Chinese labourers before the end of 1865. The law was prefaced by a number of 'considering thats' and consisted of forty-three elaborate regulations. The preamble stated that it was 'the duty of the local government to favour all serious efforts which aimed to increase the agricultural population', and that the introduction of Chinese workers 'could not cause any trouble in the country, but, on the contrary, could result in immense advantages, by example, to the "insouciante" natives', who were 'so little given to work'. The regulations stipulated that the coolies, who were not to be over forty years of age, were to be contracted for periods of up to seven years. At the end of their contracts, they were to be repatriated at the expense of the plantation company, but those who wished to renew their contracts or remain in the colony could obtain permission to do so. A house and a garden were to be provided free for each head of family. Food, medical attention, working tools, and a certain number of clothes were also to be provided free. The working day was to be of twelve hours, with a break of two and a half hours for one or two meals. In effect, Atimaono was to be a worker's paradise. The regulations added that the coolies were to be contracted under the supervision of French consular officials, and that in Tahiti they would be under the protection of the Commissioner of Immigration.

Stewart, however, did not wish to mark time until the arrival of these coolies, so he induced de la Richerie to lend him the Government gun-boat to recruit workers in the Cook Islands. Ninety-six of these islanders were brought to Tahiti on May 21, 1864, on a twelve-month contract. They were immediately set to work clearing and fencing the Atimaono property, which Stewart had graced with the name of Terre Eugénie in honour of the French Empress. By October 1, about 340 acres had been cleared and over 100 planted with cotton. An article in the Government newspaper said that work was proceeding 'with rapidity and enthusiasm' and showed results that 'should confound those who doubted the success of this unprecedented enterprise in our colony'.

On November 5, 1864, de la Richerie was replaced as Governor by Count de la Ronciere. Stewart, who was a great ladies' man and a lavish host, wasted no time in wooing the favour of the Count and his wife. The count and countess visited his remarkable plantation a week or so after their arrival, and thereafter became frequent visitors. The count was soon supporting the enterprise with even greater enthusiasm than his predecessor, while his wife showed her appreciation for Stewart's attentions by dubbing him 'le beau monsieur d'Atimaono'.

The first contingent of 329 Chinese labourers arrived at the plantation from Hong Kong on February 28, 1865. During the same month, the first sample of Tahitian sea-island cotton was exported. The brokers declared it excellent, and valued it at the remarkably high price of between 3s. 4d. and 3s. 7d. a pound. About 200,000 pounds of cotton were exported by the end of the year, and the prospects for the future of Terre Eugénie seemed bright indeed. A second contingent of 342 Chinese labourers arrived from Hong Kong on December 8, and the final batch of 339 on January 6, 1866. Seven overseers were brought out from England four months later.

With this big increase in his working force and with the money for cotton rolling in, Stewart was able to do things on a grandiose scale. The clearing of land (of which 17,000 acres were eventually acquired) and the planting of cotton went on at a prodigious rate. Two fisheries were established at Taravao and Maroa to help feed the plantation personnel, and numerous buildings were erected—some on coral blocks brought from the great *marae* at Mahaiatea despite the prayers and protestations of the natives. The buildings included a cotton ginning mill, engine and boiler house, cotton drying house, sugar mill, coffee cleaning house, boat houses, a hospital, substantial quarters for the employees, and a comfortable house for Stewart himself. Three schooners were employed to ship the cotton to Europe and bring back machinery and supplies. Plans were also laid down for a Chinese club and theatre.

The development of the plantation was a tribute to Stewart's tremendous drive, energy, and administrative ability. But what impressed everyone most was the building of a country house on a small plateau about 1,600 feet above sea-level and nearly three miles in an air line from the sea. The idea had been suggested to Stewart by Countess de la Ronciere, who remarked to him one day that such an estate as Terre Eugénie should have a health resort on the heights. Stewart replied that it was too soon for him to think of such an expense, but secretly began to make plans. He had a road made up the hill and a site cleared on the plateau, ostensibly to plant cinchona trees. All the material for a six-room house and out-buildings was cut and marked ready to erect. Most of Stewart's 1,200 labourers were then diverted from their other work to carry up the material and erect the buildings, to instal furniture, lay out a garden and transplant bushes and even small trees, which were watered from a neighbouring spring. The work was accomplished in a few weeks without the slightest hint of it reaching Papeete. When all was ready, Stewart hastened to Papeete to induce the count and countess to come to Terre Eugénie to be surprised. On their arrival at the plantation, they were carried in sedan chairs up the winding road to the house, which Stewart presented to the countess as a 'maison de campagne', complete with a staff of servants. The countess named it Montcalm, but she did not occupy it very often. By the beginning of 1867, the hostility towards Stewart among people in Papeete had become so bitter that the Governor and his wife felt it prudent to curtail their visits.

Stewart's enemies were outraged by the rumours and stories of his despotic manner of running the Atimaono plantation. It was said in Papeete that workers who incurred his displeasure were subjected to fines, reductions of rations, terms of solitary confinement, and even incarceration in fetters. Another rumour was that Stewart had actually rigged up a guillotine on the property and had executed a Chinaman after practising on a pig. While this was undoubtedly a gross fabrication, other stories were certainly true. The British Consul reported to the Foreign Office on one occasion that an Englishman called John Bible had gone insane as a result of the treatment he received at Atimaono. Another of his reports said that several English overseers had complained that Stewart had failed to fulfil the repatriation clause in their contracts. Other consular correspondence shows that the hours worked at Atimaono were often longer than the time laid down in the regulations; that overseers sometimes whipped and beat their charges; and that Stewart was lax in returning native labourers to their home islands at the end of their contracts. The most notorious case of this concerned forty-five Cook Islanders who were kept at Atimaono two years longer than their contracts stipulated, and were forced at pistol point to land on the island of Maupiha after the rascally captain of the repatriation vessel had robbed them of all they had earned during the preceding three years.

While Stewart, with the Governor's protection, could afford to ignore what people thought of him in Papeete, it was a different matter when adverse reports were published about him in the outside world. Two such reports, based on information supplied by an ex-worker on the Atimaono plantation, appeared in the San Francisco Press and the *Sydney Morning Herald* in the early part of 1867. The articles bitterly attacked the plantation as a place where slavery was the rule and atrocities were commonplace. As these allegations were also a reflection on the French administration, the Governor ordered a commission to be set up to investigate. The commission consisted of five French officials, four planters, two sea-captains, and three merchants, one of whom was Consul for Hamburg. Stewart also tried to get the British Consul to be present at the investigation, but his invitation was politely declined.

The commission met at Atimaono for several days in the first weeks of September, 1867, and questioned many of Stewart's employees. Its report completely exonerated Stewart of charges of ill-treatment, and expressed 'profound indignation at the unwarranted attacks' on the Atimaono enterprise. The only cause for complaint that the commissioners could find was that the Chinese were not allowed to hang themselves—a course one of them had apparently taken to avoid paying his gambling debts! 'There is no question of cruelty,' the commissioners said, 'and no one complains of ill-treatment, of having been beaten, or of lack of food. In short, the members of the commission express their complete satisfaction, without reserve, of everything they have seen. Some of them, who have been in English, French, and Spanish colonies declare that they have rarely seen immigrants who were the objects of such intelligent care; who have such well-arranged lodgings, such a well-equipped hospital, such good food, and such regular pay; and who are treated with so much kindness.'

Stewart was naturally delighted by the commission's report, which was undoubtedly more generous than he deserved. He made sure that it was widely circulated by printing it in a pamphlet called 'An Outline of how it came to pass that so many Absurd Stories have been circulated about the Cotton Plantation on Terre Eugénie'. A copy of the pamphlet was sent to the *Sydney Morning Herald*, which published an apologetic summary of the commission's findings. Thus, for the time being, Stewart's name was cleared. But his troubles did not end.

Early in 1868, he fell out with his brother James, who, for some years, had been running a small mercantile business in Papeete besides a store at Atimaono, which was managed by William Keane. The business at Papeete was apparently run against the advice of William, and when James experienced financial difficulties, William refused to help him. James therefore decided to sell out and quit Tahiti, and Keane came forward as a buyer of the Atimaono store. Keane, however, did not have the ready money to pay James, so he approached William for a loan. William gave him an order for 92,000 francs, payable six months after date on his Auckland agents, which Keane handed to brother James. James Stewart then proceeded to liquidate his Papeete store.

Meanwhile, William sent James a bill for 24,000 francs, which James owed him for freight on merchandise brought to Tahiti in plantation schooners. James recognized the legitimacy of this bill, but claimed that the correct amount owing was 17,000 francs. This led to another argument between the two brothers, and the matter was taken to court. Here was the opportunity for Judge Langomazino, one of William's bitterest enemies, to get his revenge. He did so by upholding James Stewart's contention that the bill should be reduced to 17,000 francs and also by ordering that the draft for 92,000 francs, which William had given to Keane and Keane to James, should be rendered payable at once. In other words, William was ordered to make an immediate payment to his brother of 75,000 francs.

William Stewart appealed against this ridiculous decision to the superior court, but came off even worse than before. M. Boyer, the president, not only upheld the decision of the lower court, but also ordered him to pay immediately a draft for 25,000 francs on his New Zealand bankers which he had given to James some time earlier. This meant that William had to make an immediate payment of 100,000 francs. William, of course, did not have such a large sum of money on hand; and when he had not made a settlement within forty-eight hours, a sheriff took possession of all the property at Atimaono and even confiscated the Chinamen's food.

At this point, Governor de la Ronciere stepped in and ordered the Caisse Agricole (Agricultural Bank) to buy 100,00 francs worth of cotton from the plantation, which enabled Stewart to pay the amount of the unjust judgment. The Governor then removed the two judges who had attempted to ruin Stewart, and banished Boyer to the neighbouring island of Moorea. Boyer, however, had influential friends in Paris, and through them, he denounced the Governor to the French Government. The result was that de la Ronciere was recalled in March, 1869, after being ordered to restore Boyer to his post. Meanwhile James Stewart, with 100,000 francs in his pocket, had slipped out of Tahiti to San Francisco, leaving debts amounting to 60,000 francs behind him. His subsequent history is unknown, but there were various reports that he died in gaol after being convicted for fraud.

William Stewart's loss in the disastrous transaction with his brother was the turning point in the fortunes of the Tahitian Cotton and Coffee Plantation Company. Although the plantation was producing over 700,000 pounds of cotton a year, the price—from 1868 onwards—dropped steadily due to the rapid recovery of the American estates at the end of the Civil War. To combat the decreasing returns, Stewart apparently decided to increase the production of the plantation—a course of action which made it necessary to import more labour.

Recruiting vessels were therefore sent out to various islands and several hundred Gilbert, Ellice, and Cook Islanders were brought back between 1869 and 1872. But the callous methods of the masters of these vessels (who included the notorious 'Bully' Hayes) did the plantation more harm than good. The most injurious voyage was that of the *Moaroa*, commanded by Captain Blackett.

The *Moaroa* left Tahiti in April, 1869, and collected about 180 natives at various islands in the New Hebrides before meeting the *Anne*, of Melbourne, off Nukunau on July 4, 1869. The *Anne* had 159 natives on board who had been recruited as labourers for Fiji. But the captain was afraid of landing them in those islands due to a report that a British man-of-war was lying in wait for unauthorized 'blackbirders'.

When it was learned that the *Moaroa* was in search of labourers for Tahiti, the captain of the *Anne* offered to sell his natives to Captain Blackett at £5 a head. The sale was agreed upon, but as Blackett did not have the ready cash, J. B. Laffin, the supercargo of the *Anne*, transferred to the *Moaroa* to collect the money in Tahiti. With over three hundred natives on board, the *Moaroa* steered for Tahiti, but she had not cleared the New Hebrides when the natives revolted. Blackett, Laffin, and six others were killed, and four were wounded. The natives were in complete possession of the ship when Steenalt, the Danish mate, remembered some gunpowder that was on deck. Creeping forward from his hiding-place in the hold, he emptied seventeen pounds of it into a butter firkin and blew up the deck. A large number of natives were killed in this explosion and many others were maimed. The rest jumped overboard and made for the shore, but many of them did not reach safety for Steenalt & Co. fired on them with rifles and the sharks did the rest. An official inquiry into this bloody outrage was held in Papeete when the *Moaroa* returned, but Steenalt concocted an acceptable excuse, and no action was taken against anyone.

Despite the fact that the Protectorate Government sent an agent on subsequent recruiting voyages for the Atimaono plantation, there were rumours on each vessel's return that the natives had been captured by foul means and that further massacres had taken place. These rumours, with others from other parts of the Pacific, eventually became so persistent that on June 27, 1872, the British Parliament passed a law making it illegal for British subjects to recruit native labour without the permission of the Governor of an Australian colony or a British Consul.

By this time, however, Stewart could not afford the expense

of importing additional labourers. The Atimaono plantation was in serious difficulties. The price of cotton at the end of 1871 had fallen to 1*s*. 5*d*. a pound and the prospects for 1872 were even worse. There was no hope of saving the plantation from disaster.

The beginning of the end came on September 22, 1872, when Stewart's bankers in Auckland put a mortgage into force that they had secured on the property the previous year. Two months later, Stewart was forced to sell a business he had in Papeete to a firm in San Francisco, and on January 31, 1873, he was replaced as manager of Terre Eugénie by an agent for the mortgagors. He was reinstated on March 28, but again replaced on June 17. The plantation's affairs were now in a hopelessly irretrievable state, and Stewart's health was failing rapidly. His phenomenal career ended with startling suddenness. On September 23, 1873, he, personally, was declared bankrupt and forbidden to leave his house at Atimaono without permission. Next night, he died of a violent hæmorrhage, undoubtedly brought on by chagrin. Almost all the friends to whom he had extended hospitality had deserted him, and he was utterly penniless. Everything he had, had been put into the plantation to keep it going.

The collapse of the Tahitian Cotton and Coffee Plantation Company was now imminent. On August 22, 1874, it was declared insolvent by the Tahitian Court; and the Atimaono estate was put up for auction twelve months later at a price of 500,000 francs. The price, however, was far too high for anyone to pay, and within two years the estate was fast falling into ruin. A visitor in 1877 said that 'the bulk of the large village of wooden houses, once tenanted by master and men, now stands empty. The plantation is utterly neglected, the cotton fields are all overgrown with guava scrub, and the whole place is a picture of desolation. . . .'

Nowadays, all that remains of Stewart's magnificent enterprise is a tall mango tree which he planted on the plateau near the site of Countess de la Rónciere's 'maison de campagne'. The house itself and all the other buildings have long since fallen down or been removed, and most of the estate has returned to its virgin state. Even the name of William Stewart has been forgotten. But the legacy he left Tahiti is everywhere apparent. This legacy is the island's thriving Chinese population.

In the last chaotic year of Stewart's life, officialdom conveniently forgot that the Chinese labourers at Atimaono were due to be sent home. So the Chinese stayed on, and as their master's empire fell in ruins around them, they took to growing vegetables for the Papeete market. Gradually they acquired wealth, shifted to Papeete and elsewhere, and became merchants. Nowadays, almost all the small stores of Tahiti and the other islands of French Polynesia are in the hands of the eight thousand descendants of Stewart's coolies and later Chinese immigrants. A lot of other business is also in their hands.

42. A TAHITIAN IDYLL

ON January 29, 1872, Julien Viaud, a young French naval officer, arrived in Tahiti on board the frigate *Flore*. Eight years later, he was to make himself famous as the author of *Le Mariage de Loti*—a romantic novel describing an idyllic love affair between himself and a young native girl called Rarahu. This book was the first of the still endless stream of modern novels, travel books, magazine articles, films, picture postcards, travel brochures, and travelogues glamourizing Tahiti and the South Seas.

Young Viaud was a dreamy, sensitive, romantic youth, who was scarcely cut out for the naval life. His childhood had been sheltered and pampered in an old house at Rochefort, and he had grown up preferring to collect shells, catch butterflies, and read travel books rather than indulge in the more rugged pastimes of normal boys. He had joined the navy not because he wanted to be a sailor, but because he longed to see the strange, exotic places which his sailor-brother Gustave had described to him.

Viaud had been in the navy for about four years when he arrived in Tahiti. He had seen a good deal of the world by then and had filled numerous journals with descriptions of what he had seen. He had had a good many love affairs, too, for he was a good-looking youth and rather fancied himself as a ladies' man.

In fact, making love was the great passion of his life; and after that, writing about it.

On reaching Tahiti, he was just getting over an affair with 35-year-old Carmencita, of Valparaiso, and was ready for another. The result was the idyll of Rarahu, the details of which he recorded in his journal and later used as the basis of his first novel. In the novel, however, he changed his nationality from French to English; gave himself the name of Harry Grant (although he soon adopted the name of Loti which the Tahitians gave him); put himself on board the *Reindeer* instead of the *Flore*; and made the *Reindeer* stay in Tahiti for over a year instead of a few weeks.

Le Mariage de Loti is a loosely knit novel, and was evidently written rather hastily, at odd moments, in between the author's other duties. There is little attention to form. The plot weaves slowly in between long, extraneous pen pictures of Tahiti and Tahitian life. The story is sometimes related in the first person and sometimes in the third. Even the tenses are not always the same. Nevertheless, *Le Mariage de Loti* is an extremely readable book. No other writer has succeeded in recreating the peculiar (almost indescribable) atmosphere of Tahiti as well as Loti did. The love-story, however, is rather too sentimental for modern tastes, but it is interesting if only to see how tastes in literature have changed.

As Loti's famous novel is not easily procurable in English nowadays, a digest of it is given in the following pages. Apart from one or two connecting sentences and explanatory phrases, and the changing of a tense or person here and there, the digest is in the author's own words, as translated by Clara Bell.

Rarahu was born in January, 1858, in the island of Bora Bora. At the moment when this tale begins, she had just completed her fourteenth year. While very young, her mother had sent her away in a long canoe with sails which was making for Tahiti. Rarahu's mother had her brought to Tahiti to make a present of her to a very old woman of the Apire district to whom she was distantly related. This time-honoured exchanging of children is one of the quaint peculiarities of Polynesian manners.

Rarahu was a little creature unlike anyone else, although

she was a perfect specimen of the Maori race which has peopled the Polynesian archipelagos, and which is one of the finest types of humanity. A very distinct race, too, whose origin and birthplace remain an unsolved mystery.

Rarahu's eyes were of a tawny black, full of exotic languor and coaxing softness, like those of a kitten when it is stroked; her eyelashes so long and so black that you might have taken them for painted feathers. Her nose was short and delicate, like the nose in some Arab faces; her mouth, rather too thick and too wide for a classic model, had deep corners deliciously dimpled. When she laughed, she showed all her teeth, somewhat large teeth of brilliantly white enamel, not yet polished by the wear of years but showing the striations of young growth. Her hair, scented with sandalwood oil, was long, straight, and rather harsh, falling in heavy locks on her bare shoulders. Her skin was of the same hue all over, from her forehead to the tips of her toes; a dusky brown, verging on brick-red, like that of old Etruscan terra-cotta pottery. Rarahu was small, beautiful in proportion and mould; her bosom was purely formed and polished; her arms as perfect as an antique. Round her ankles a pattern was tattooed to imitate anklets; across her lower lip were three faint blue lines like those of the women of the Marquesas; and on her forehead a still paler tattoo suggested a coronet. The feature most characteristic of her race was the small space between her eyes, which like the eyes of all Maoris were by no means deep set. When she was laughing and gay this gave her face the mischievous shyness of a marmoset; when she was grave or sad, there was something about her which can only be described as Polynesian grace.

Rarahu, from her earliest infancy, had scarcely ever left the cabin inhabited by her old adoptive mother, who lived in the Pare district by the brook Fautaua. Her business in life was very simple: to dream, to bathe—especially to bathe—to sing, and to wander through the woods with Tiahoui, her inseparable companion.

It must not, however, be supposed that Rarahu was wholly unlearned; she could read her Tahitian Bible, and write in a large and very firm hand the soft words of her native tongue; nay, she was strong in spelling by the rules of orthography as laid down by the Picpus brothers, who constructed a conventional code of syllables in the Latin character to represent Polynesian sounds.

It was about noon, on a calm and scorching day, when I first saw my little friend Rarahu. I had gone to the Fautaua falls with some friends from the *Reindeer*. The young Tahitian women who frequented the falls—drowsy with the heat—were lying on a grassy bank close to the stream, their feet dipping in the clear, cool water. The same green shade lay over us, vertical and motionless; large black velvet butterflies marked with lavender eyes fluttered languidly past, or rested on us, as though their sheeny wings were too heavy to bear them; the air was charged with heady and unfamiliar perfume; quite unconsciously, I abandoned myself to this enervating existence, overborne by the Oceanian spell.

The undergrowth of mimosa and guava trees in the background of the picture was suddenly parted; there was a gentle rustle of leaves, and two little girls peered forth, studying the situation like two mice peeping out of a hole. They were crowned with head-dresses of leaves to shelter their heads from the heat of sun; they were girt with *pareus* (sarongs) of dark blue with broad yellow stripes; their slender dusky bodies were otherwise bare; their long black hair hung loose. No Europeans were to be seen; there was nothing to scare them. The two children, feeling quite safe, stole out to lie under the waterfall, which tumbled and splashed noisily about them. The prettier of the two was Rarahu; the other was Tiahoui, her friend and confidante.

Then Tetouara (a humorous Melanesian woman) roughly seized my arm—my navy blue sleeve with its gold braiding—and held it up high above the long grass in which I was lying, displaying it to them with an indescribable twinkle of mischievous fun—shaking it like a scarecrow.

The two little things, startled like two birds who catch sight of a baboon, fled in a panic. And that was our introduction, our first interview.

During the next month, I got to know Rarahu quite well, and one day, while playing cards with Queen Pomare (who was a great cheat), the Queen suggested that Rarahu and I should marry in the Tahitian fashion.

Rarahu's old foster-parents had ideas on such subjects which are not current in Europe, and I was not slow to discover this. They said that a great girl of fourteen was no longer a child and was not created to live alone. She did not walk the streets of Papeete, and that was all they asked of her propriety. They thought Loti better than many another—Loti, who, like her, was young, who seemed gentle-tempered, and appeared to be fond of her. So after due reflection, the old folks approved.

In order to be able to talk to Rarahu in her own tongue, to understand her thoughts, even the deepest or the strangest, I made up my mind to learn Maori. . . .

The hours, days, months, flew in this land as they do nowhere else; time slipped on without leaving any trace, in the monotony of perpetual summer. It was as though I were in an atmosphere of unchanging calm, where the turmoil of the world had ceased to exist!

Oh! those delicious hours—the summer hours, sweet and warm, which we spent, day after day, by the Fautaua brook, in that nook in the woods, so shady and out of ken, which was the nest of Rarahu and Tiahoui.

But there was one thing which Rarahu was already beginning to feel, and which she was fated to feel bitterly later—a thing she was incapable of formulating with any precision in her own mind, and yet more of expressing in the terms of her primitive tongue. She apprehended vaguely that there must be gulfs in the intellectual order fixed between Loti and herself, whole worlds of undreamed-of ideas and knowledge. She already appreciated the difference of our race, of our notions, of our lightest emotions. On the most elementary details of life, our ideas differed widely. Loti, though dressed as a Tahitian and speaking her language, was still to her a *popaa*—that is to say, one of the men who come from the impossible lands beyond the ocean. Then, too, she knew that Loti would soon go away, never to return—go away to his own remote country. She had no conception of those bewildering distances. She never thought of herself as being in Loti's eyes—child of fifteen as she was—anything more than a strange little being, a plaything for a time, soon to be forgotten.

But she was mistaken. I was beginning to be aware that I had a feeling for her of a less vulgar stamp. I was beginning to love her, really love her. I remembered my brother George, whom the Tahitians had called Roueri, who had carried home with him ineradicable memories of this land, and I felt that I should do the same. It seemed to me quite possible that this love-affair might leave deep and permanent traces on my whole life. . . .

There were numberless mysterious affinities between Rarahu and myself, born at opposite extremities of the earth. Both of us had the habit of seclusion and contemplation; both were used to woods and Nature's solitudes; both were quite happy spending long hours in silence, reclining on moss and flowers; both were passionately addicted to day-dreams, music, fine fruit, flowers, and running water.

And for the present, there was not a cloud on the horizon. We still had five long months before us. It was quite useless to look forward to the future. . . .

In May, 1872, however, the *Reindeer* weighed anchor for a month's cruise of the Marquesas, and the idyll was ended. Against all human anticipation, those hours of peace and delight that we had spent on the shore of the brook of Fautaua were gone, never to return. When the *Reindeer* returned, Rarahu's adoptive father was dead, and Rarahu came to live with me in a hut behind the Queen's gardens in Papeete.

The days went by very gently under the towering coconut palms which shaded our dwelling.

To rise every morning soon after the sun, go past the boundary of the Queen's garden, and there plunge into the stream that flows past the palace and take a long bath under the acacias—it was delicious in the pure fresh morning air of Tahiti! The bath, in fact, was spun out by easy chat with the women about the court, and carried us on till the midday meal. Rarahu's dinner was always extremely frugal; now, as at Apire, she was content with baked breadfruit and a few sweet cakes which the Chinese brought round for sale every morning.

Then sleep filled up the greater part of the day. We hung up hammocks of New Zealand flax under the veranda and spent hours in them, dreaming or sleeping to the soothing chirp of the grasshoppers. In the afternoon, Teourahi would generally drop in to play cards with her friend, Rarahu.

Then we had coral-fishing out on the reef. Rarahu and I would often go out on these excursions in a native canoe, and would poke and grope in the warm blue water and fish up madrepores and cowries. . . .

It was the same exotic, peaceful, sun-lit existence which my brother Roueri had formerly led here, the life I had pictured and longed for in those strange dreams of my boyhood, which had so constantly carried me to these distant lands of the sun. Time glided on, and all about me grew those thousand inextricable little threads, twined of the charms of the South Sea shores, which at last are knotted into a dangerous web, veiling the past, casting a shroud over home and our native land, till it has so closely enwrapped the dreamer that he cannot escape. The sweet habits of our domestic life bound us more closely day by day; and yet the life of this delightful today had no possible tomorrow. It must be cut short by separation and absence—the most utter separation, which would put continents and oceans between us— the awful diameter of the whole earth!

I was very fond of the poor little thing, and the Tahitians always called her Loti's little wife. She was to all intent my little wife; I loved her truly. And yet there was a great gulf between us—a great gate for ever shut. She was a little savage; between us two, who were one flesh, there was the radical difference of race and utter divergence of views on the first elements of things. If my ideas and conceptions were often impenetrably dark to her, so were hers to me; my childhood, my native land, my home and hearth would ever remain to her incomprehensible and strange. I remembered what she had once said to me: 'I am afraid lest the same God did not create us both.' In truth, we were the offspring of two types of nature, absolutely apart and dissimilar, and the union of our souls could only be brief, imperfect, and stormy.

Meanwhile, nothing could be more gentle and more peaceful than my little Rarahu; she never fell into her old childish rages; she was almost always silent, calm, and submissive. She was gracious and attentive to everyone. Anyone coming to the house and seeing her sitting in the shade of the veranda in a happy, careless attitude, smiling on all with the mystic smile of her race, would have said that our little hut and tall trees were the abode of a perfect poem of peaceful and entire happiness.

There, she had hours of passionate tenderness for me; it seemed as though she craved to cling to her only friend and mainstay in the world. At such moments, the thought of my departure made her shed many silent tears; and then I would again recur to the insane notion of remaining here with her for ever. At other times, she would bring out the old Bible she had carried from Apire; she would pray ecstatically, and a simple fervent faith shone in her eyes.

But, then, she very often withdrew from my society, and I could see on her lips the same doubtful and distrustful smile which I had first noticed one evening on returning from Afareahitu. She seemed to gaze far away and see mysterious things in the distance; strange ideas came back to her from her savage childhood, and her sudden questions about the strangest and deepest subjects showed the disorder of her imagination and the chaotic confusion of her ideas. Her Maori blood burned in her veins; she had days of fever and utter prostration when she hardly seemed to be the same creature. Poor little thing, she was hardly responsible for the aberrations of her strangely ardent and vehement nature.

In appearance, she had, as yet, none of the symptoms which, in Europe, betray disease of the lungs. Her figure was full and as perfect as a Greek statue. But the characteristic short cough, just like that of the Queen's children, became more frequent, and the blue circles round her eyes grew darker. She was, in fact, a sad and pathetic personification of the Polynesian race as it gradually dies out under contact with our civilization and our vices, soon to be no more than a memory in the history of Oceania.

Then the day of departure came. The melancholy gleam of dawn came in at the open windows. For a moment, I looked at Rarahu where she slept, and then I woke her with a kiss. 'Ah, yes, Loti,' she said. 'It is the day, you have woke me, we must be off.' Rarahu dressed with many tears; she put on her best tunic and crowned her head with the faded wreath and the *tiare* (gardenias) she had worn yesterday, vowing that she would wear no others till my return. Then I opened the door to the garden and cast a farewell glance at our trees and thicket of flowers. I pulled a branch of acacia, and a trailing clump of pink peri-winkle—and the cat crept after us, mewing as it used to do when we went to the bathing place at Apire. Before the sun had risen, my little savage wife and I, hand in hand, sadly made our way to the strand for the last time.

A silent but numerous throng had already collected; all the Queen's women, all the damsels of Papeete, whose friends or lovers the *Reindeer* was about to snatch away, were there seated on the ground; some were weeping, others simply watched us as we came. Rarahu sat down with the rest without shedding a tear. And the last of the ship's boats carried me on board.

At about eight in the morning the *Reindeer* weighed anchor. It was a lovely morning, calm and soft, as they are in Oceania; there was not a breath of air; heavy clouds were gathering high up among the mountains and forming a great dark vault beneath which the morning sun blazed down on the Tahitian shore, the green coconut palms, and the figures of the women in their white robes. The thought of departure lent the charm of melancholy to this grand picture, so soon to be lost to sight.

When the group of Tahitian women was no more than an in-distinguishable mass, my brother's deserted home, where he had lived with his Tahitian girl, was still for a long time visible on the shore of the sea, and my eyes lingered on the speck as it vanished among the trees. The clouds gathering about the hilltops came down rapidly over Tahiti; they fell like a huge curtain, in which the whole island was presently wrapped. The sharp peak of the precipice of Fautaua was still to be seen through the rent in the shroud, till at last all was lost in the gloomy mass; the trade wind rose to a gale, the sea turned green and surfy and a storm of rain began to fall.

I went below into my dingy cabin and flung myself down in my berth, covering myself with a blue *pareu*, torn in many places by the thorns of the forest, which Rarahu had worn long ago in her home at Apire. There I lay all day, lulled by the monotonous noises of the rolling ship as she laboured on, the sad reiteration of the waves which beat in irregular succession on the hollow walls of the *Reindeer*. All day—sunk in the melancholy reverie which is neither sleeping nor waking, in which pictures of Oceania were strangely mingled with the dim memories of my boyhood.

In the green twilight which came in through the thick bull's-eye that closed my port-hole, I could make out all the queer objects in my room—head-dresses of Oceanian chiefs, the abortive shapes of Maori idols, grinning gods, branches of palm, branches of coral, branches of many kinds snatched at the last hour from the trees in our garden; faded but still fragrant wreaths worn by Rarahu—and that last bunch of pink periwinkle pulled at the door of our little abode.

Soon after sunset, I was to take the watch, so I went up the companion. The keen, open air, the breeze which lashed my face, brought me back to the realities of life and a full comprehension of our departure. Two dim outlines—Tahiti and Moorea—were still to be seen as scarcely visible clouds on the horizon. I had long lost the habit of tears, but for the last twenty-four hours, I had longed to shed them, and in the darkness, I wept like a child.

Three weeks after this, the *Reindeer* put into Honolulu, the chief town of the Sandwich Islands, where for two months we spent a very jolly time. Then followed six months cruising along the coast of California, Canada, and American Russia (*sic*), and on November 1, 1873, the *Reindeer* left San Francisco to return home via Tahiti and Cape Horn.

On November 25, under a strong gale, we made the Tuamotu Islands. The tropical wind was blowing hard and the sky was dirty. At noon on the 26th, land—Tahiti—was in sight ahead to port. A dim outline among the clouds: the peak of Faaa. A few minutes later, the heights of Moorea were in sight to starboard above a transparent low mist. The flying fish rose in hundreds. The 'delicious island' was there, close at hand—and a strange feeling came over me for which I have no words.

The breeze was already loaded with Tahitian perfumes, gusts of scent from orange-trees and gardenias in bloom. A heavy pile of clouds lay over all the island, and soon we could distinguish greenery and coconut palms under this dark hanging. The mountain tops glided swiftly by; Papenoo, the great bluff in Mahina, Fautaua, then Point Venus, Fare-ute and the harbour of Papeete.

I had feared some disillusion, but the view of Papeete was

enchanting. All the golden-tinted verdure had a magical beauty in the evening sunlight.

It was about seven o'clock when we dropped anchor. There was no one on the beach to see us arrive, and by the time I set foot on shore it was dark. The Tahitian scent which distils at night under the leaves was intoxicating. It was a strange joy to find myself once more in this land.

Eventually I found Rarahu, who clasped me in her arms with all her might. We spent the evening wandering aimlessly about the avenues of Papeete or in the Queen's gardens. Sometimes, we loitered down an alley, the first that came; sometimes we threw ourselves on the scented grass among the thick undergrowth of shrubs. They were hours of transient intoxication which we never forget as long as we live—an intoxication of the heart and senses, spell-bound by the indefinable charm and strange influences of Oceania. And in spite of everything, we were sad in the midst of our happiness at meeting again; we both felt that this was indeed the end, that very soon we must part for ever.

Rarahu had altered; in the darkness I could feel that she was more frail, and the terrible little cough was more frequent. Next day I saw that her face was paler, and pinched; she was now nearly sixteen; she was still delightfully young and childlike; but she had acquired more than ever of the mysterious stamp which, in Europe, we call distinction. There was really exquisite and perfect distinction in her little savage physiognomy. Her face seemed to have gained the ultra-terrestrial charm of those doomed to die.

During my absence, she had learnt to speak English, and I cannot express the strange effect it had on me to hear her speak it. She was fully aware of this, and never used it excepting when she was very sure of what she meant to say and wished me to be greatly impressed by it. At such moments, her voice had an indescribable sweetness, and a quaint, penetrating charm of sadness. Some words and phrases she pronounced very well, and then I could fancy her a daughter of my own race and blood; it seemed suddenly to bring us closer together in a mysterious and unexpected way. She saw now that it was vain to think of keeping me with her; that this notion was past and gone like a dream of childhood; that all this was quite impossible and done with for-

ever. Our days were numbered. At most could I talk of returning, and she had ceased to believe me. What she had done during
my absence I knew not; she had taken no other sailor lover, and
this was all I asked. I had not lost a sort of prestige over her
imagination; absence had not broken it, and no one else could
have exerted it. On my return, she had lavished on me all the
love that a passionate little being of sixteen has to give; and yet,
I saw it clearly as time flew on, day by day, Rarahu was slipping
from me. She smiled with the same quiet smile, but her heart, I
knew, was full of bitterness, of disenchantment, of obscure wrath,
and all the seething passions of a savage child. And I loved her
all the time, God knows! It was torture to leave her and know
that she was lost.

'My sweet little girl,' I would say to her, 'you must be very
good when I am gone. God willing, I will come back to you.
You, too, believe in God; then pray, at any rate, pray, and we
shall meet again beyond the grave.'

'You must go away,' I said on my knees to her. 'Go far away
from this town of Papeete. Go and live with your little friend,
Tiahoui, in a country district, far away from any Europeans.
You will marry as she has done, and have a family like a Christian
woman; and then, with little ones belonging to you and which you
will bring up yourself, you will be happy.'

Then, and always, her lips wore the same inscrutable smile;
she hung her head, but made no reply. I knew full well that when
I was gone, she would be one of the wildest of the lost among the
damsels of Papeete. Good God! what misery it was when she,
silent and absent-minded to all I could say to her of passionate en-
treaty, only smiled that smile of mournful indifference, of doubt
and irony. Is there any suffering to compare with this—of loving
and feeling you are no longer listened to? That the heart which
has been yours is closing against you, do what you will? That
the dark, unaccountable side of her nature is reasserting all its
claims and all its power? And, all the time, to love with all your
soul, which is slipping from you?

And then Death lurks in the background; it must lay hands
ere long on that beloved form, flesh of your flesh. Death without
resurrection or hope, since the one who is doomed to die has lost
all faith in salvation and another life. . . .

So the day before the *Reindeer*'s final departure came, Rarahu and I went to sit by the falls at Fautaua.

'Loti,' said Rarahu, 'I am your—I am your little wife, am I not? Do not be afraid for me; I believe in God; I do pray; I will pray; I will do all you ask me, everything. Tomorrow when you go I will leave Papeete and never be seen there again. I will go to live with Tiahoui; I will have no other husband, and till I die, I will pray for you. . . .'

Here sobs cut short her words, and Rarahu put her arms round me and laid her head on my knees. I shed tears too, but they were tears of comfort; I had found my little girl as she had been of old; she was crushed, but she was saved. I could bear to leave her now—for fate must part us inexorably and irrevocably; but the parting was less full of bitterness and heart-rending terrors. I could leave her with a doubtful but consoling hope of returning, and perhaps with a vague hope of eternity. . . .

That evening, there was a grand ball at the palace, a farewell entertainment to the officers of the *Reindeer*. In spite of everything, the ball was a sad function. The greater number of the guests were the ship's officers, and this cast a gloom of departure and parting which nothing could lift. There were young men who were leaving behind a life of careless enjoyment; and there were old men, too, old hands who had been to Tahiti two or three times in the course of their lives and who knew that the end had come, with a chill at their heart as they reflected that they would return no more.

Some time before dawn, I kissed Rarahu for the last time and returned to the ship. Rarahu set out to join her friend, Tiahoui.

Back in England two years later, I met a friend who gave me news of Rarahu. He said that six or eight months after the *Reindeer*'s departure, she had returned to Papeete prettier than ever—more of a woman and more fully formed. Her great sadness gave her added charm; she had the grace of an elegy.

She went to live with a young French officer, whose passion for her was quite out of the common; he was jealous even of Loti's memory. This lasted two or three months, during which she was the most elegant and remarkable-looking woman in Papeete. But an event occurred at court which gave rise to a quarrel between Rarahu and her lover; and as, in fact, she did not care for him, she made it a reason for parting from him. From then on, she stayed at Papeete and led a wholly dissolute life.

A year or so later, I learned from a naval officer in Malta who had just arrived from Tahiti that Rarahu had fallen very low—wreaths of flowers, always fresh, on a death's-head face. She had no home of her own, and wherever she went she dragged an old cat at her heels, a feeble thing with rings in its ears to which she was devoted. This cat followed her everywhere with lamentable mewings. She was dying of consumption, and as she had taken to drinking brandy, the course of the disease was rapid.

One day, in November, 1875, I heard that she had set out with her infirm old cat for her native island of Bora Bora to die. She lived, it would seem, only a few days.

43. END OF AN ERA

ON September 17, 1877, an event occurred in Tahiti which soon brought the end of another era in the island's history. This was the death of Queen Pomare.

The old Queen—she was sixty-four—had been ruler of Tahiti for over fifty years. Her rule, however, had been purely nominal for the greater part of the French protectorate. The Tahitian Legislative Assembly, of which she was the head, rarely met to consider the laws proposed by the Protectorate Government, and the pretence of promulgating laws in her name had long been abandoned.

The Queen's last years were embittered by the death of her eldest and favourite son; and when she died, she was succeeded by her second son, Ariiaue. Ariiaue, who took the title of King Pomare V, was totally unfitted for the duties of even nominal kingship. He was easy-going, dissolute, and drunken. He lived beyond his means, had discarded his wife, and cared nothing for the affairs of state. He had, moreover, passed all his life among the French and so had none of his mother's pride in trying to preserve the glories of the past.

The French authorities took advantage of this weak King to get Tahiti entirely into their own hands. Survey work on the Panama Canal had just begun, and the authorities imagined that the island would eventually become a valuable possession as the first stopping-place west of the canal. They wanted to have undisputed authority in Tahiti when the canal was opened.

It was not difficult for them to get Pomare to abdicate after promising him a number of cash benefits. These benefits included the payment to him of an annual pension of 60,000 gold francs; the payment of similar pensions to his wife and two brothers; the completion of a new palace, begun in the 'sixties; and the payment of his mother's debts. The French authorities also promised that Pomare could conserve his title of King and all the privileges and honours that went with it.

For the King to abdicate, it was necessary to obtain the consent of the leading chiefs of the districts, but their consent was obtained under Government pressure. On June 29, 1880, a declaration of abdication was drawn up 'au palais du gouvernement', signed by 'Le Roi Pomare V' and twenty chiefs. It was provisionally accepted by the French Governor. Three days later, Pomare read the following proclamation to his people assembled on the wharf at Papeete:

Tahitians:

I would have you know that in agreement with Monsieur the Commandant Commissioner of the Republic and the chiefs of the districts, I have declared Tahiti and its dependencies united to France. It is a testimony to the recognition and confidence which I desire to give to the nation, which, for nearly forty years, has covered us with its protection. Henceforth, our archipelago and its dependencies form with France but one and the same country.

I have transferred my rights to France.

I have reserved yours, that is to say, all the guarantees of ownership and liberty which you have enjoyed under the government of the Protectorate. I have even required new guarantees which increase your happiness and prosperity.

Our resolve, I am sure, will be received with joy by all those who love Tahiti and sincerely desire its progress.

We were already Frenchmen at heart. Today we are that in fact. Vive le France. Vive Tahiti.

The French Governor's acceptance of Pomare's abdication was ratified by the French Senate and Chamber of Deputies on December 30, 1880. The century-old rule of the Pomare dynasty was thus brought formally to an end and Tahiti became a fully fledged French colony. By the same Act of Parliament, France also took possession of the myriad islands of the Tuamotu Archipelago.

PART VII

MODERN TAHITI

44. *DOLCE FAR NIENTE*

IN the first six decades after the abdication of the last Pomare there were few events of political, economic or social importance in Tahiti. Having gained undisputed control over the island after governing it as a protectorate for forty years, the French did nothing with it. The rapidity of recall of the French Governors and other officials—there were 38 Governors between 1880 and 1940—prevented any continuity of administrative policy or schemes of reform. Almost nothing was done either in Tahiti or the surrounding islands to develop their greatest natural resource, their agriculture. 'Despite the fact that these fertile islands will produce almost anything, there are comparatively few plantations,' Stewart's *Handbook of the Pacific Islands* recorded in 1908. It went on: 'The chief items of export are copra, vanilla and mother-o'-pearl. The output of copra in 1903 was 8,500 tons, in 1904 5,616 tons and in 1905 6,782 tons. . . . The exports from Tahiti to all countries for 1905 amounted to the sum of £114,133 as against £140,325 in 1904. . . .' The opening of the Panama Canal in 1914 made a small difference to Tahiti's economy, but it certainly did not convert it into the rich and important shipping centre that the authorities of the 'seventies had visualised.

The fact that the French officials lived in houses of colonial splendour, collected large salaries and did very little before they 'leap-frogged' to some new retreat in the French Empire was increasingly criticised in Tahiti as the years passed. There was a strong feeling locally that not enough Tahitians were employed in the various administrative services, and there was considerable resentment over the fact that the officials from France were much better paid than the locals, who were prevented from rising to the higher administrative jobs. In short, it was generally felt that those how knew the country best were governed by those who knew it least.

However, the Tahitians made the best of things and settled down peaceably under their French rulers. Their *joie de vivre* gradually returned to them; and their declining birth rate, which threatened them with extinction for over a century, was halted and they began to increase again. Although many of their ancient customs had been discarded long before the abdication of their last king, much still remained of the old Tahitian way of life.

Despite the efforts of three generations of foreign, straitlaced missionaries, Tahiti remained an uninhibited island of love. The old Tahitian outspokenness and freedom in sex matters never changed; and after years of performing their erotic dances in secret, they brought them into the open again. The Tahitians, however, have remained strong church-goers; yet there are still many lingering beliefs in the old spirits and gods.

Although Tahiti seldom figured in the newspaper headlines of the outside world until the early 1960's, its fame continued undiminished. From 1880 onwards, it was visited by an ever-swelling stream of novelists, artists, yachtsmen, anthropologists, poets, film-makers and tourists of one sort and another who have sung its praises in their own sweet way. In recent times, a year has rarely passed without the publication of at least a couple of travel books on Tahiti and the surrounding islands. Many of their titles speak for themselves.

The following chapters are concerned with the most notable visitors Tahiti has had since it came under the full control of the French, and other matters of recent date that have made the island what it is today.

45. AN INVALID SCOTSMAN

ON September 4, 1888, a tall, graceful, 94-ft. schooner put into Papeete. On board was the most famous literary figure in the English-speaking world—Robert Louis Stevenson. Stevenson, who had already written *Treasure Island*, *Kidnapped*, and *Dr.*

Jekyll and Mr. Hyde, was cruising the South Seas in search of health. He was accompanied by his wife, Fanny, his 64-year-old mother, and his step-son, Lloyd Osbourne. His schooner, the *Casco*, was commanded by a Captain Otis, and manned by a cosmopolitan crew of five.

The *Casco* had been hired for Stevenson by the representative of an American newspaper syndicate which wanted him to write a series of fifty South Sea letters for 10,000 dollars. The vessel belonged to a Californian millionaire physician. She was the last word in luxury—white sails, glittering, polished brasswork, white and gold panels and mirrors, crimson carpets, soft rugs, and velvet, upholstered seats. The natives of Fakarava, where the *Casco* had spent a fortnight at anchor before coming on to Tahiti, had called her 'Pahi Muni', meaning 'silver ship'.

The *Casco* had sailed from San Francisco on June 27. Stevenson had spent the previous winter convalescing from catarrhal consumption in the Adirondacks near the Canadian border. By the time he reached Tahiti, he was much improved in health and his thin frame was almost as brown as a native's. For several weeks, Stevenson and his family lived in a house in Papeete next to the Calabooza Beretane where Melville had been imprisoned. It was 'a little, bare, one-twentieth furnished house surrounded by mangoes, etc.' But the climate of Papeete did not agree with the invalid author. He caught a bad cold and began to suffer again from his old affliction of hæmorrhages. Thinking that the end was near, he calmly arranged his affairs and said farewell to Captain Otis. But after a while, his health improved again and when he had recovered sufficiently, he was taken aboard the *Casco* which left immediately for Taravao.

Twice on the journey to Taravao, the schooner narrowly escaped being battered to pieces on the reef. She managed, however, to anchor in an enclosed harbour without suffering damage, and Stevenson and his family were put ashore. This place proved to be even worse than Papeete. The climate and mosquitoes were so disagreeable that Stevenson was rushed to Tautira, about sixteen miles away, in a wagon hired from a Chinaman. The journey was a trying one over a difficult road crossed by a number of streams. By the time Stevenson reached Tautira, he was in a state of collapse.

For several days, the sick Scotsman lay in a semi-coma in a native house. He had a burning fever, his lungs were congested, and he was unable to eat. To the members of his family, it seemed that he had but a short time to live. Then, one day, there appeared at the door a tall, graceful, native woman, whose bearing indicated her noble birth. The woman was Princess Moe, ex-queen of Raiatea and daughter-in-law of the late Queen Pomare. Princess Moe said she had heard there was a sick foreigner in the village who would not eat, so she had brought him a plate of raw fish, prepared with miti sauces, which she had made herself. Fanny slipped a few morsels into her husband's mouth.

Several times a day from then on, the princess came with other specially prepared native dishes. Within a week, the patient had recovered. He expressed his gratitude in a charming little poem, 'To An Island Princess':

> I threw one look to either hand,
> And knew I was in Fairyland.
> And yet one point of being so,
> I lacked. For, Lady (as you know),
> Whoever by his might of hand
> Won entrance into Fairyland,
> Found always with admiring eyes
> A Fairy princess kind and wise.
>
> It was not long I waited; soon
> Upon my threshold, in broad noon,
> Fair and helpful, wise and good,
> The Fairy Princess Moe stood . . .

To make things more agreeable for the Stevensons, Princess Moe invited them to take over the home of a local chief, Ori-a-Ori. This chief was a huge, broad-shouldered man, who was quickly nicknamed 'The Colonel'. He and Stevenson became warm friends. In the cool of the evenings, they would sit together exchanging stories. Ori related episodes in the history of his own tribe, the Teva clan; and Stevenson replied with tales of his own clansmen in Scotland. Stevenson became so interested in the stories of his host that he found it difficult to concentrate on *The*

Master of Ballantrae which he was then writing. Several times he laid it aside to work on poems describing the doings of Ori's ancestors. The poems were called 'The Song of Rahero' and 'The Feast of Famine'. They were Stevenson's only writings on Tahitian subjects apart from his poem on Princess Moe and a few letters. In the letters, he described Tautira as 'an earthly heaven', 'fairyland', and 'Hans Christian Andersenville'. He regarded the two months he spent there as among the happiest of his life.

Before leaving to continue his voyage in the *Casco*, Stevenson held a huge feast to express his gratitude for the natives' overwhelming hospitality. His departure was a moving one. Oria-Ori, with tears in his eyes, bade him farewell and pleaded with him to return to Tahiti soon. Stevenson, equally moved, promised that he would. His letters for two or three months afterwards indicate that he had every desire to carry out his promise. But he never did. After extensive wanderings in many parts of the Pacific, he settled, at last, at Vailima, Samoa, where he died in 1894.

46. A HISTORIAN AND A PAINTER

HENRY ADAMS had no notion of writing the history of Tahiti's ancient Teva clan when he arrived in Papeete with his painter-friend, John La Farge, on February 4, 1891. But, like Stevenson, he fell under the Teva spell.

Adams, whose grandfather and great-grandfather had been presidents of the United States, was 'seeking relief from the sorrows and tensions' of his own life. The suicide of his wife five years before had been a shattering blow to his emotions; and the exacting work on his *History of the United States* had left him physically and mentally exhausted. He needed to rest and to get away from it all in entirely different surroundings.

Adams and La Farge left San Francisco on a trip round the world in August, 1890. They had already visited Hawaii and

Samoa when they arrived in Tahiti. Despite bouts of sea-sickness, Adams was beginning to relax. The discovery that there was no hotel in Papeete was somewhat 'staggering', but the American Consul greeted them kindly and found them a house. Through the Consul, they met a number of well-known island residents, including ex-Queen Marau, Pomare's divorced wife. On the first evening, 'with some remnant of energy', they tried to find the Calabooza Beretane where Herman Melville had been imprisoned. But there was no one to help them in their search, and no one remembered anything. La Farge said that 'buildings occupied the spaces of woodland that Melville saw about him', and nothing remained but 'the same charm of light and air which he, like others, tried to describe and bring back home in words'.

In a letter to his niece, Adams said that, after having read about Tahiti from childhood, he was 'half-angry' to find it was a 'real place and not a pantomime'. Papeete, he found, was 'a little French provincial town, pretty as can be, but neither Polynesian nor European, and quieter than any town you ever imagined'. The natives, who wore clothes, 'looked commonplace after Samoa'. And the whole island was 'melancholy' even when the sun was brightest and the sea really blue. 'I do not mean that the place is gloomy,' he went on, 'but just quietly sad, as though it were a very pretty woman who had got through her fun and her troubles and grown old, and was just amusing herself by looking on. She has retired out of the world and sees only her particular friends, like me, with the highest introductions; but she dresses well and her jewels are superb.'

Adams and La Farge called on King Pomare. 'He wore green goggles; smiled kindly; and was at the club next evening, very drunk and noisy.' Adams noted that the Governor was a Martinique negro, and that the people who lived in Papeete seemed to have no nationality in particular. 'There are four or five thousand natives,' he said, 'or whatever the number may be; but they do nothing except get drunk and die. They don't even seem amused. Evidently there is something the matter with the place....'

After staying in Papeete for a month, Adams and La Farge shifted to Tautira. On the way, they spent three days at the Papara home of Tati Salmon, the principal chief of the island. Tati, who spoke French and English, was the son of an English

Jew who had married the chiefess Arii Taimai, the head of the Teva clan. Adams said that Arii Taimai was 'a pure native' and spoke no foreign language. She was sixty-eight years old and refused to sit at a table for meals, but sat on the floor in the old native way. She was 'a very good person indeed'. 'In the evenings,' Adams said, 'we lay down on mats about her and she told us of the old Tahiti people, who were much more interesting than now. She told us, too, long native legends about wonderful princesses and princes, who did astonishing things in astonishing ways, like Polynesian Arabian Nights. We drove to see the old family temple, a big enclosure with a huge hill of coral rocks piled up in the middle of it. There every head of a family had a stone to sit on, as though they were in church; and they sacrificed men by way of entertaining their gods. . . .'

In Tautira, the historian and painter stayed in the house of Ori-a-Ori, Stevenson's old friend. Soon after they had settled in, Ori received a volume of Stevenson's poems which the Scotsman had dedicated to him. He brought it to the Americans at once to find out what was in it.

Adams found Tautira 'a good place to work in', but it offered 'no exciting amusements'. The scenery was pretty, but the days were hot and the walks were short, for there were streams on both sides to wade through. Adams spent most of his time writing letters. La Farge painted. They led a very lazy life. By April 6, they were back at Papara again listening to Arii Taimai's stories of the past. Arii Taimai conferred the family names on them, according to an old Tahitian custom. Adams became Tauraatua, and La Farge, Teraaitua.

After a visit to the neighbouring island of Moorea, the historian and painter returned to Papeete where they 'coldly' took possession of the American Consulate—the Consul having gone to Washington on leave. Adams confessed to a correspondent on April 27 that his stay in Tahiti had done him 'a lot of good'. 'I am more like a sane idiot than I have known myself to be in these six years past,' he said. 'Tahiti is so unreal, so totally like a different planet. I can sit for hours dozing on the porches, waking up only to a sense of wonderful air and light, and lovely scenery, but thinking of nothing at all. The pigs are prodigies of nervous energy compared with me. Even the natives can teach me little in laziness. La Farge works, but I only doze, even when I pretend to be doing something. . . .'

Adams, however, was not as indolent as he made himself out to be. He had become intrigued by the story of Arii Taimai's Teva clan. The old chiefess had also come to Papeete and was living in a house across the yard from the American Consulate with ex-Queen Marau and her sisters, Piri and Manihinihi. La Farge said that he and Adams called on their new family as often as their fears of intrusion would allow. Adams went there more frequently than he did, and had 'returned to congenial and accustomed studies' by working at the genealogy of the Teva family and helping them 'to get it into written shape'. The fact was that Arii Taimai had 'begun to open the registers of memory and to correct and make clear things kept obscure. . . .' She had begun to explain the complicated story of the native wars which had baffled and annoyed the early explorers and missionaries, and had led, with their support, to the supremacy of the Pomare family with its subsequent tragic results. The Pomare family, it seemed, could never be accepted by the powerful Teva clan as the ruling family throughout Tahiti. Tahiti, in fact, had never had a system of supreme kingship before the arrival of the Europeans. It was because the Europeans had tried to impose such a system on the natives, that the island seldom knew peace from the time of the *Duff* to several years after the establishment of the French protectorate. It was because the missionaries had supported drunken Pomare II that the war broke out in 1808 which compelled him and them to leave the island. And it was because they had supported his daughter, Queen Pomare IV, that the chiefs of the Teva clan had welcomed the Catholic priests and had conspired with Moerenhout to obtain the help of the French. It was not until it was too late that the Tevas realized that in seeking French assistance they stood in danger of losing their island altogether. And it was not until the French had occupied Tahiti that the Tevas joined forces with the Pomares to try to throw the Frenchmen out. The two families had only give up after Arii Taimai had realized that the struggle was useless and had prevailed on Queen Pomare to return from Raiatea and submit quietly to French rule. And it was only when Arii Taimai's daughter,

Marau, had married Queen Pomare's son, Pomare V, that the two families had become united and settled their differences. By then, of course, Tahiti was irretrievably lost.

Such, in brief, was the tragic story which Henry Adams learned from Arii Taimai. If the Europeans had understood it from the first, the history of Tahiti would undoubtedly have been very different. As it was, the only thing Adams could do was to write it down. 'Everything conspires,' La Farge said, 'for getting some definite record just before the last veil closes over a past already dim enough.'

When the two Americans left Tahiti after a stay of exactly four months, Adams had filled a number of notebooks with the details of the old chiefess's story. On returning home a year or so later, he supplemented his notes with material from the narratives of the early missionaries and explorers. In 1893, he published 'ultrissimo privately' the *Memoirs of Marau Taaroa, Last Queen of Tahiti*. This title was not really accurate as the ex-Queen had merely been the interpreter of her mother's story. Adams corrected it in 1901 when he published a revised version of the book, again in a very small private edition. The title was then changed to *Memoirs of Arii Taimai*.

Although several other editions have appeared since then, the number of copies printed in every case has been small, and the interesting little book of America's famous historian and man of letters has remained little known. It is, however, an important contribution to the literature on Tahiti.

47. PAINTER OF NOBLE SAVAGES

FEW names are more famous in the annals of Tahiti than that of Paul Gauguin, the prosperous French stockbroker turned penurious painter, who came to the island in 1891. Gauguin's fame is partly due to the quality and vision of his Tahitian canvases (which now change hands at fabulous prices), and partly to the bizarre circumstances of his life.

Gauguin was born in Paris in 1848. His father was a journalist, and his mother the grand-niece of a rich ex-viceroy of Peru. When Gauguin was three years old, his father decided to migrate to Peru where he hoped to improve his meagre fortune by starting a newspaper of his own. Gauguin, senior, however, died on the voyage in the Straits of Magellan, and his widow and two children continued their journey alone. They stayed in Peru for four years, and then returned to France to settle at Orleans in reduced circumstances. Paul Gauguin was placed in a religious school, where he remained until he was seventeen. It was then decided that he should enter the French Merchant Marine, but sea life was not to his taste and he left it after four years to become a stockbroker. In this profession, Gauguin was highly successful—his income sometimes reaching 30,000 or 40,000 francs a year. At twenty-five, he married a young Danish girl, Mette Gad, and settled with her in a comfortable home in the Rue Lafitte. Five children were born to them during the next few years, and there seemed no reason to suppose that Gauguin would not remain a respectable, industrious, bourgeois citizen. Then came a change.

Through a friend, Gauguin became interested in art. At first it was only a hobby which occupied his holidays and week-ends. But gradually, as his interest deepened, it began to take up his evenings as well. After leaving the noisy halls of the Stock Exchange, Gauguin would wander into the artists' quarter of Montmartre to eat and talk in smoky cafés with painters of the Impressionist school. He met Pissarro, Monet, and Dégas; learned the tenets of the new painting; and occasionally bought a few pictures.

Eventually, after eleven years on the Stock Exchange, Gauguin found that he was not content with being a spare-time painter. He decided to give up his job, his social connections, and his comfort to devote himself solely to art. His wife, not surprisingly, was horrified. But, hopeful that he would be able to sell his pictures, she accompanied him first to Rouen and then to her parents' home in Copenhagen. After months of hard work in Denmark, Gauguin held an exhibition. It was a complete failure. This made it impossible for him to live with his wife's people, and after a violent scene with his wife, he returned to Paris with Clovis, his six-year-old son.

Gauguin was determined to make a living by art, and when he did, he wanted his wife and family to join him. But his paintings in Paris did not sell, and he was forced to live a hand-to-mouth existence in humble quarters. Sometimes he nearly starved. After a year of this life, he went to Pont-Aven, in Brittany where, still penniless, he continued to paint in the Impressionist manner. He returned to Paris in 1886. 'My sufferings have almost passed the limit of human endurance,' he wrote to his wife.

Soon after this, Gauguin sailed for Panama to take a job offered to him by his brother-in-law. But this job came to nothing, and he went, with the help of a friend, to the tropical island of Martinique. He was very contented there. The colours, scenes, and people excited him. His eye took up the challenge, and his hand began to find itself. Little by little, he acquired a new artistic philosophy. It was a sort of latter-day Rousseauism—a desire to return to the simplicity of primitive life. The style of the Impressionists fell away from him, and the colours in his canvases became brighter. But the climate of Martinique was foul. Gauguin caught dysentery and malaria, and within a year he returned to France as a seaman in a sailing ship.

In France, Gauguin lived mainly on the generosity of friends and continued to paint in the new manner he had discovered in Martinique. He painted at Pont-Aven, Paris, and Arles, where he lived for a time with Vincent Van Gogh. He worked always with the illusion that success was just around the corner, and that his wife and family would soon be able to join him. But although his paintings were admired and talked about in the art world of Paris, few people thought they were worth paying money for. Always being poor and always living on friends made Gauguin bitter about civilization. Every now and then he would long to get away from it all—to go again to the colourful, primitive tropics. For some time, he nurtured the thought of going to Madagascar where life was supposed to be ridiculously cheap. Then a copy of *Le Mariage de Loti* fell into his hands, and the reading of this made up his mind. He decided to go to Tahiti.

To obtain money for the voyage, he held a sale of all his paintings and belongings at the Hotel Druout. The sale realized 9,850 francs, thanks to a kindly newspaper article by Octave Mirabeau which attracted a large crowd. Mirabeau said that

Gauguin was 'fleeing from civilization and voluntarily seeking oblivion and silence' so that he would know himself better and so that he could 'hear more clearly the inner voices' which were drowned in the noise of passions and disputes. 'He feels,' Mirabeau continued, 'that he has not given all that is in him. In his soul there is confusion. He gropes vaguely, but with power, towards more abstract and mysterious ways of expression. His thoughts go back to the lands of light and mystery that he has visited before. There, he believes, he can find new untouched elements in art conforming with his dreams. . . .'

Gauguin sailed for Tahiti at the beginning of April, 1891. His wife was particularly chagrined that he took all the proceeds of the Druout sale with him. 'My heart is filled with bitterness that Paul could be so criminally selfish,' she wrote to a friend. 'I have never seen or heard anything like it.' The artist, however, continued to regard himself as a 'faithful lover and husband', and his early letters from Tahiti were full of affection and hope for the future. Writing on June 4, 1891—three days after his arrival—Gauguin said he thought he would soon have some well-paid commissions for portraits. 'I am bombarded with requests to do them,' he said. 'In any event, I think I can earn money here, a thing on which I did not count.' Gauguin added that he had been well received by the Governor and the Secretary for the Interior, and that they could not do too much for him.

But the official attitude soon changed. When the Governor learned that Gauguin had a commission for paintings from the French Government, he decided that this was only a synonym for espionage. 'I tried in vain to undeceive him,' Gauguin wrote, 'but everyone about him shared his belief, and when I said that I was receiving no pay for my mission, no one would believe me.'

After this setback, Gauguin quickly tired of life in Papeete.

> It was Europe [he said] the Europe which I had thought to shake off—and that under the aggravating circumstances of colonial snobbism. There was the imitation—grotesque, even to the point of caricature—of our customs, fashions, vices, and absurdities of civilization. Was I to have made this far journey only to find the very thing which I had fled?
>
> Nevertheless, there was a public event which interested me.

King Pomare was mortally ill, and the end was daily expected. Little by little, the city assumed a singular aspect. All the Europeans—merchants, functionaries, officers and soldiers—laughed and sang on the streets as usual, while the natives, with grave mien and lowered voice, held converse among themselves in the neighbourhood of the palace. In the roadstead, there was an abnormal movement of orange sails on the blue sea. The natives of neighbouring islands were hastening hither to be present for the last moments of their king and at the definite taking possession of their empire by France. . . .

All the Tahitians dressed in black, and for two days they sang dirges of grief and laments for the dead. It seemed to me that I was listening to the Sonata Pathétique. Then came the day of the funeral. At ten in the morning, they left the palace. The troops and the authorities were in white helmet and black dress-coat; the natives in their mourning costume. All the districts marched in order, and the leader of each one bore a French flag. At Arue, they halted. There, an indescribable monument rises—a formless mass of coral stones bound together by cement. It forms a painful contrast with the natural decorative beauty of vegetation and atmosphere. Lacascade (the Negro Governor) pronounced a discourse of conventional pattern which an interpreter translated for the benefit of the Frenchmen present. Then the Protestant clergyman delivered a sermon to which Tati, the brother of the Queen, responded. That was all. They left. The functionaries crowded into the carriages. It reminded one somewhat of a 'return from the races'.

In the confusion of the way, the indifference of the French set the key, and the people—for a number of days so grave—recovered their gaiety. The *vahines* again took the arms of their *tanes*, chattered actively, and undulated their hips, while their strong bare feet stirred up heavily the dust of the road. Close to the River Fatu, there was a general scattering. Concealed among the stones, the women crouched here and there in the water with their skirts raised to the waist, cooling their haunches and legs, tired from the march and the heat. Thus cleansed, with bosom erect, and with two shells covering the breasts rising in points under the muslin of their corsage, they again took up the way to Papeete. They had the grace and elasticity of healthy young animals. A mingled perfume, half animal, half vegetable, emanated from them—the perfume of their blood and of the gardenias (*tiare*) which all wore in their hair. '*Teine merahi noa noa* (now very fragrant),' they said.

The inhabitants of Papeete, both native and white, soon forgot the dead king. Those who had come from the neighbouring islands to take part in the royal obsequies left; thousands of orange sails again crossed the blue sea. Then everything returned to the customary routine. It was only one king less. But with him disappeared the last vestiges of ancient traditions. With him, Maori history closed. It was an end. Civilization, alas!—soldiers, trade, officialdom—triumphed.

Soon after the King's funeral, Gauguin resolved to leave Papeete and live in one of the country districts. He felt that by 'living intimately with the natives in the wilderness', he would gradually gain their confidence and come to know them. He set out to find himself a suitable hut with a half-French, half-Tahitian girl called Titi who had attached herself to him. They found one at Mataiea, about thirty miles from the town, and moved in. But Gauguin soon sent Titi back to Papeete. She had 'nothing to give of that special happiness' he sought.

I told myself [Gauguin said] that in the country I would find that which I was seeking. It would only be necessary to choose. Meanwhile, I felt very lonely. The inhabitants of the district and I mutually watched each other, and the distance between us remained the same. By the second day, I had exhausted my provisions.

What to do? I had imagined that with money I would be able to find all that was necessary for life. I was deceived. Once beyond the threshold of the city, we must turn to Nature in order to live. She is rich; she is generous; she refuses to no one who will ask his share of her treasures, of which she has inexhaustible reserves in the trees, in the mountains, and in the sea. But one must know how to catch fish, and how to dive to tear loose the shellfish attached to stones at the bottom of the sea. One must know how; one must be able to do things.

Here was I, a civilized man, distinctly inferior in these things to the savages. I envied them. I looked at their happy, peaceful life round about me, making no further effort than was essential for their daily needs, without the least care about money. To whom were they to sell when the gifts of Nature were within the reach of everyone?

In the meantime, it was so simple to paint things as I saw them; to put, without special calculation, a red close to a blue. Golden figures in the brooks and on the seashore enchanted me. Why did I hesitate to put all this glory of the sun on my canvas? Oh! the old European traditions! The timidities of expression of degenerate races!

Gauguin became friendly with his neighbours. When he was not working, he shared their life of 'indolence and joy'. He began to understand the language. His feet became hardened to pebbles, and his skin to the sun. 'I am in the process of regaining my beautiful figure of yore without becoming too lean,' he told his wife in March, 1892. 'I eat very little and then scarcely anything except roots and fish, like the natives. On the other hand, I have gone very grey.'

Gauguin's grey hair had undoubtedly been brought on by his long years of poverty and worry about the future. But he was convinced that he was following the path of destiny. 'I am a great artist and I know it,' he told his wife. 'It is because I am such that I have endured such sufferings. To do what I have done in any other circumstances would make me out as a ruffian, which I am, no doubt, to many people. Anyhow, what does it matter? What distresses me most is not so much the poverty as the perpetual obstacles to my art which I cannot practise as I feel ought to be done, and as I could do if relieved of the poverty which ties my hands. . . . Every month, I have been expecting money from (my friend) Morice, with whom I left it, plus the proceeds of pending picture deals, but I have had neither money nor news from him. In spite of all these vexations, I am working hard, and believe that on my return, I shall have collected enough material to paint for a long time.'

Meanwhile, Gauguin did a lot of thinking about the Tahitian way of life. His thoughts, which he recorded in *Noa Noa*, help to explain his art.

Among the people that go naked, as young animals, the difference between the sexes is less accentuated than in our climates. Thanks to our cinctures and corsets, we have succeeded in making an artificial being out of woman. She is an anomaly, and Nature herself, obedient to the laws of heredity, aids us in complicating and enervating her. We carefully keep her in a state of nervous weakness and muscular inferiority, and in guarding her from fatigue, we take away from her possibilities of development. Thus modelled on a bizarre ideal of slenderness to which, strangely enough, we continue to adhere, our women have nothing in common with us, and this, perhaps, may not be without grave moral and social disadvantages.

On Tahiti, the breezes from the forest and sea strengthen the lungs; they broaden the shoulders and hips. Neither men nor women are sheltered from the rays of the sun nor the pebbles of the shore. They engage in the same tasks together with the same activity or the same indolence. There is something virile in the women and something feminine in the men. This similarity of the sexes makes their relations the easier. Their continual state of nakedness has kept their minds free from the dangerous pre-occupation with the 'mystery' and from the excessive stress which among civilized people is laid upon the 'happy accident' and the clandestine and sadistic colours of love. It has given their manners a natural innocence, a perfect purity. Men and women are comrades—friends rather than lovers—dwelling together almost without cease, in pain as in pleasure, and even the very idea of vice is unknown to them.

Gauguin became more and more attuned to his new surroundings. But he was restless and his work suffered. It was several months since he had separated from Titi. He missed the 'melodious babble' of her conversation. He was unhappy without a permanent female companion. He wanted a substitute for his far-off wife. In the end, he decided to go on a tour of the island to see if he could find his heart's desire. He took the road to Taravao and reached the tiny village of Faaone. A good-looking woman of forty-odd accosted him.

'Where are you going?' she asked.

'I am going to Itia.'

'What for?'

'To find a wife.'

'There are many pretty women at Faaone. Do you want one?'

'Yes.'

'Very well! If she pleases you, I will give her to you. She is my daughter.'

'Is she young?'

'Yes.'

'Is she pretty?'

'Yes.'

'Is she in good health?'

'Yes.'

'Good. Go and bring her to me.'

The woman went away and came back with a girl of thirteen or fourteen. Her name was Tehura. Gauguin was impressed by her; and she was eager to go with him. After a meal, they left together for Mataiea. Then began a life 'filled to the full' with happiness. 'Happiness and work rose up together with the sun, radiant like it,' Gauguin said. 'The gold of Tehura's face flooded the interior of our hut and the landscape round about with joy and delight. We lived, both of us, in perfect simplicity.'

Gauguin made study after study of his new *vahine*. Among these were 'Vahine No Te Tiare', 'Tahitienne', and 'Reverie'. A year after Tehura had joined him, he wrote to his wife that he had completed 'forty-four important canvases which ought to bring in a yearly income of 15,000 francs'. Many of these canvases were as good as any he had ever done.

But although Gauguin's life with Tehura was productive and in many ways idyllic, the painter often felt frustrated and neglected. His wife—to whom he sent his paintings—rarely wrote to him, and never sent him a penny for the paintings she sold. Most of his friends were equally poor correspondents. At the end of eighteen months, Gauguin was disheartened and almost destitute. He went into Papeete to apply to the Governor for free repatriation. He believed that if his Tahitian canvases were to be sold, it was necessary for him to return to France to attend to the business himself. It was April, 1893, before he could go. He managed to survive until then through the generosity of a friend, who—moved by his tales of woe—sent him three remittances totalling 1,300 francs. Gauguin still had a fair amount of this money when he left Papeete, but it dribbled away during the voyage, and when he reached Marseilles early in August, he was down to his last four francs.

In Paris, after he had raked some money together, he settled in a studio in the Rue Vercingetorix. He wrote to his wife asking her to join him (provided she paid the fare from Copenhagen), but she would not. He held an exhibition of his paintings at the Durand-Ruel Gallery, but only five Tahitian pictures were sold. Visitors to the exhibition were either baffled or amused by the strangely brilliant colours that Gauguin had used when excesses of tobacco and sex had weakened his eyesight. His red dogs, yellow mountains, and green houses were regarded as an enormous joke. Hard things were also said about his fat, unshapely women. Nevertheless, the adverse comments put Gauguin in the public eye and made him much talked about in art circles.

Gauguin tried to live up to his new reputation as an eccentric. He took to wearing weird clothes; decorated his studio with exotic Tahitian bric-à-brac; installed a half-Javanese girl (with a parakeet and a monkey) as a model and mistress; and put a notice on the door saying, 'Here, one loves.' Gauguin held regular gatherings of his artistic friends, and Paris was soon whispering of orgies in his studio. He drank hard and smoked too much. The only important work he did during this period was to write *Noa Noa*, the story of his Tahitian sojourn.

In the spring of 1894, Gauguin went to Pont-Aven, in Brittany, with the half-Javanese girl, the parakeet, and the monkey. The fantastic entourage greatly offended the respectable Bretons. Gauguin got into a fight with some fishermen, fell over, and broke his leg. The local doctor failed to set the bone correctly, and the wound would not heal. Gauguin was in bed for weeks.

While thus immobilized, Gauguin's mistress went up to Paris, and ransacked his studio. This blow decided him to return to Tahiti for good.

At the end of the year, he organized another sale of his paintings at the Hotel Druout, but the sale yielded a profit of only 500 francs. It was at this time that Gauguin realized that his wife had no intention of living with him again, and was only interested in extracting money from him. In a fit of despair, he picked up a prostitute in Montparnasse and took her to his studio. When he left for Tahiti in February, he was suffering from syphilis.

In Tahiti, Gauguin acquired some land at Punaauia and settled there with a new *vahine*—Pahura. After four months of inactivity, he began painting. But he had scarcely taken up his brush when his dreadful disease began to assert itself. Sores broke out on his injured leg and spread to the other. His sight began to weaken and he could only sleep for an hour or two at night with the aid of drugs. He was in and out of hospital. His *vahine* gave birth to a child. His wife wrote to him that his favourite daughter, Aline, was dead. And on top of everything, he was practically broke.

By the end of the year, he had decided to kill himself. But first of all, he was determined to paint a masterpiece embodying all his philosophy. He painted 'D'où venons-nous? Que sommes-nous? Où allons-nous?' and sent it to Paris early in 1898. He then dragged himself into the mountains and took a large dose of arsenic. The poison made him violently sick but did not kill him. He crawled home again next day.

For several weeks, Gauguin lay in bed unable to eat and in great pain. When he had recovered somewhat, he went to the Office of Public Works and begged for a job. He got one at six francs a day, drawing plans and copying specifications. He stuck to it for nine months. The money he saved enabled him to get treatment at the hospital. During this period, Gauguin painted several more pictures. Among them was one of his greatest—'Les seins aux fleurs rouges'—for which his *vahine*, Pahura, served as model. By the end of 1899, however, Gauguin had almost reached the end of his painting career. He had ventured into the more profitable field of journalism.

Gauguin contributed articles to a weekly paper called *Les Guêpes* (The Wasps) which a merchant friend of his had started.

Later, he became the paper's manager and practically wrote it all himself. The paper was anti-church and anti-government. Gauguin used its columns for savage onslaughts against the administration. 'To colonize,' he wrote on one occasion, 'is to cultivate a country, to make an undeveloped area produce things that are useful above all to those who live there. That is a noble cause. But to conquer that area and erect a flag, and to put a parasitical administration over it at enormous cost for the sole glory of the conquering power is uncivilized and shameful stupidity.'

Gauguin was equally critical of the government and church in a paper he founded called *Le Sourire*. The paper was hand-written and illustrated by drawings, and was printed by a special process. It was meant to be amusing and sometimes was, but it never sold more than twenty or thirty copies each month. Gauguin, however, was no longer entirely dependent on his journalistic efforts. Money was at last arriving from France for his paintings. They had begun to sell.

After further bouts of sickness, Gauguin decided to move to the Marquesas Islands. He sold his hut and land for 5,000 francs—his most profitable deal since being a stockbroker—and sailed for Hiva-oa in August, 1901. He built himself a hut and decorated it with carvings and paintings. During the next twenty-two months, he was in frequent trouble with the French authorities for siding with the natives in various matters. On March 23, 1903, his activities earned him a sentence of three months' imprisonment and a fine of 1,000 francs. He asked for the right of appeal in Papeete. But his health by this time had greatly deteriorated, and he died on May 7, 1903, before his appeal could be heard. His furniture, pictures, books, and sculptures were sent to Papeete for auction to pay his fine. His last painting was held upside down and sold as the Niagara Falls for seven francs.

Gauguin was buried in the missionary cemetery at Hiva-oa. At the time of his death, his paintings were almost unknown in Europe except in the art circles of Montparnasse. It was nearly twenty years before they became known to a wider public.

48. SEEKER OF 'LOST GAUGUINS'

G AUGUIN had been dead just over ten years when a fair-haired
young Englishman—as English an Englishman as you could
find anywhere—walked down a steamer's gang-plank at Papeete.
His name: Rupert Brooke. Occupation: poet. Object in coming
to Tahiti: to look for 'lost Gauguins'.

Brooke at that time was twenty-five years old. He was not yet
famous as a poet, although a small volume of poems which he had
published at the end of 1911, after a brilliant scholastic career at
Cambridge, had elicited much favourable comment in literary
circles. Brooke had left England for a long period of travel in
May, 1913. With a contract from the *Westminster Gazette* for a
series of articles, he had visited New York, Boston, Canada, San
Francisco, Hawaii, Samoa, Fiji, and New Zealand.

From Fiji in December, 1913, he wrote to a friend: 'I've been
making inquiries about Tahiti, and I discover a predecessor
taking my tour. He passed through Fiji lately and is now heard
of in Tahiti. Who but Stephen Haweis! He writes that he has
found things of Gauguin in Tahiti. So I'm forestalled by three
months. Isn't that sickening? However, I shall go along and
if Stephen Haweis is still there, knock him on the head, and take
the boodle. I hear he's quite a small man.'

Whether the said Stephen Haweis was still in Tahiti when
Brooke arrived in January, 1914, does not appear to have been
recorded. Brooke, at any rate, did not succeed in finding any
'lost Gauguins'. But he did find 'the ideal place in the world
to live and work in', and there he wrote three of his finest poems.
The 'ideal place' was a house in the district of Mataiea, about
thirty miles from Papeete and close to the spot where Gauguin
had lived. It had a wide veranda over a blue lagoon, with a
wooden pier running into water that was clear and deep for
diving. The house belonged to a native woman, Madame Tetuanui, who had a handsome young daughter called Maaua. Brooke
moved there after spending a few days in a 'hovel' at the back of

the Hotel Tiare in Papeete, which was filled by night with 'flitting figures of girls with wreaths of white flowers keeping assignations'.

At Madame Tetuanui's, Brooke was given the native name of 'Pupure', meaning 'fair'. He took to wearing a native *pareu*, and the result was that his back got terribly sunburnt. Maaua (or Mamua, as he called her) used to anoint him with vinegar and coconut oil, but it was difficult to get him to sit still. He was physically active most of the time. He bathed with the children; tramped up the river with the men to spear shrimps in the native fashion; and went into the mountains for a day or two and camped out. On one occasion, he walked right down the peninsula of Tahiti-iti. But his favourite exercise was swimming. He swam by day and by night. And he was quicker in the water than Maaua herself.

The romantic, indolent, tropical life appealed to him. 'Tonight,' he wrote to a friend on one occasion, 'we will put scarlet flowers in our hair and sing strange, slumbrous South Sea songs to the concertina, and drink red French wine, and dance and bathe in a soft lagoon by moonlight, and eat great squelchy tropical fruits, custard apples, papaia, pomegranate, mango, guava and the rest. Urana! I have a million lovely and exciting things to tell you—but not now.'

Despite all the exciting distractions around him, Brooke did not neglect his work. On the wide veranda overlooking the lagoon, he spent several hours each morning working at poems and writing his articles for the *Westminster Gazette*. Three of the poems which he completed there were 'The Great Lover', 'Retrospect', and 'Tiare Tahiti'. The last of these was particularly lovely:

> Mamua, when our laughter ends,
> And hearts and bodies, brown and white,
> Are dust about the doors of friends,
> Or scent a-blowing down the night,
> Then, oh! the wise agree,
> Comes our immortality.
> Mamua, there waits a land
> Hard for us to understand.
> Out of time, beyond the sun,

All are one in Paradise,
You and Pupure are one,
And Tau, and the ungainly wise.

    ·   ·   ·   ·   ·

Tau here, Mamua,
Crown the hair, and come away!
Hear the calling of the moon,
And the whispering scents that stray
About the idle warm lagoon.
Hasten, hand in human hand,
Down the dark, the flowered way,
Along the whiteness of the sand,
And in the water's soft caress,
Wash the mind of foolishness,
Mamua until the day.
Spend the glittering moonlight there
Pursuing down the soundless deep
Limbs that gleam and shadowy hair,
Or floating lazy, half-asleep,
Dive and double and follow after,
Snare in flowers, and kiss, and call,
With lips that fade, and human laughter
And faces individual,
Well this side of Paradise! . . .
There's little comfort for the wise.

Brooke stayed in Tahiti three months, prolonging his visit
from time to time partly through lack of funds and partly because
he was too contented to move. 'I'm cut off from everything till
I can tear myself from Tahiti,' he told a friend, 'and that won't
be for a long while. It's too fascinating, at first sight. And
Gauguin grossly maligned the ladies. Oh, I know all that about
expressing their primitive souls by making their bodies squat and
flat. But it's blasphemy. They're goddesses. He'd have done a
Venue of Mili thus. . . .'

A few days later, he wrote to a cousin that he had been ill:

I got some beastly coral poisoning into my legs, and a local
microbe on top of that, and made the places worse by

neglecting them and sea-bathing all day—which turns out to be the worst possible thing. I was in the country when it came on bad, and I tried native remedies which took all the skin off and produced such a ghastly appearance that I hurried into town. I have been lying on my back for eight or nine days, suffering intensely, while I swab my skinless flesh with disinfectant. However, I have got over it now and have started hobbling about. I think I have been doing too much. . . .

I have been nursed and waited on by a girl with wonderful eyes and the walk of a goddess and the heart of an angel, who is, luckily, devoted to me. She gives her time ministering to me, I mine to probing her queer mind. . . .

The poet went on to complain about the difficulty of getting money 'in this damned place', and he spoke of sending 'frantic cables all over the world' for a few pounds to save him to civilization. Tahiti was beginning to pall. He longed to get back to England again. 'The Game is Up, Eddie,' he told his friend, Edward Marsh. 'If I've gained facts through knocking about with Conrad characters in a Gauguin entourage, I've lost a dream or two. I tried to be a poet. And because I'm a clever writer and because I was forty times as sensitive as anybody else, I succeeded a little . . . I'm what I came out here to be. Hard, quite hard. I have become merely a minor character in a Kipling story.'

Brooke sailed for San Francisco early in April, 1914. 'I resigned myself to the vessel and watched the green shores and rocky peaks fade with hardly a pang,' he wrote. 'I've been away long enough. I'm older than I was. I've left bits of me about —some of my hair in Canada, and one skin in Honolulu, and another in Fiji, and a bit of my third in Tahiti, and half a tooth in Samoa, and a bit of my heart all over the place. I'm deader than I was. *Partir, c'est toujours mourir en peu. . . .*'

Twelve months later, the poet was dead altogether. Two months after returning home, the First World War broke out and Brooke obtained a commission in the Royal Naval Division. He sailed for the Dardanelles on February 28, 1915. But before he left England, he assured himself of immortality by writing his famous war poem, 'The Soldier':

If I should die, think only this of me:
That there's some corner of a foreign field
That is for ever England . . .

On the way to the Dardanelles, Brooke's troopship called at Port Said, where the poet caught amoebic dysentery. The illness was caused by another 'local microbe' penetrating his body while swimming. The course of the illness was short, and Brooke died on board a hospital ship in the Bay of Skyros, Greece, on April 20, 1915.

Another lover of Tahiti who died in the smoke of battle which began at Gallipoli five days later was George Calderon. Calderon had visited Tahiti in 1906, and had collected a great deal of material for a book. But afraid that the book might be too highly coloured if he wrote it immediately, he waited for six years before beginning his task. Most of the book was finished when the war began. It was published by his widow in 1921 as *Tahiti* by 'Tihoti'. It was one of the most sensitive books ever written about the island.

49. GERMAN RAIDERS

ALTHOUGH Tahiti provided a contingent of native soldiers to fight for France in the muddy trenches of European battle-fields, it also had a taste of the First World War at close hand. A few weeks after the outbreak of the war, Papeete was bombarded by two German raiders, the *Scharnhorst* and the *Gneisenau*, which were cruising eastwards across the Pacific. This episode followed a visit by the raiders to the near-by island of Bora Bora.

The *Scharnhorst* and *Gneisenau*, commanded by Admiral Von Spee, anchored off Bora Bora on September 21, 1914. They flew no flags and Von Spee had given orders that only officers speaking French or English should receive visitors. Soon after their arrival, the German vessels were visited by two European resi-dents—the 'brigadier de gendarmerie' in charge of the island and a settler. The brigadier and his companion found two officers on deck arguing volubly in English.

'What news of the war?' one of them asked, breaking into French.

'None, captain,' the brigadier replied. 'We heard from a visiting English vessel that you had declared war on Germany, but I do not know if France has joined in or not.'

'Oh, France is not in it,' one pseudo-English officer said. 'Indeed, I fear that the enemy squadron may have already captured Papeete where we hope to obtain coal. Can you tell us anything?'

On this, the brigadier launched into a full description of the defencelessness of Papeete. The local garrison, he said, consisted of only twenty-five colonial infantry and twenty gendarmes. Although the gunboat *Zelee* was moored in the harbour, her guns had been taken ashore and were the only artillery the French had there. The stock of coal, however, was large. Besides the 5,000 tons which were always kept on hand, 3,000 tons had just been taken from a captured German collier.

Still under the impression that the German raiders were English cruisers, the Bora Borans supplied them with what provisions they could. It was not until they were leaving port that Von Spee hoisted the German colours in acknowledgement of the brigadier's farewell salute.

Meanwhile, at Papeete, precautions had been taken against a possible raid by two other German warships which were believed to be at Apia, Samoa. Lieutenant Destremau, the commander of the *Zelee*, had landed all but one of his vessel's guns—four 2½-inch and one 4-inch—and placed them in a battery on a hill about three hundred feet above the town. He had then sailed to the island of Makatea and captured the German vessel *Walküre* which was loading phosphates there. On his return, he had collected all the French reservists in the Society Group and raised a volunteer corps of Tahitians; mined the beacons which guided vessels through the reef; dug trenches across the roads of Papeete; and set up observation posts at various points on the island, plus one on the neighbouring island of Moorea.

At 6.30 a.m. on September 22, the observation post at Moorea sighted the *Scharnhorst* and *Gneisenau* about nine miles off shore. Destremau immediately gave orders to blow up the guiding beacons, set fire to the stock of coal, get steam up on board the *Zelee* and sink her in the passage through the reef. When the cruisers were within a mile of the reef, three salvoes were fired from the battery above the town, which was obscured from the Germans by a heavy fog. The salvoes from the hidden battery made the German commander cautious, and instead of making an immediate attempt to enter Papeete harbour, he patrolled the reef for more than an hour trying to discover the battery's position.

About 7.45 a.m., the cruisers opened a searching fire on the hills, but without success. Fifteen minutes later, they seemed to be making for the gap in the reef. Destremau then ordered the *Zelee* to be sunk at her moorings as she could not be moved to the harbour entrance for lack of steam.

At this point, Von Spee decided that Papeete was not worth the risk of losing men. He had been unable to discover where or how strong the battery was; and the stock of coal, which he badly wanted, was burning merrily. Before leaving, however, Von Spee—either to express his annoyance or to impress the natives—ordered forty-nine shells to be fired on the town. Two of these helped to send the sinking *Zelee* to the bottom; others did extensive damage to the town, and killed one or two natives. The *Scharnhorst* and *Gneisenau* then continued their voyage eastward and were subsequently sunk by British warships off the Falkland Islands.

Until quite recent times, Papeete still wore at least one scar of its brief career as a battlefield of World War I. Behind a picture in the old Yacht Club restaurant was a hole where an unexploded shell passed through, felling a coconut palm on the way out.

50. FINDER OF 'LOST GAUGUINS'

IN 1916, the famous English novelist, W. Somerset Maugham, arrived in Tahiti to gather material for a novel inspired by the life of Paul Gauguin. Maugham had first heard of Gauguin when he went to Paris in 1904. With a painter-friend who later became president of the Royal Academy, he visited Montparnasse and there heard much talk of Cezanne, Van Gogh, and Gauguin. He met men who had worked with Gauguin at Pont-Aven, and he read the only biography of the painter that had then appeared. What he learned seemed interesting material for a novel.

Maugham bore the idea in mind for over ten years until the opportunity came to go to Tahiti. He went there with the definite intention of finding out what else he could of Gauguin's life. He came across a number of people who had been associated with the painter in some way. He jotted down whatever they had to tell him, and was soon ready to begin his book.

Maugham stayed in Tahiti only a few days. He lodged at the Hotel Tiare in Papeete, where the hostess was an enormous half-caste woman of about fifty called Lovaina Gooding. Madame Lovaina, who died soon after in a fierce influenza epidemic which swept the island, was one of the most famous personages of modern Tahiti. Maugham described her in *A Writer's Notebook*. She was 'not merely fat', he said, but 'huge and shapeless'. She had 'a ready smile and a hearty fat laugh'. She took 'a motherly interest in all young people'; was 'a good cook and very hospitable'. Anyone in want of a meal could always get one at the Hotel Tiare. Maugham liked Lovaina so much that he made her a character in his novel. He called her Tiare Johnson.

Maugham had a stroke of rare good fortune in Tahiti. He found some of the 'lost Gauguins' which Rupert Brooke had searched for in vain. At the house of a chiefess about thirty-five miles from Papeete, he learned there were some Gauguin paintings in another nearby. It proved to be 'a very shabby frame house, grey and dilapidated', reached from the road by 'a swampy grass path'. The house was bare of furniture except for a few mats, and the veranda was 'swarming with dirty children'. Maugham was invited in by the master of the house—'a flat-nosed smiling native'—whose parents had apparently looked after Gauguin when he was sick. Gauguin had repaid this kindness by painting pictures on the glass panels in the upper part of three doors in one of the bungalow's rooms. The children, however, had since picked away at two of these pictures so that hardly anything of them remained; but the third picture was in 'tolerable preservation'. Maugham said that the owner of the house 'took no interest in the pictures as such, but merely as remembrances of the dead guest'. He was not unwilling to sell the third picture when Maugham pointed out that he could keep the other two, but said it would mean buying a new door. The price of this would be a hundred francs. Maugham offered him two hundred, and so clinched the deal. But just in case the native should change his mind, Maugham thought he had better take the old door with him. So they got out the tools of the car he had come in, un-screwed the hinges, and carried the door away. The lower part of the door was later sawn off at the house of the chiefess, and the panel with the picture taken back to Papeete. In this manner, Maugham acquired what was probably the last 'lost Gauguin' in Tahiti. (He resold it in 1962 for £17,000.)

Maugham published his Gauguin-inspired novel, *The Moon and Sixpence*, in 1919. Gauguin's paintings at that time were still practically unknown outside of the art circles of Montparnasse. *The Moon and Sixpence* was not meant to be a biography of the artist told as fiction, but it adhered to the basic essentials of the artist's life. It was not surprising that the reviewers did not realize that the hero (Charles Strickland) was actually a real person. One reviewer, in fact, complained that the author had 'wilfully handicapped himself with improbabilities'. Another thought that the idea of the story was 'fantastic'. And a third said that the author's 'primitive man' was 'too much of a brute to be true to nature'. Nevertheless, the reviews were generally ex-tremely favourable and the book had (and continues to have) a wide sale.

It was not long, of course, before a few readers woke up to the fact that *The Moon and Sixpence* was basically a true story. One of the first results of this discovery was the publication in New York of *Noa Noa*—an English translation of a series of articles which Gauguin had written describing his first Tahitian sojourn. The publication of a collection of Gauguin's letters from Tahiti, in English and French, soon followed. Interest in Gauguin and his work steadily increased, and paintings which were sold in the artist's lifetime for a few francs began to change hands at fabulous prices. In February, 1926, a painting of Gauguin's Tahitian hut ('Te Fare Maori') was sold at Christie's for £798. Two other pictures of Tahitian subjects sold in France in the early 'thirties fetched a total of 145,600 francs; and three auctioned in New York in the early 'forties brought a total of 14,600 dollars. Others sold privately brought even higher prices.

Somerset Maugham can thus claim a fair amount of the credit for popularizing Gauguin, and, in so doing, keeping Tahiti famous as an isle of romance. A film version of his novel, with George Sanders as Strickland, was released in 1943.

51. CAPTAIN BLIGH WALKS AGAIN

IN the years immediately following the First World War, Tahiti was deluged by a great number of visitors—writers, artists, businessmen, yachtsmen, and so forth—who were trying to escape from the stresses and strains of a war-shattered world. The residents of Tahiti called them 'white shadows'. This was an apt name, for most of them, after spending their money or losing their illusions, disappeared again, 'leaving not a wrack behind'. But there were two 'white shadows' who were destined to become permanent fixtures on the Tahitian landscape, and whose work was to make Tahiti well known to millions of people all over the world. These very substantial shadows were two young Americans, Charles Nordhoff and James Norman Hall. Through them, Captain Bligh and his mutinous crew walked again, and the romance of the *Bounty* was re-enacted on celluloid.

Nordhoff and Hall were wartime pilots who met in Paris in the autumn of 1918. Both were members of the all-American Lafayette Squadron, and both had been flying more or less continuously since the beginning of the war. They were awaiting orders from home when the founder of the Lafayette Squadron called them into headquarters, introduced them to each other, and asked them to write a history of their corps. The two pilots agreed, and thus began one of the most remarkable partnerships in modern literature. After collecting the grim records of their gallant squadron, Nordhoff and Hall sailed for home. There they locked themselves in a cottage at the top of Martha's Vineyard and got to work. By the end of the summer, the history was complete, and their thoughts turned to what Hall called 'the simple life'. They decided to carry out a plan, discussed in Paris several months earlier, of visiting Tahiti and other islands of the South Seas.

Armed with a contract from Harper Bros. and some advance payments for a series of articles, they sailed from San Francisco late in January, 1920. Tahiti and its neighbouring island of Moorea came in sight on 'a clear, windless February morning'. After gathering material in the Cook Islands and some of the islands of the Society Group, the two Americans settled at the Hotel Tiare (then run by Lovaina's son) to write their articles for Harper's. These articles were later published in book form as *Faery Islands of the South Seas*. After this first joint venture in Tahiti, Nordhoff and Hall went their separate ways—Nordhoff writing two novels for boys, and Hall two volumes of essays and sketches. But none of these books had much success, and by 1929 it was obvious to both of them that they were not making much progress in their literary careers. It was then that Nordhoff suggested that they should again collaborate. He wanted to make the hero of his boys' books a pilot in the Lafayette Flying Corps and carry him through a series of adventures in World War I. Hall agreed to help him, and between the two of them, they produced a novel called *Falcons of France*. The success of this decided them to keep on writing together, and they began to look around for another story that would interest them both. One day, Hall asked his friend if he had ever heard of the *Bounty* mutiny.

'Of course,' said Nordhoff. 'Who hasn't who knows anything about the South Seas?'

'Well, what about that for a story?'

Nordhoff shook his head. 'Someone must have written that long since.'

'I doubt it,' Hall replied. 'The only book I have seen is Sir John Barrow's factual account of the mutiny. Barrow was secretary of the British Admiralty at that time. His book was published in 1831.'

'By the Lord, Hall!' Nordhoff said. 'Maybe we've got something there! I wish we could get hold of a copy of Barrow's book.'

'I have it,' Hall said. 'I bought it in Paris during the war.'

Nordhoff took the book home and read it, and was back next day in what Hall described as 'a dither of excitement'.

'What a story! What a story!' he said, walking up and down on Hall's veranda.

'It is three stories,' Hall said. 'First, the tale of the mutiny; then Bligh's open boat voyage; and third, the adventures of Fletcher Christian and the mutineers who went with him to Pitcairn Island. It's a natural for historical fiction. Who could possibly invent a better story?'

'You're right,' Nordhoff said, 'but . . .' He shook his head glumly. 'It must have been written long since. It's incredible that such a tale should have been waiting a century and a half for someone to see its possibilities. . . .'

But a thorough investigation showed that no one had ever written up the story of the *Bounty* affair as fiction, so Nordhoff and Hall decided to do it. Through the late Mr. Ellery Sedgwick, editor of the *Atlantic Monthly*, they obtained photostatic copies of all the old Admiralty records concerning the *Bounty* and all the Court-Martial proceedings, which, at that time, were not easily accessible in printed form. A retired British naval officer in England prepared an exact model of the *Bounty*, as well as blue-prints of her deck plans and sail and rigging plans. Mr. Sedgwick also sent them the complete works of Tobias Smollett, England's eighteenth-century novelist of the sea, so that they could become familiar with the naval language of the period. A heavily laden van containing all this material rumbled up to Hall's home in Arue one day in 1931. The two men started work at once.

After months of preparation—reading and re-reading their material, endless discussions, the laying out of chapters, and so forth—they began the actual writing at the Aina Pare in Papeete. The first book of their trilogy, *Mutiny on the 'Bounty'*, was published in 1933. It was soon followed by *Men Against the Sea* and *Pitcairn's Island*. The three books met with a remarkable response, particularly *Mutiny on the 'Bounty'* which was written in graceful language evocative of the eighteenth century. The authors told the story of the mutiny through the mouth of a fictional midshipman called Roger Byam. Byam's counterpart in the *Bounty* was young Peter Heywood, who lived through the mutiny, the wreck of the *Pandora*, and the Court Martial to become a captain in the Royal Navy. Heywood's name was omitted from Nordhoff and Hall's list of officers. Apart from this deviation, the authors stuck almost religiously to the facts, although they made Bligh out to be a far greater tyrant than he probably was.

Mutiny on the 'Bounty' had not been on the market long before the film rights were bought by Metro-Goldwyn-Mayer. Their version of the Nordhoff and Hall story, released in 1935, was one of the greatest triumphs in the history of Hollywood and was shown on screens throughout the world. Charles Laughton played the most memorable part of his career as the tyrannical Captain Bligh; Clark Gable captured millions of hearts as a hard-done-by Fletcher Christian; and Franchot Tone acted well in the less colourful role of Roger Byam.*

M-G-M went to great trouble to make the film authentic. Two small replicas of the *Bounty* were made. The flogging scenes were recreated from the descriptions in Bligh's logbook. And Charles Laughton even went to London to have a water-resistant uniform made up by Bligh's own tailors in Bond Street. While the stars of the film remained on location at California's Catalina Island, fifty technicians and minor actors made the 4,000-mile journey to Tahiti for background shots in forty native villages. They took with them 500 'native canoes, a vast array of spears and bows and arrows, a great number of costumes, and four electric generators to produce stupendous waves on the high seas. About 2,500 natives were employed in Tahiti in the crowd scenes. The director of the film resorted to a good many trick and 'process' shots to weld together the scenes taken in Tahiti and the action filmed in California. When Clark Gable, for instance, was shown speaking to some of the native girls, he was on Catalina Island and they were in Tahiti. Exactly 652,228 feet of film were shot for the picture, but only 12,000 feet were finally used.

The success of *Mutiny on the 'Bounty'* as a novel and film made Nordhoff and Hall rich men and almost legendary figures in the literary world. But success rather embarrassed them, and when passenger liners arrived in Papeete with dozens of tourists eager to

---

* This was the second film version of the *'Bounty'* story. The first, which was not based on the Nordhoff and Hall classic, was made by an Australian producer, Charles Chauvel, in the early 'thirties. Errol Flynn, then unknown, played the lead. It was his first film role.

seek them out, they remained in hiding in their country houses. The two authors continued to write in collaboration until Nordhoff died in 1947. But only one book, *The Hurricane*, which was also filmed, had anything like the success of the *Bounty* trilogy. The collaborators never again found a story which excited the same degree of interest and enthusiasm in both of them.

Hall was easily the 'senior' member and guiding force of the unusual writing team. He was an extremely modest man—gentle, studious, cultured, and a great favourite with the natives among whom he lived. He liked to call himself 'a wood-shed poet'. As a writer in his own right, he was an accomplished essayist and stylist. He was a little out of place in the modern world, which undoubtedly accounted for his and his partner's successful handling of the *Bounty* story. 'I am one of those men,' he once declared, 'who think "yesterday" a beautiful word; who love change only in its aspect of imperceptible decay. . . . I am beginning to fear that there are no past-minded men any more in America, so rarely are they heard from.'

When Hall died at his home in Arue in 1951, his passing was lamented as a major calamity by the natives of Tahiti. For two days, the natives thronged round his home giving vent to their grief. Mourners in great numbers, clad in white according to the custom of the island, followed his coffin to the graveside. The Secretaire-General of the colony (representing the Governor, who was absent in another island), many high officials, and the British and Chinese Consuls were also present. There were several addresses of eulogy, the most notable being that of the famous native orator, Terieroo, chief of Papenoo.

Hall was buried on the lovely slope of a steep hill directly overlooking Matavai Bay, where Captain Bligh anchored the *Bounty* in 1789. His grave is marked by a bronze plaque inscribed with a verse which he himself had written:

JAMES NORMAN HALL
April 22, 1887–July 6, 1951.
Look to the Northward, stranger,
Just over the hillside, there
Have you in your travels seen
A land more passing fair?

A friend of Hall's who was present at the funeral was probably right when he said: 'I think it is not far-fetched to say that in these days another Vailima has been established, and that many a pilgrim will in future years visit the hill called by Tahitians Ferai. . . .' There are many, indeed, who think that Hall and his friend, Nordhoff, deserve a greater place in the literature of the South Seas than Robert Louis Stevenson. It is certain, at any rate, that no other authors have done so much to keep the name of Tahiti green.

52. WORLD WAR II AND AFTERWARDS

WHEN France capitulated to Germany on June 17, 1940, the government of Tahiti—as with governments in all other French territories—was faced with an agonizing choice. Should it continue to accept instructions from the legitimate and constitutional government of Marshal Petain, which had negotiated the surrender? Or should it join forces with the rebellious Free French Movement which General de Gaulle started in London five days after the surrender?

In far-off Tahiti, where news of the happenings in Europe was sometimes vague and confused, the choice fell to Governor Chastenet de Gery. Governor de Gery, who had been in office for a little over three years and who was described at the time as "one of the best governors Tahiti has ever known", decided it was his duty to stick with Petain. But in a proclamation issued on June 25, he made it clear that, in his view, the people of Tahiti and the rest of French Oceania were still at war as allies of Great Britain.

The governor's proclamation was in keeping with the sympathies of the people. But his contradictory acceptance of the Petain government was not; and when various regulations, manifestly emanating from Petain in Vichy were put into force, the Tahitians became tense, restless and suspicious. At the same time, there was a strong response to General de Gaulle's broadcast appeals for Frenchmen everywhere to fight on.

On July 13, 1940, three days after Petain abolished the Third French Republic, five hundred Tahitians went to the British consulate in Papeete and volunteered to fight with the Australian forces. Eight days later, the Vichy government ordered the consulate to be closed—for the first time since its establishment in 1837—and the consul was banished to a country district 20 miles out of town and placed under house arrest.

Incidents of this kind led to the formation in Tahiti of a Committee of Free France which forced the government to hold a plebiscite in that island, Moorea and the neighbouring islands to determine the people's views. The poll took place in mid-August. The result was remarkable. Only 18 people voted to remain under the Petain government, while 5,564 cast their votes for de Gaulle. In the circumstances, Governor de Gery had no option but to resign, and he left for Europe soon afterwards.

The government was then taken over by four prominent local people—Edouard Ahnne, Georges Lagarde, Emile Martin and George Bambridge—until Commandant Edmond Mansard, an old comrade of General de Gaulle, was appointed governor. However, ill-health soon forced Mansard to resign in favour of a 32-year-old French doctor, Emile de Curton, who had been in the territory for several years.

Dr. de Curton immediately got to work on the territory's two most pressing problems—defence and economic affairs. Within a few months, a contingent of 300 volunteers had been raised and trained to join the Free French Forces fighting overseas. They sailed from Papeete in April, 1941, and later fought with distinction in the Battle of Bir Hakeim (Libya), in Italy and in France. Meanwhile, with the promise of help from the British, Australian and New Zealand Governments, Dr. de Curton did what he could to reorganise the territory's economic life, which, before the war, had been almost entirely dependent on France, both for transportation and the sale of its products.

Dr. de Curton was managing Tahiti's affairs to the complete satisfaction of the local people when a strange top-level envoy from General de Gaulle arrived on the scene. Within a few days, Tahiti was in turmoil again. The Gaullist envoy was Commandant Richard Brunot, a former French Commissioner in the Cameroons, who had been appointed French Governor-General in the Pacific. He reached Papeete on June 6, 1941, and was received with full military honours by Governor de Curton. However, the Governor's welcome was apparently not as profuse as Brunot expected; and Brunot seems to have concluded from this that the Governor and his staff were plotting against him in some way. The result was that 10 days after his arrival, Brunot announced—to the amazement of everyone in the colony—that he had assumed the governorship of French Oceania and had signed a decree authorising the arrest of Dr. de Curton, his aide, two senior administrators, and the local troops commander. A second decree ordered the internment of more than a dozen other senior officials for the duration of the war, and a third dissolved the Papeete municipal council and appointed an 11-man commission to run the town's affairs. Thirty other decrees, almost equally sweeping, were issued in the course of what became known as the "Brunot revolution".

The extraordinary Brunot revolution came to an end after three months following the arrival in Papeete of an almost equally strange Gaullist envoy, Rear-Admiral Georges Thierry d'Argenlieu. The admiral, who had been a Carmelite monk between the wars, and who had been serving as a French naval commander when the Germans invaded France, had joined de Gaulle in London after a daring escape from a German prison camp in Cherbourg. After serving de Gaulle in various capacities, he was sent to the Pacific as de Gaulle's personal representative with the title of High Commissioner for Free France. He arrived in Papeete on September 23, 1941, apparently with the express purpose of taking control of the Brunot revolution. He wasted no time. Immediately after his arrival, he suspended the Brunot administration, released the arrested and interned officials on parole, and appointed a commission to investigate the plot that Brunot claimed he had uncovered. Within a few days, d'Argenlieu announced that the commission had found nothing in the nature of a plot and that the measures taken by Brunot were 'unjustified'. The admiral added that anyone who considered that he had suffered material loss as a result of Brunot's action could file a claim for reparations.

The Brunot revolution having thus been ended, Admiral d'Argenlieu appointed Lieutenant-Colonel Georges Orselli to the governorship and departed in a warship for New Caledonia. There, almost unbelievably, he staged exactly the same kind of palace revolution as Brunot had done when he arrested and deported New Caledonia's highly popular Governor Henri Sautot. The upshot in this case was that the American military commander had to intervene to avoid civil war, and de Gaulle had to recall his monkish envoy to London.

Meanwhile, the unfortunate Dr. de Curton had joined de Gaulle's staff in London, and he there wrote the only book on Tahiti to be published during the war. There were editions in both French and English, the English edition being called *Tahiti and French Polynesia: Fighting French Territory*. The book bore the unusual imprint of Fighting French Publications, 4 Carlton Gardens, London, S.W.1 Its object was to provide Fighting French volunteers and the public generally with "concise, trustworthy and up-to-date information" concerning Tahiti and the other islands, which, in answer to General de Gaulle's call, "rejected the armistice and now continue the struggle for the liberation of the motherland". Many of the book's illustrations were provided by Dr. de Curton himself, and they show the author to have been a better-than-average photographer. As history, however, the book leaves much to be desired, as there is not even a hint of the extraordinary drama in which the author, personally, was involved.

As for Dr. de Curton's successor in Tahiti, Lieutenant-Colonel Orselli, he remained in the governorship for the rest of the war. There were no more palace revolutions or *coups d'etat*. Tahiti, in fact, was as peaceful as any island can be in times of war. It was even mildly prosperous, for a huge force of Americans was eventually stationed on neighbouring Bora Bora, and these men were eager buyers of every artifact and curiosity that Tahiti's souvenir industry could turn out.

But the Americans at Bora Bora did not only bring dollars

to French Oceania. They also brought new ideas. And these ideas, allied with others picked up by Tahiti's contingent of soldiers overseas, began to manifest themselves soon after the war was over. Trade unionism, for example, a notion unthought of in Tahiti before the war, spread through the island like the proverbial wild fire. Each profession—machinists, stenographers, school teachers, stevedores, etc.—organised a 'syndicate', and by mid-1947 there were no less than 26 of them. There was also talk of nationalism.

One of the most active figures in this new, more aggressive Tahiti was a Huahine-born man, Marcel Pouvanaa a Oopa, whose blue eyes and fair complexion were an inheritance from a Danish grandfather. The fall of France in 1940 and the subsequent uncertainties in the government of Tahiti had diminished the prestige of France in his eyes and had caused him to become a Tahitian nationalist. Being a persuasive orator, with a flair for Biblical allusions, his ideas soon won a band of followers, and in February, 1947, a Comite Pouvanaa was formed. Three months later, the committee began publishing a regular journal, *Te Ara'tai*, to air and disseminate its views. The committee's aim, the first issue of the journal said, was to "conduct Tahiti and its archipelagoes towards more political, economic, administrative and cultural freedom". Articles in the paper were strongly anti-colonialist and anti-capitalist, and in favour, among other things, of the "Tahitianisation" of the public service.

On the morning of June 22, 1947, the Pouvanaa committee showed that it had already won wide support when it led a huge crowd of demonstrators to the Papeete waterfront to oppose the landing of three new French officials, who had arrived from Marseilles in the liner *Ville d'Amiens*. Many of the demonstrators were ex-servicemen, and so large were their numbers that the local police and troops were powerless to intervene. For two days, they prevented the new officials from landing; and finally, the Governor (now Mr J. C. Haumant) ordered the *Ville d'Amiens* to anchor offshore for fear that things might take a nastier turn. This move succeeded in taking some of the heat out of the situation; and after two more days, a couple of Navy launches were able to spirit the officials and their families ashore in the early hours of the morning. Soon afterwards, the governor proclaimed a state of emergency, closed the office of the Pouvanaa committee, and arrested Pouvanaa and a dozen of his men.

Pouvanaa and company were held in custody for five months before being brought to trial on a series of charges involving a challenge to governmental authority. The trial aroused intense public interest, and it was clear from the outset that the people's sympathy was with the accused. A priest, Father Calixte, who spoke on behalf of the prisoners, declared that it was evident from the medals of World Wars I and II that some of them (including Pouvanaa) wore on their chests that they were not anti-French. Later, when the foreman of the jury told the court that there was nothing to prove that the accused were anti-French, or that they had planned to overthrow the government or foment disorder, the spectators cheered heartily. Needless to say, a verdict of 'not guilty' was announced.

Pouvanaa's long imprisonment before his trial, and then his acquittal, earned him a martyr's crown, which made him more popular than ever. Two years later, when elections were held for a deputy to represent French Oceania in the French Parliament, he won the seat hands down with 9,818 votes to 4,679 for his nearest opponent. He was re-elected by equally impressive margins in subsequent elections in 1952 and 1956. Meanwhile, the Comite Pouvanaa had blossomed into a fully-fledged political party, the Rassemblement Democratique des Populations Tahitiennes (RDPT), or Tahitian People's Democratic Assembly. The RDPT put forward candidates in elections for the Territorial Assembly (local parliament) in 1953 and 1957, and won a majority of seats on both occasions. Pouvanaa did not stand for election in 1953. But in 1957 he did so and gained a seat.

Pouvanaa's entry into the Territorial Assembly followed hard on the heels of a law passed by the French Parliament which introduced sweeping reforms in France's possessions around the world. These reforms represented an effort by the tottery French Government to silence the growing cries of nationalism that were then being heard, particularly in Africa. Under the new law, French Oceania was reconstituted as French Polynesia from August 10, 1957; the membership of its Territorial Assembly was increased from 25 to 30; and the Assembly's powers to make laws were considerably extended. In addition, a council of government (cabinet), was created, with local people holding ministerial posts. The governor of the territory was *ex-officio* president. Pouvanaa was named vice-president, and was thus its effective head.

The creation of the council of government represented Tahiti's biggest political advance in nearly 80 years as a French colony. But it was not destined to last for long, for a series of events soon occurred which caused the governor to suspend its operation indefinitely 'in the interests of public order'. The first event was an announcement by Pouvanaa in April, 1958, that his party (which controlled the Territorial Assembly by 17 votes to 13) intended to secede from France and form an independent Tahitian republic. Shortly afterwards, Pouvanaa's party, the RDPT, introduced an income tax law in the Assembly, designed particularly to raise revenue from the (mainly Chinese) merchants and traders. Not surprisingly, both the secession proposal and the income tax plan were strongly opposed by the thirteen members of the opposition Democratic Union, which had the support of the trading community. And it turned out that when it came to a showdown, Tahiti's moneyed class could shout much louder than Pouvanaa's followers, many of whom were scattered through the outlying islands.

When a shopkeepers' strike was organized on April 29, 1958, as a protest against the proposed income tax, everyone in Papeete stopped work and thousands of idle workers gathered before the Territorial Assembly building on the waterfront. Insults were shouted at the seventeen RDPT members who were upstairs. Some demonstrators tried to force their way into the building, but were repulsed by militia and gendarmes. Pouvanaa tried to placate the crowd by loudspeaker from a window of the building. But he only inflamed the demonstrators more when he said that the income tax law would be repealed when Tahiti became independent. The demonstration got out of hand when three trucks, laden with stones, provided ammunition for the demonstrators to bombard the building. Assembly members and officials cowered inside as about sixty windows were broken. They finally escaped with a heavy police escort when the fire brigade, which had been called out, turned its hoses on the demonstrators.

About four thousand people then marched to the residence of the newly-arrived governor, Dr Henri Bailly, where the Assembly members had been given sanctuary. They demanded the repeal of the new income tax law, and an assurance that the RDPT-dominated Assembly would not sever Tahiti's connection with France. Meanwhile, other demonstrators stoned the house of Pouvanaa a Oopa.

Next day, the shopkeepers' strike continued. About five thousand people gathered grimly outside the Governor's residence while the council of government met to consider the situation. Tension eased when Pouvanaa came out and announced that the income tax law would be abrogated. Later, the demonstrators sang the *Marseillaise* as the Assembly met and hurriedly repealed the law.

On May 3, thirty-one leading Tahitians, including the Assembly's thirteen Democratic Union members, signed a declaration affirming that, for them, the idea of a Tahitian republic was 'an aberration'. The document conceded the right of French territories in Africa to seek independence, but claimed it was nonsense for French Polynesia to do the same. 'We have enough freedom and have no need for more,' the signatories agreed.

While business in Papeete returned to normal after Tahiti's first serious political disturbances since the *Ville d'Amiens* affair, one of the RDPT leaders cabled President Coty in Paris that the RDPT was 'indefectably attached to France'. This, however, did not conform with the general view, and another member, Senator Florisson, was sent post-haste to Paris to present the party's real views.

Four weeks after this, General de Gaulle again became leader of France. On September 27, elections for his new Constitution were held. These gave the eighteen French colonies throughout the world the chance to obtain independence simply by voting for it. In French Polynesia, the poll was indicative of the discord prevailing there. Only sixty-four per cent of the people voted to remain in the French Union—the smallest 'yes' vote in any colony except French Guinea, which overwhelmingly voted 'no'.

Pouvanaa, who had a strong influence on the big 'no' vote with a campaign of 'Tahiti for the Tahitians, and the French into the sea', found himself in trouble within a few days of the referendum. On October 11, he and a number of his followers were arrested on a variety of charges, including having thrown 'Molotov cocktails' in the streets of Papeete, and of having plotted to burn the town down. Pouvanaa's house, the government claimed, was found to be defended like a blockhouse and to contain a large stock of 'Molotov cocktails' and other weapons.

Pouvanaa was held in gaol for just over a year before being brought to trial in Papeete on charges of attempted murder, arson and the illegal possession of arms. His trial, which was delayed by complicated legal disputations, lasted three days. On October 23, 1959, he was sentenced to eight years' imprisonment and was banished from Papeete for fifteen. (This meant that he was banned from the Tahitian capital until he was seventy-nine, as he was sixty-four when the sentence was imposed.) Fifteen confederates of Pouvanaa were tried at the same time. His right-hand man got six years' gaol and was banned from Papeete for fifteen years; another leader got six years' gaol and five years' banishment; and the others received prison sentences of up to six years.

Although the Tahitians took a lively interest in the trials, the verdicts were received calmly. This, on the surface, seemed to suggest that the Tahitians believed that Pouvanaa and his confreres had had fair trials and that they deserved the sentences they got. This, however, was by no means the case, for it has since become clear that, in the eyes of many Tahitians, the entire case against Pouvanaa and his followers was a fabrication, engineered by officialdom to get a set of troublesome politicians out of the way.*

Certainly, the disappearance of Pouvanaa from Tahiti's

* When President de Gaulle visited Tahiti in September, 1966, John Teariki, then deputy for French Polynesia in the French Parliament, presented a submission to the President on the territory's problems. In this he referred at length to Pouvanaa's case and compared

political scene brought a calm to Tahiti that it had not known since the war. Debates in the Territorial Assembly became more restrained and much less radical; and as the Governor had suspended the council of government after Pouvanaa's arrest, the Tahitians were again without executive power in their own government.

Meanwhile, two decisions of great moment had been made which were to have far-reaching repercussions on everyone in Tahiti. One was a decision by Metro-Goldwyn-Mayer to make a new film version of the Nordhoff and Hall classic, *Mutiny on the Bounty*, with Marlon Brando starring in the role of Fletcher Christian. The second was a decision by the French Government to build an international airport near Papeete so that a serious effort could be made to build up a tourist industry in Tahiti, and so provide employment for the increasing population.

Work on Tahiti's airport got under way in mid-1959, and by October of the following year, it was ready for use. Three international airlines—TAI, TEAL and South Pacific Airlines (American) —immediately began using it, making four landings each week with plane loads of up to 66 passengers. Simultaneously, Metro-Goldwyn-Mayer began flying in actors and technicians for the filming of *Mutiny on the Bounty*. By mid-November, 1960, well over 100 MGM personnel were in Tahiti, and hundreds of Tahitians were on the MGM payroll as actors, extras, musicians, dancers, advisers, canoe-makers, and general assistants.

The increased influx of tourists as a result of the opening of the new airport and the arrival of the 100-odd MGM personnel placed a heavy strain on Tahiti's available accommodation and sent rents for houses, flats and rooms sky-rocketing. Wages spiralled at the same time, for MGM paid its employees on a scale previously unheard of in Tahiti. MGM's munificence

it with that of Maurice Lenormand, Pouvanaa's counterpart in New Caledonia, who was stripped of his political posts in 1964 after being convicted of a charge involving sabotage. Teariki told de Gaulle: "The fate of our former deputy, Pouvanaa a Oopa . . . still weighs heavily and bitterly in the hearts of Tahitians. Since his conviction, the events which have followed here—and elsewhere—have underlined the political character of the 'affair' which placed him in prison and exile. Pouvanaa a Oopa was no more an arsonist than Maurice Lenormand, deputy of New Caledonia, was a saboteur. Defenders of democratic freedom and territorial rights, both fell in the same way and in the same cause . . ."

knocked the bottom out of the local labour market, and one plantation owner complained, typically, at the time: 'I used to be able to get my trees aluminium banded for five francs apiece. Now I offer 10 francs and 20 francs and nobody's interested. They're all working for MGM.'

Due to temperamental actors, disagreements over the direction, mismanagement, the weather, and a variety of other factors, the making of the *Bounty* film dragged on for over a year and brought wealth directly or indirectly to almost every Tahitian family. One of the results was that the Tahitians discarded their old push bicycles and slow-moving ways, and took to riding motor-scooters, motor-cycles and small cars at frightening speed. Meanwhile, with tourism continuing to boom, land for hotels, shops, snack bars, etc., began to change hands at fabulous prices; and with fewer people working the land than previously, the prices of such commonplace products as coconuts, papaws, mangoes, bananas, taro, bread-fruit and avocados soared in unison. Not surprisingly, many a tourist who went to Tahiti expecting to find it still more or less as it was in Captain Cook's day was disappointed to find that the cost of living was even higher than it was at home, and that the Tahitians, perforce, were just as eager as anyone else to make a fast franc.

The Tahitians had scarcely had time to settle down to a more normal, less hectic mode of life following the departure of the MGM team when the French Government leaked news that it planned to use one of the islands of French Polynesia as a nuclear testing base. It was rumoured at first the Mangareva, in the Gambiers, would be the site of the base. But in April, 1963, after eight months of speculation, the Government announced officially that Mururoa Atoll, some 800 miles south-east of Tahiti in the Tuamotus, had been chosen as the site. Four other atolls—Anaa, Hao, Fangataufa and Tureia—were to have roles in the testing project, the announcement said. Governor Aime Grimald told a specially-convened meeting of the Territorial Assembly and the Papeete Municipal Council that Tahiti would play an important role in the project, as it would serve as a disembarkation point for men and supplies. The existing maritime traffic of 80,000 tons a year would increase by at least 50 per cent, he said, and to cope with this, the port of Papeete would be modernised at a cost of nearly $6 million (Australian). Governor Grimald added that at least 1,000 houses would be built in Tahiti to house the project's technicians, and that workshops and laboratories would also be built. Everything would be of great economic value to Tahiti.

The words were scarcely out of the Governor's mouth when Tahiti began to swarm with officials and technicians concerned with the planning and execution of various aspects of the new project. News that two battalions of Foreign Legionnaires were to come to the island as labourers brought a unanimous protest from the Territorial Assembly. The Assembly complained in a resolution sent to President de Gaulle that 'grave inconveniences' could follow the contact of a peace-loving population with 'elements noted for their violence'. The French President, however, ignored the Tahitians' protests, as he did all other protests that emanated from their Assembly. Indeed, when Pouvanaa's party, the RDPT, and an off-shoot of it, the Pupu Tiama Maohi, circulated petitions in Tahiti in November, 1963, protesting against the invasion of the island by French troops, President de Gaulle promptly outlawed both of them. To do this, the President made use of a 27-year-old law which forbade 'all associations or groups whose aim is to assault the integrity of the national territory'. The law also forbade such associations or groups to reconstitute themselves under different names. However, the individual members were allowed to retain their seats in the Territorial Assembly.

Organised political opposition to the nuclear testing project thus became impossible on the part of the parties which were most closely identified with the Tahitian people, and the French plans rolled forward more or less according to schedule. Although at heart many Tahitians shared the views of the outlawed party members, they found the high wages paid to workmen on the nuclear testing project and its associated works programmes too enticing to resist. In 1965, for example, wages for Polynesian workmen on the various projects amounted to some $3 million (Australian), and so many Tahitians had been lured from the land that their agricultural industry was in chaos. Meanwhile, the tourist industry continued to expand, with new hotels going up everywhere, more cruise ships arriving, and more and bigger planes coming in following the extension of the new airport to take jet aircraft. The number of tourists (excluding cruise ship passengers) in 1966 was 16,200 compared with 14,830 in 1965, 13,085 in 1964, 14,135 in 1963, 10,406 in 1962, and 1,472 in 1959.

The new port of Papeete, which had been created by reclaiming some 35 acres of coral reef, was officially opened at the end of June, 1966. Three days later, the first of a series of nuclear devices was exploded at Mururoa Atoll to the accompaniment of protests from all round the world. President de Gaulle, himself, visited Tahiti in September, 1966, en route to Mururoa to see one of the explosions. While in Tahiti, he learned at first hand that there was still intense resentment against the nuclear project. In a submission he received from John Teariki, the territory's deputy in the French parliament, de Gaulle and his government were accused of deliberately exploiting the economic situation in the territory so that the *Centre Experimental du Pacifique* (the organisation responsible for the nuclear tests) would become dominant. 'Likewise,' the submission said, 'our crushing budgetary problems have been adroitly manipulated to increase the power of the State over the local administrative services, leading irresistibly towards the disappearance of our last territorial freedom...' Mr Teariki went on to say that most Polynesians did not wish to be separated from France, but they did wish that their relations with her might be 'cleansed and regularized' by a revision of the territory's constitution. Article 73 of the Charter of the United Nations, he said, placed an obligation on France 'to respect the primacy of our interests locally as well as our political aspirations in the progressive development of our free institutions'. He added that he could not prevent himself from telling President de Gaulle, in the name of the people of his territory, of the bitterness and sadness they felt at seeing France—fortress of the Rights of Man and home of Pasteur—brought to disgrace by becoming a party to what Jean Rostand had called the 'Atomic Gang'.

Evidence that Tahitians generally agreed with what their

deputy said was provided in the following month when the Union Communale, a group of Tahitians opposed to the nuclear project, emerged triumphant in elections for the Papeete Municipal Council. Although Teariki lost his seat in the French Parliament soon afterwards, his successor, Francis Sanford, soon proved to be a man of similar ideals and forthrightness. In fact, Teariki and Sanford have been close allies ever since and have jointly fought for the same causes as leaders of two political parties, Here Ai'a (Patriots' Party) and E'a Api (The New Way). In elections for the Territorial Assembly in September 1967, they and their supporters won 17 out of 30 seats after campaigning vigorously on a platform of internal self-government for French Polynesia.

As soon as the new Assembly was convened, the Sanford-Teariki coalition pushed through a resolution to set up a commission to study the self-government question and to submit a plan for constitutional reform to the French Government. A few weeks later, the coalition combined to pass a resolution asking France to appoint a six-man commission, including representatives of the United States, New Zealand and Japan, to control radio-active pollution from the nuclear tests. 'We have no confidence in French scientists who say there is no pollution,' one of Teariki's supporters said. Sanford himself told the Assembly that he would withdraw his support for President de Gaulle in the French Parliament if the French Government ignored the resolution and failed to take heed of the Assembly's views on internal self-government. And when, as frequently happened later, the government treated Tahiti's deputy with a lofty disdain, Sanford resigned from one of the French centre parties, and thereby deprived the President of his parliamentary majority.

From that time onwards, there was little love between the French Government and Sanford, Teariki & Co.; and the Tahitians used every opportunity to hammer home their desire for self-government and their opposition to nuclear tests. In February 1968, they went as far as to discuss self-government with a senior United Nations official who happened to visit Papeete. And in the following month, Sanford, Teariki and two of their lieutenants went to Paris to raise the matter with the government, and also to urge it to allow Pouvanaa to return home because of failing health. The delegation did not get much of a hearing. The Minister for Overseas Territories, General Billotte, refused even to see them, and pointedly confirmed an earlier statement by the French Premier, Georges Pompidou, that France had no intention of granting internal self-government to French Polynesia. Despite this setback, the delegation did get a certain amount of newspaper publicity for their cause, and Sanford seized the chance to reiterate the view that Pouvanaa had been 'framed'. 'It is astonishing,' he said, 'that Pouvanaa should be treated as a common law criminal when, in fact, he is a political prisoner.' He added that, in Parliament, he would formally ask for his release.

Meanwhile, France was preparing for its first thermo-nuclear tests in the Pacific, and these were held in August and September, 1968. When a pro-Gaullist minority group in the Territorial Assembly introduced a resolution congratulating French scientists on the success of the tests, the Sanford-Teariki alliance quickly defeated it by 12 votes to five. 'Science without conscience is the ruin of the soul,' one member of the alliance said.

Although protests about 'the bomb' and appeals about self-government fell on deaf ears, the Tahitians' efforts to obtain Pouvanaa's release were finally crowned with success. On 11 November 1968, President de Gaulle used the occasion of the fiftieth anniversary of the end of World War I to sign a decree of pardon for Pouvanaa, permitting him to return home after serving nine years of his 15-year term of exile, of which three were spent in prison. Several thousand well-wishers went out to Faaa Airport to welcome the veteran leader on his return to Tahiti. It was an emotional home-coming, but there were no verbal fireworks—no promises of new battles in the future. Now 73, tired from his long journey, and partly paralysed from a stroke, Pouvanaa greeted the crowd with a restrained speech, then almost immediately disappeared from the public gaze. Some six months later, when his civil rights were restored to him, he was briefly in the news again. But otherwise little was heard of him until September 1971 when the Sanford-Teariki forces nominated him for French Polynesia's seat in the French Senate. Pouvanaa won the seat in an electoral college vote by 74 votes to 34. It was a sensational comeback for a man of 76; a colossal rebuff to the French Government; and a symbolic victory for those Tahitians who had long felt that they could and should govern themselves.

Meanwhile, Sanford and Teariki had been doing all they could to show their disapproval of the French Government. In April 1969 when President de Gaulle unsuccessfully staked his political future in a referendum on his social and economic policies, they strenuously urged their supporters to vote against him—which they did. Later, when de Gaulle's former Premier, Pompidou, contested the presidency against Senate president Alain Poher, Sanford and Teariki again campaigned for an anti-Gaullist vote. The fact that, in this case, most Tahitians backed a loser did not augur well for any change in the French Government's attitude towards them. Nevertheless, the radical alliance kept up their battle for reform.

When severe credit restrictions in France forced the government to cancel its proposed nuclear tests at Mururoa in 1969, causing a huge loss of income in Tahiti, Teariki was quick to point out that the island's economy was 'too fragile.' In a speech in the Territorial Assembly, Teariki said that because of the tests, Tahiti had learned to live beyond its means. The tests had also brought various social evils in their train, as thousands of people had flocked to Tahiti to work on the various projects associated with them. Many of the people had crowded into the area between Point Venus and Punaauia, where a commission of inquiry on urbanism had counted nearly 4,000 unhealthy dwellings sheltering some 22,400 people. 'The inhabitants of these shanties do not seem to enjoy the economic euphoria so often described by officialdom,' Teariki said. 'Fifteen per cent of them receive salaries of less than 7,500 Pacific franc [about $A75] per month. Thirty per cent earn less than 10,000 francs; and 50 per cent less than 15,000 francs. Only 5 per cent gain more than 25,000 francs per month.' Teariki said that most of the shanty-dwellers were immigrants from the outer islands who had previously lived healthier lives on the products of their lands and their fishing. Their children made up the biggest group of juvenile delinquents in the territory.

The radical leader went on to urge the government yet again to allow the Tahitians a greater measure of political autonomy.

'Up to now,' he said, 'no colonial power has been able to oppose successfully the universal movement for freedom which followed World War II in the overseas countries, and which continues to this moment. French Polynesia is taking part in this general movement. Our young elite grow in numbers year by year as they return from France at the end of their studies. These young people have a role to play—a role which cannot be limited to the blind execution of orders from France. The direction of the territory's affairs must be in their hands. It is necessary therefore to give French Polynesia the institutions which the times, our geographical position and our degree of evolution demand—in a word, internal self-government.'

As on previous occasions, this new plea for self-government produced no discernible reaction from the French Government. Indeed, France's policy at this time was to ignore all speeches and resolutions from the radical side of the Territorial Assembly, and even to claim that the Sanford-Teariki coalition was not representative of territory opinion. Not surprisingly, this policy increasingly exasperated the members of the alliance until, in the end, their annoyance reached boiling point.

In August 1970, Sanford wrote an open letter to the Papeete Press in which he accused the Government of treating the Tahitians with contempt over the self-government issue and of making a mockery of their elected representatives. 'For three years,' he said, 'my friends and I have fought to obtain internal self-government for the territory. We have sought nothing more than an executive entirely elected by a regional assembly which would be competent to handle its own affairs . . .* For three years the Central Government has refused to discuss the matter.'

A few days after this letter was published Sanford-Teariki supporters held a meeting at which they agreed to demonstrate in various ways during a visit to Tahiti by a new Minister for Overseas Territories, Mr. Henri Rey. Their aim was to emphasise their demands for internal self-government. The main tactics decided on were that they would boycott the Minister's arrival at

---

* Full details of the proposed plan for self-government were set out in a 43-page document presented to the Governor by the Territorial Assembly in February 1969. Under the plan, the Governor would become French High Commissioner; the chief executive would be a prime minister chosen by the Assembly; and there would be a governing council comprising the prime minister as president, a vice-president, and five to seven ministers chosen by the prime minister.

Faaa Airport; that during his visit they would parade in the streets with the red and white flag of independent Tahiti (last used before the island became a French protectorate in 1842); that they would drive in the daytime with their car headlights switched on; and that they would carry signs demanding internal self-government.

When the Minister arrived in Tahiti on September 11, one of his first acts was to announce a French Government plan to create a series of communes in the territory, each of which would handle its own affairs. The autonomists immediately denounced this as a device to divide and rule; and members of the Sanford-Teariki coalition held a meeting in the Territorial Assembly building while the flag of independent Tahiti was hoisted outside. Although the Governor promptly promulgated a decree forbidding the flying of flags, other than the French flag, on public buildings and monuments, there was another incident involving the Tahitian flag on the morning of the Minister's departure. On that occasion, about 50 vehicles bearing Tahitian flags drove to the airport to 'farewell' Mr. Rey; and when the Minister entered the terminal building, one of the autonomists dramatically unfurled a Tahitian flag in front of him. Almost immediately, the chief of police grabbed the flag, broke the staff across his knee, threw it on the ground, stamped on it, and said for all to hear: 'Where is the WC?' This provoked another autonomist to throw down a French flag and stamp on that.

Inevitably, there were some lively exchanges afterwards between the autonomists and the government. The autonomists demanded that the police chief and another official involved in the flag incident should be recalled to France. 'No genuine Tahitian,' they said, 'can remain insensitive to the treatment of his old flag, because French Polynesia is Polynesian first and then French.' Sanford, for his own part, denounced the Governor's flag decree as dictatorial, and said that although he and his followers had lowered their flags, they were ready to raise them again. 'The government is now trying to push us to extremes,' he added, 'and one day we will be obliged to appeal to the United Nations to conduct an honest referendum in the territory.'

Despite bitter statements such as these—despite the fact that Sanford returned all his medals to the government because, he said, he was too ashamed to wear them, the government continued to antagonise the autonomists. When elections were held for the Papeete Municipal Council in May 1971, the government used a variety of questionable means to try to defeat the autonomist candidates, but with signal lack of success. The president of the Territorial Assembly, Mr. Jean Millaud, said afterwards: 'We are taking part in a general confrontation, an impassioned struggle, in which pressures, misleading information, fanciful accusations, divisions, and, inevitably, hatred, take precedence over all other considerations. One is "French" and is treated with consideration and favouritism, or one is "anti-French", scorned and liable to reprisals, according to whether one is for or against the nuclear tests, or for or against internal self-government.' Millaud said it was time Tahiti's politics were cleansed of this abscess, and he went on to call for a dialogue between the government and the territory's political leaders on the territory's future. 'To refuse this dialogue is a negative attitude which will not suppress the problem and will not lead to any solution,' he added.

Whether it was Millaud's speech that did it, or whether it was a combination of all the speeches and denunciations of the preceding four years, the French Government finally decided to take notice of what Tahiti's leaders were saying. In September 1971, when yet another Minister for Overseas Territories, Mr. Pierre Messmer, visited Tahiti to open the Fourth South Pacific Games, he surprised and delighted everyone by announcing that the government was at last willing to hold discussions on the political, social and economic future. However, he made it clear that the government had no plans to replace the territory's present *statut* or constitution, nor did it intend to grant it complete independence. Nevertheless, additions and changes to the constitution were possible and desirable in the light of honest, realistic discussions. On the other hand, the Minister thought that the territory's principal problem was to find a 'solid and durable base' for its economy—something to replace the artificial economy based largely on 'the bomb'. In his view, tourism would be the economic mainstay of the future; and he said that the government in Paris would do everything possible to develop it.

By 1975, he added, Tahiti and the surrounding islands could be receiving as many as 150,000 tourists a year.

Although the Minister's statement brought the first ray of sunshine to Tahitian politics for several years, not everyone was happy at the prospect of some 150,000 tourists, or perhaps 500,000 tourists, descending on the island in a single year. 'It is necessary that Tahiti should die that the Tahitians may live,' proclaimed *Le Journal de Tahiti* in a review of the tourist industry early in January 1972. However, those 150,000 tourists, or 500,000, or whatever the number may be, have not reached Tahiti yet, and the island is still far from dead. Indeed, despite all that has happened there over the years—despite explorers, mutineers, beachcombers, missionaries, whalers, traders, empire builders, poets, painters, novelists, film-makers, atomic scientists, French troops and politicians—Tahiti lives on as Everyman's idea of paradise.

In its way, if you can afford the prices, it still is a paradise, for it still has the same attractive people, delicious scenery, lush vegetation, sweet flowers, balmy air, and incredible blueness of sea and sky that it had when Captain Wallis arrived there in HMS *Dolphin* just over two hundred years ago. Add to all that its richly diversified history of the past two centuries, and it is easy to agree that, as Charles Darwin said in 1835, Tahiti must 'for ever remain classical to the voyager in the South Seas.'

BIBLIOGRAPHY

AND INDEX

BIBLIOGRAPHY

(The figures in brackets after each reference indicate the chapters or parts of this book for which each reference served as a guide or source of material.)

MANUSCRIPTS—IN MITCHELL LIBRARY, SYDNEY

Anonymous, *Letter from Member of 'Daedalus' crew dated December 29, 1792*, (18).

Bolton, W. W., *Papers*, (Parts I–VI).

Burney, James, *Journal 1776–9*, (8).

Hassall, Rowland, *Letters and Papers*, (20–3, 25–6).

Haweis, Thomas, *Papers*, (18–19).

British Consulate, Tahiti, *Letters and Papers, 1826–88*, 25 vols., (27–32, 34–41).

COPIES OF MANUSCRIPTS—
IN MITCHELL LIBRARY, SYDNEY

Young, J. L., Atimaono, Copy of Manuscript dated 1926 with notes by W. W. Bolton, in Bolton Papers, (41).

British Foreign Office, London, Photostat Copies of Correspondence with British Consulate, Tahiti, 1822–44, 14 vols., (27–31, 34–9).

PRINTED BOOKS, ETC.

Adams, Henry, *Letters to a Niece*, London, 1920, (46).

Adams, Henry, *Tahiti: Memoirs of Arii Taimai* (Ed. R. Spiller), New York, 1947, (3, 46).

Agate, James, *Around the Cinemas* (Second Series) London, 1946, (50).

Amezaga, C. de, *Viaggio di Circumnavigazione*, 2 vols., Rome, 1885, (43–4).

Anderson, C. R., *Melville in the South Seas*, Columbia University, 1939, (33).

Anonymous, *Omiah's Farewell: Inscribed to the Ladies of London*, London, 1776, (6).

Anonymous, *An Epistle from Oberea*, London, 1773, (4).

Anonymous, *Histoire des Révolutions de Taiti par Mademoiselle B.D.B.D.B.*, Paris, 1782, (3).

Banks, J., *Journal* (Ed. Sir Joseph D. Hooker), London, 1896, (4).

Barrow, Sir John, *The Mutiny and Piratical Seizure of HMS 'Bounty'*, London, 1831, (10–11, 13–14, 18, 24).

Baston, Abbé G. A. R., *Narrations d'Omai*, 4 vols., Rouen, 1790, (6).

Beaglehole, J. C., *The Exploration of the Pacific*, London, 1934, (Parts I–II).

Beechey, Frederick William, *Narrative of a Voyage to the Pacific*, 2 vols., London, 1831, (24, 26–7).

Bellingshausen, Thaddeus von, *Voyage to the Antarctic Seas*, 2 vols., London, 1945, (26).

Bennet, Frederick Debell, *A Narrative of a Whaling Voyage Round the Globe*, 2 vols., London, 1840, (26–7).

Bligh, William, and others, *A Book of the 'Bounty'*, (Everyman Series), London, 1938, (10–11, 13–14).

Bligh, William, *Second Voyage to the South Sea* (Ed. Ida Lee), London, 1920, (16–17).

— *The Log of the 'Bounty'*, London, 1937, (10).

— *A Narrative of the Mutiny on board HMS 'Bounty'*, London, 1790, (10, 14).

— *A Voyage to the South Sea*, London, 1792, (10).

Boswell, James, *Life of Dr. Samuel Johnson*, (Ed. G. B. Hill), Oxford, 1934, (6).

Bougainville, Louis Antoine de, *Voyage autour du Monde*, Paris, 1771, (3).

— *A Voyage Round the World*, (English translation by John Reinhold Forster), London, 1772, (3).

Bowden, Keith Macrae, *George Bass*, Melbourne, 1952, (22).

Bricaire de la Dixième, *Le Sauvage de Taiti aux Français*, Paris, 1770, (3).

Brooke, Rupert, *Collected Poems*, New York, 1948, (48).

Brosses, Charles de, *Histoire des Navigations aux Terres Australes*, 2 vols., Paris, 1756, (1).

Broughton, William Robert, *A Voyage of Discovery*, London, 1804, (18).

Buck, Peter H., *Explorers of the Pacific*, Honolulu, 1953, (Parts I–II).

— *Vikings of the Sunrise*, New York, 1938, (Intro.).

Burney, Fanny, *Early Diary*, (Ed. A. R. Ellis), 2 vols., London, 1889, (6).

Caillot, A. C. E., *Histoire de la Polynésie Orientale*, Paris, 1910, (Parts I–VI).

Calderon, George, *Tahiti by 'Tihoti'*, London, 1921, (48).

Cameron, Hector Charles, *Sir Joseph Banks*, London, 1952, (4, 10).

Cater, Harold Dean, *Henry Adams and his Friends*, Boston, 1947, (46).

Clark, Thomas Blake, *Omai, First Polynesian Ambassador to England*, San Francisco, 1940, (6).

Colman, George, *Random Records*, 2 vols., London, 1830, (6).

Commerçon, Philibert, *Letter*, *Mercure de France*, Paris, November, 1769, (English translation in Corney, q.v.), (3).

Cook, James, *Journal*, (Ed. W. J. L. Wharton), London, 1893, (4).

— *Voyages of Discovery*, (Everyman Series), London, 1948, (3, 6, 8).

— *A Voyage Towards the South Pole*, 2 vols., London, 1777, (6).

Cook, James, and King, James, *A Voyage to the Pacific Ocean*, 3 vols., London, 1784, (8).

Corney, Bolton G., (Ed.), *The Quest and Occupation of Tahiti by Emissaries of Spain*, 3 vols., London, 1913–18, (3, 5, 7–8).

Covit, Bernard, *Official Directory and Guide Book for Tahiti*, San Francisco, 1951, (Parts I–VII).

Cowper, William, *Poetical Works* (Ed. Rev. H. F. Cary), London, 1851, (6).

Cradock, J., *Literary and Miscellaneous Memories*, London, 1828, (6).

Cumming, C. F. Gordon, *A Lady's Cruise Aboard a French Man of War*, London, 1882, (41, 43).

Dakin, W. J., *Whalemen Adventurers*, Sydney, 1934, (24).

Danielsson, Bengt, *Love in the South Seas*, London, 1956, (Parts I–VII).

Darwin, Charles, *Voyage of the 'Beagle'*, (Ed. N. Barlow), London, 1945, (27, 52).

D' Auvergne, E. B., *Pierre Loti*, London, 1926, (42).

Davies, John, *Journal*, published in *Journal of William Lockerby*, London, 1925, (23).

Delano, Amasa. *A Narrative of Voyages and Travels*, Boston, 1817, (24).

Delessert, E., *Voyages dans les Deux Océans*, Paris, 1848, (28–39).

Desgraz, C. L. F. and Vincendin-Du Moulin, C. A., *Exposé des Faits qui ont accompagné l'Aggression des Français*, Paris, 1843, (28–32).

Diderot, Denis, *Supplément au Voyage de Bougainville*, (Ed. G. Chinard), Baltimore, 1935, (3).

Du Petit-Thouars, Abel Aubert,*Voyage autour du Monde sur la Frégate 'La Venus'*, 4 vols., Paris, 1840–5, (29–30).

D'Urville, Dumont, *Voyage au Pole Sud*, 10 vols., Paris, 1841–6, (30).

Edwards, Edward, and Hamilton, George, *Voyage of HMS 'Pandora'*, (Ed. Sir Basil Thompson), London, 1915, (14).

Ellis, William, *A History of the London Missionary Society*, London, 1844, (19–23, 25–7).

Ellis, William, *Polynesian Researches*, 2 vols., London, 1829, (19–23, 25–7).

Ellison, Joseph W., *Tusitala of the South Seas*, New York, 1953, (45).

Fahnestock, Bruce and Sheridan, *Stars to Windward*, London, 1939, (51).

Fichter, Joseph H., *Roots of Change*, New York, 1939, (1).

Fisher, John., *Midmost Waters*, London, 1952, (42).

Forster, George, *A Voyage Round the World*, 2 vols., London, 1777, (6).

Furnas, J. C., *The Anatomy of Paradise*, New York, 1948, (Parts I–VII).

Gaffarel, P., *L'Affaire Pritchard*, Société Bourguignonne de Géographie et d'Historie, Paris (?), 1912, (38).

Gauguin, Paul, *Letters to Georges Daniel de Monfried*, London, 1923, (47).

— *Letters to His Wife and Friends*, Cleveland and New York, 1949, (47).

— *Noa Noa*, New York, 1920, (47).

Godwin, George, *Vancouver*, London, 1930, (15).

Greville, Charles C. F., *Journal of the Reign of Queen Victoria from 1837 to 1852*, 3 vols., London, 1885, (37).

Guizot, F. P. G., *Memoirs of Sir Robert Peel*, London, 1857, (37).

Hall, James Norman, *My Island Home*, Boston, 1952, (51).

— *Under a Thatched Roof*, Boston, 1942, (51).

Hanson, Lawrence and Elizabeth, *The Noble Savage*, London, 1954, (47).

Harding, George L. and Kroepelien, B., *The Tahitian Imprints of the London Missionary Society*, Oslo, 1950, (26).

Hawkesworth, John, *An Account of the Voyages of Capts. Byron, Wallis, Carteret and Cook*, 3 vols., London, 1773, (1–2, 4, 24).

Henry, Teuira, *Ancient Tahiti*, Honolulu, 1928, (Parts I–III, V).

Heyerdahl, Thor, *American Indians in the Pacific*, London, 1952, (Intro.).

Hort, Dora, (Mrs. Alfred), *Tahiti, The Garden of the Pacific*, London, 1891, (41).

Jacolliot, L., *La Vérité sur Tahiti*, Paris, 1869, (41).

Jore, L., *Essai de Bibliographie du Pacifique*, Paris, 1931, (Parts I–VII).

— *George Pritchard, l'Adversaire de la France*, Paris, 1940, (27–32, 34–9).

— *Un Belge au Service de la France*, Paris, 1944, (27–32, 34–9).

Jose, A. W., 'The Royal Australian Navy', Vol. 9 of *Official History of Australia in the War* (Ed. C. E. W. Bean), Sydney, 1928, (49).

Keable, Robert, *Tahiti : Isle of Dreams*, London, n.d., (48).

Kotzebue, Otto von, *A New Voyage Round the World*, 2 vols., London, 1830, (26).

La Farge, John, *Reminiscences of the South Seas*, London, 1914, (46).

La Place, Cyril Pierre Theodore, *Campagne de Circumnavigation de la Frégate 'l'Artémise'*, 6 vols., Paris, 1841, (30).

Lesson, René Primavere, *Voyage autour du Monde sur la Corvette, 'la Coquille'*, 2 vols., Paris, 1838–9, (27).

Lloyd, Christopher, *Pacific Horizons*, London, 1946, (Part I).

Loti, Pierre, *Le Mariage de Loti*, Paris, 1880, (42).

— *The Marriage of Loti*, (English translation by Clara Bell), London, 1925, (42).

Lovett, Richard, *History of the London Missionary Society*, London, 1899, (Parts III, V–VI).

Lucett, Edward, *Rovings in the Pacific*, London, 1852, (39).

Lutteroth, Henri, *O'Taiti, Histoire et Enquête*, Paris, 1845, (28).

Mackaness, George, *Life of Vice-Admiral Bligh*, Sydney, 1931, (10–11, 13–14, 24).

Marshall, Donald Stanley, *A Working Bibliography of the Society Islands, particularly Tahiti* (multigraphed), Auckland, 1951, (Parts I–VII).

Maugham, W. Somerset, *Selected Novels*, Vol. II, London, 1953, (50).

— *The Moon and Sixpence*, London, 1919, (50).

— *A Writer's Notebook*, London, 1949, (50).

Melville, Herman, *Omoo*, New York, 1847, (Intro., 33).

Menzies, Archibald, *Journal of Vancouver's Voyage*, Victoria, B.C., 1923, (15–16).

Moerenhout, J. A., *Voyage aux Îles du Grand Océan*, 2 vols., Paris, 1837, (27).

Montgomerie, H. S., *William Bligh of the 'Bounty'*, London, 1936, (10–11, 13–14).

Morrison, James, *Journal*, London, 1935, (10–11, 13–14).

Mullot, —, *Voyage en Océanie*, Bulletin de la Société des Études Océaniennes, Papeete, September, 1932, (36).

Nordhoff, Charles, and Hall, James Norman, *Faery Lands of the South Seas*, New York, 1921, (51).

— *The Hurricane*, London, 1936, (51).

— *Mutiny on the 'Bounty'*, New York, 1933, (51).

— *Pitcairn's Island*, New York, 1935, (51).

O'Brien, Frederick, *Mystic Isles of the South Seas*, New York, 1921, (48).

Parkinson, Sydney, *Journal of a Voyage to the South Seas*, London, 1773, (4).

Perkins, Edward, *Na Motu, or Reef Rovings in the South Seas*, New York, 1854, (40).

Pochhammer, Hans, *La Dernière Croisière de l'Admiral von Spee*, Paris, 1929, (49).

Pritchard, George, *The Missionary's Reward*, London, 1844, (Parts III, V–VI).

Pritchard, W. T., *Polynesian Reminiscences*, London, 1866, (36–7).

Ramsden, Eric, *William Stewart and the Introduction of Chinese Labour in Tahiti*, Journal of Polynesian Society, Vol. 55, Wellington, 1946, (41).

Reybaud, L., *'L'Artémise' à Tahiti*, Paris, 1840, (30).

Ribourt, P., *État de l'Île Taiti pendant les Années 1847–48*, Papeete, 1863, (40).

Richerie, E. Gaultier de la, *Souvenirs de Tahiti*, Bulletin de la Société de Géographie, Paris, 1866, (41).

Richerie, E. Gaultier de la, *Établissements Françaises de l'Océanie*, Paris 1865, (41).

Roberts, Stephen H., *History of French Colonial Policy*, Vol. 2, London, 1929, (44).

Robertson, George, *The Discovery of Tahiti* (Ed. Hugh Carrington), London, 1948, (2).

Rousseau, Jean Jacques, *The Social Contract and Other Essays* (Everyman Series), London, 1913, (1).

Scherzer, Karl von, *Narrative of the Circumnavigation of the Globe by the Austrian frigate 'Novara'*, 3 vols., London, 1861, (40).

Shillibeer, John, *A Narrative of the Briton's Voyage to Pitcairn Island*, London, 1813, (24).

Shipley, Conway, *Sketches in the Pacific*, London, 1851, (39).

Singer, Kurt, *The Charles Laughton Story*, London, 1954, (51).

Smith, Bernard, *European Vision and the South Pacific*, (Parts I, III, V).

Sparrman, Anders, *A Voyage Round the World*, London, 1944, (6).

Stevenson, Robert Louis, *Works* (Intro. A. Lang), Vols. 14 and 24, London, 1911–12, (45).

Stewart, William, *An Outline of How it Came to Pass that So Many Absurd Stories have been Circulated about Terre Eugénie*, Papeete, 1867, (41).

Stringer, Arthur, *Red Wine of Youth*, New York, 1948, (48).

Taitbout, *Essai sur l'Île d'Otaheite*, Paris, 1779, (3).

Taylor, C. R. H., *A Pacific Bibliography*, Wellington, 1951, (Parts I–VI).

Taylor, Fitch W., *The Flag Ship*, New York, 1840, (30).

Tinker, Chauncey Brewster, *Painter and Poet*, Cambridge, Massachusetts, 1938, (6).

Turnbull, John, *A Voyage Around the World*, 3 vols., London, 1805, (22).

Tyerman, Daniel, and Bennet, George, *Journal of Voyages and Travels*, 2 vols., London, 1831, (26–7).

Vancouver, George, *A Voyage of Discovery*, 3 vols., London, 1798, (15–16, 18).

Vason, James, *An Authentic Narrative of Four Years' Residence at Tongatapoo*, London, 1810, (19).

Voltaire, *Œuvres Complètes*, Vol. 49, Paris, 1882.

Walpole, Frederick, *Four Years in the Pacific*, Paris, 1850, (39).

Ward, Sir A. W., and Gooch, G. P., (Eds.), *The Cambridge History of British Foreign Policy*, Vol., 2, Cambridge, 1923, (28–32, 34–8).

Ward, John M., *British Policy in the South Pacific*, Sydney, 1948, (Parts III, V–VI).

Watts, John, *Journal*, published in *The Voyage of Governor Phillip to Botany Bay* (Ed. John Stockdale), London, 1789, (8–9).

Webber, James, *Views in the South Seas*, London, 1808, (8).

Wheeler, Daniel, *Memoirs of the Life and Gospel Labours of the Late Daniel Wheeler*, London, 1842, (28).

Wilkes, Charles, U.S. *Exploring Expedition*, 9 vols., Philadelphia, 1845–8, (30).

Wilkinson, C. S., *The Wake of the 'Bounty'*, London, 1953, (10–11, 13–15, 24).

Williams, John, *Narrative of Missionary Enterprise in the South Sea*, London, 1837, (26).

Williamson, James Alexander, *Capt. Cook and the Opening of the Pacific*, London, 1946, (4, 6, 8).

Williamson, R. W., *The Social and Political Systems of Central Polynesia*, 3 vols., Cambridge, 1924, (Intro.).

Wilson, James, *A Missionary Voyage to the South Pacific*, London, 1799, (19).

Wise, Henry, A., *Los Gringos: or An Inside View of Polynesia*, New York, 1849, (40).

Annals of the Propagation of the Faith, No. 1, Paris, 1838, (28–9).

Annuaire de Tahiti, Papeete, 1863 and 1877, (41).

Annuaire de Tahiti, Papeete, 1892, (43).

Annual Register, London, 1774, (6).

Annual Registers, London, 1844 and 1845, (37–8).

Art Prices Current, London, 1907–56, (50).

Australasian Encyclopedia, (Parts I–VII).

Book Review Digest, New York, 1904–56, (Part VII).

Bulletin de la Société d'Études Océaniennes, Papeete, 1917–56, (Parts I–VII).

Correspondence Relative to Tahiti, 1825–43, presented to the House of Commons, London, 1843, (27–32, 34–6).

Correspondence Relative to the Removal of Mr. Pritchard from Tahiti, presented to both Houses of Parliament, London, 1845, (36–7).

Correspondence Relative to the Society Islands, 1822–47, printed for the Confidential Use of the British Cabinet, London, 1847, (27–32, 34–9).

Dictionary of National Biography, London, 1885–1950, (Parts I–VII).

Encyclopedia Americana, (Parts I–VII).

Encyclopedia Britannica, (Parts I–VII).

Evangelical Magazine and Missionary Chronicle, London, 1795–1820, (19–23, 25–6).

Galerie des Pritchardistes, par 'Le National', Paris, 1846. Reprinted from *Le National* of July 12–21, 1846, (38).

Hansard of House of Commons and House of Lords, London, 1844–45, (35, 37).

Historical Records of Australia, Series I, (Parts I–III, V–VI).

Historical Records of New South Wales, (Parts I–III, V–VI).
Journal of the Polynesian Society, Wellington, 1892–1956, (Parts I–VII)
Le Messager de Taiti, (weekly newspaper), Papeete, 1862–75, (41).
Les Guêpes, (weekly newspaper), Papeete, 1899–1900, (47).
Marshall, John, *Royal Naval Biography,* 8 vols., London, 1823–35, (10–11, 13–14, 24).
Missionary Sketches, London, 1810–40, (25–7).
Omai, or A Trip Round the World, London, 1785–86. Playbills in Mitchell Library, Sydney, (6).
Pacific Islands Monthly, Sydney, 1930–58, (Parts I–VII).
Pacific Islands Year Book, (Ed. R. W. Robson), Sydney, 1932–56, (Parts I–VII).
The Advertiser, Adelaide, May 8, and October 9 and 15, 1958, (51–2).
The Times, London, 1838–45, (30–2, 34–8).
Transactions of the Missionary Society, 4 vols., London, 1804–32, (19–23, 25–6).
Twentieth Century Authors (Ed. Kunitz, S. J., and Haycraft, H.), New York, 1942, (48, 51).

ADDITIONAL BIBLIOGRAPHY (Chapter 52)

Curton, E. de, *Tahiti, terre francaise combattante,* London, 1942.
— *Tahiti and French Polynesia: Fighting French Territory,* London, 1943.
Farwell, George, *Last Days in Paradise,* Adelaide, 1964.
O'Reilly, Patrick and Reitman, Edouard, *Bibliographie de Tahiti et de la Polynesie francaise,* Paris, 1967.
O'Reilly, Patrick and Teissier, Raoul, *Tahitiens: Repertoire bio-bibliographique de la Polynesie Francaise,* Paris, 1962, and *Tahitiens: Supplement,* Paris, 1966.
Journal de Tahiti, Papeete, 1963– to date.
Journal of Pacific History, Canberra, Vol. II, 1967.
Pacific Islands Monthly, Sydney, 1959– to date.

INDEX

Aberdeen, Lord, 146, 158-9, 160-2, 171, 172, 173, 174
Actaeon, HMS, 139
Adams, Henry, 219-23
Adams, John (Alexander Smith), 109, 110-11, 112, 128
Adventure (sloop), 31
Afareaitu, 120
Aguila (Spanish frigate), 29-30, 38-42
Ahonu, 91, 93
Aimata—*see* Pomare IV, Queen
Aitutaki island, 63, 70
Albion (whaler), 94
Amat y Jimient, Viceroy Manuel de, 29-30, 38, 42
Anne ('blackbirder' ship), 194
Aotourou, (Tahitian youth), 22-3
Areoi Society, 26, 89
Ariiaue—*see* Pomare V
Arii Taimai, 182, 221, 222-3
Artemise (French frigate), 143-4, 145
Artemise Bank, 30, 143
Arue, 169, 246
Assistance, HMS, 76, 78
Atehuru, 99
Atimaono Cotton Plantation, 186, 187-92, 194-6; Chinese labourers imported into, 188, 189; building of Terre Eugenie, 190; Cook Islanders in, 191, 193-4; adverse reports on, 191; collapse of, 195-6

Bailly, Dr. Henri, 250
Baker, Captain James, 76
Balboa, Vasco Nunez de, 9, 28
Banks, Sir Joseph, 24, 25, 26, 27-8, 51, 52, 56, 58
Barrow, Sir John, 108, 110, 245
Basilisk, HMS, 167, 168, 169, 179, 180
Bass, George, 96*n.*
Beagle, HMS, 130
Beechey, Captain F. W., 111, 124, 128
Bethia, HMS—*see* Bounty.
Betsey, 93, 94
Bible, John, 190
Bicknell, G., 121

Bicknell, Henry (missionary), 85, 91, 92, 100, 115, 116, 120
Blackett, Captain, 194
Bligh, Captain William, 63, 65, 86, 248; first sails with Christian, 51; commands *Bounty,* 51 *et seq.;* his treatment of crew, 53-7; abuses Christian, 58-9; seized and cast adrift, 60-2, 106; returns to England, 68, 73; publishes *Narrative,* 68; commands fresh breadfruit expedition, 76-8; comments on change in island, 77-8; Governor of New South Wales, 99; Laughton's portrayal of, 247
Bloody Bay, 64
Blossom, HMS, 111, 124
Boenechea, Captain Domingo de, 29-30, 38-41
Bora Bora island, 26, 70, 119, 197, 209, 239-40
Boudeuse (French ship), 19-23
Bougainville, Captain Louis Antoine de, 19-23, 27, 31
Bounty, HMS, 18; sails on breadfruit expedition, 51-3; mishaps and discontent in, 53-60; mutiny in, 60-2, 68; Bligh cast adrift from, 61-2; return of, 63-4; at Tubuai, 63, 64, 65; return to Tahiti, 65-6, 71; destroyed, 106; mutineers from, on Pitcairn Island, 105-12; Nordhoff and Hall's book on, 245-7; films of, 247, 258
Boussole (French frigate), 154, 155
Brando, Marlon, 258
Briton, HMS, 109-10
Brooke, Rupert, 235-9, 242
Broomhall, Benjamin (missionary), 85, 90, 91, 93, 95
Brosses, Charles de, 9
Broughton, Lieutenant William Robert, 73-5, 78, 79
Brown, John, 67, 70
Brown, William (*Bounty* gardener), 53, 62, 66, 67
Bruat, Captain Armand, 165, 167, 169, 170, 174, 181, 182, 183
Bunker, Captain Ebor, 94, 95

Magellan, Ferdinand, 9
Main, Edward (missionary), 85, 90, 91
Mamaia sect, 127-8, 129
Mangareva island, 135-6
Marau, ex-Queen, 220, 222, 223
Margaret (ship), 96
Mariage de Loti, Le (Loti), 196, 197-209, 225
Maroa, 189
Martin, Isaac (*Bounty* seaman), 53, 60, 62, 66
Mary Ann (whaler), 75
Masserano, Prince of, 28-9
Mataiea, 186, 187, 189, 228, 231, 235
Matavai Bay, 13, 14, 19, 24, 25, 43, 44, 46, 63, 64, 67, 68, 74, 76-7, 78, 85, 88-93, 95, 96, 98-101, 120, 248
Matilda (whaler), 75-6, 77, 78
Maugham, W. Somerset, 241-4
Maupiha island, 191
Mehetia Island, 11, 56, 75
Melville, Herman, 151-3, 217, 220
Memoirs of Arii Taimai (Adams), 223
Mercury (brig), 64-5, 67
Messmer, Pierre, 267, 268
Millaud, Jean, 267
Miller, George, 187
Mills, John (*Bounty* gunner's mate), 52, 60, 62, 66
Millward, John (*Bounty* seaman), 53, 57, 62, 67, 73
Mirabeau, Octave, 225-6
Moaroa (trading ship), 194
Moe, Princess, 218-19
Moerenhout, Jacques Antoine, 143, 144, 150, 155, 222; becomes American Consul, 129-30; and Catholic priests, 137, 138-9, 140, 141; dismissed as consul, 141; becomes French Consul, 142; intrigues for protectorate, 146-7, 154, 163, 222
Moon and Sixpence, The (Maugham), 243, 244
Moorea, 98, 100, 115, 116, 117, 118, 119-21, 122, 124, 128, 147, 149, 150, 151, 153, 193, 221, 240
Morrison, James (*Bounty* boatswain's mate), 52, 55, 58, 62, 63, 66, 67, 69, 70, 73
Mortimer, Lieutenant George, 64, 65
Motu-utu island, 141
Murphy, Colomban, 135-6, 151

Muspratt, William (*Bounty* seaman), 53, 57, 62, 66, 67, 73
Mutiny on the 'Bounty' (Nordhoff and Hall), 246-7

Namuka, 58
Nautilus (ship), 90-1, 93
Nelson, David (*Bounty* botanist), 52, 56, 60, 63
Nicolas, Commodore John Toup, 155-8, 160, 168, 170
Nilopolis, Etienne Rochouse, Bishop of, 135, 136
Noa Noa (Gauguin), 230, 232
Nordhoff, Charles, 244-8
Norfolk (armed brig), 95-6
Norman, Charles (*Bounty* carpenter's mate), 52, 62, 66, 71
Norton, John (*Bounty* quartermaster), 52
Nott, Henry (missionary), 85, 91, 100, 115, 117, 119, 120, 125, 126, 129

Oakes, Francis (missionary), 85, 89
Oberea, Queen, 17, 18, 27
Omai ('noble savage'), 31-7, 42-3, 44, 47
Omoo (Melville), 151-3
Oponohu, 121
Ori-a-Ori, Chief, 218-19, 221
Orsmond, J. M. (missionary), 120, 121, 122, 125
Osbourne, Lloyd, 217
Otis, Captain, 217
Otoo (later Pomare I, *q.v.*), 39, 44, 46, 65, 67, 74
Otoo (son, later Pomare II), 74, 86, 90, 95, 96-7

Paete, Chief, 146
Pahura (Gauguin's companion), 233
Palmerston, Lord, 143, 145, 146, 161, 181
Palmerston Island, 71
Pandora, HMS, 68-72
Papara, 120, 152, 186, 187, 220, 221
Papeete, 137, 140, 141, 144, 150, 151, 153, 154, 165, 168, 172, 180, 182, 192, 195, 242, 246, 247; mission at, 120; seat of government, 128; Chinese labourers at, 196; Loti and, 201-4, 205-9; Stevenson at, 217; Henry Adams and, 220, 221-2; Gauguin and, 226-8, 232; in World War I, 240-1

Papenoo, 182, 205
Papetoai, 117
Paraita, Chief, 146, 147, 148, 150, 182
Pare, 67, 76, 89, 100, 116
Parry, William, 34
Paulet, Lord George, 180
Peacock (American warship), 125
Peckover, William (*Bounty* gunner), 52
Peel, Sir Robert, 171, 173
Penrhyn Island, 47
Perez, Francisco, 40-1
Perseverance (ship), 100
Picpus, Society of, 135, 199
Pipon, Captain, 110
Pirates, The, or Calamities of Captain Bligh, 68
Pitcairn Island, 18; *Bounty* mutineers on, 105-12; descendants brought to Tahiti, 128
Point Venus, 13, 25, 46, 56, 86, 205
Polynesian Plantation Company, 186
Pomare I (formerly Otoo, *q.v.*), 74, 90, 93, 94-5, 97
Pomare II (formerly Otoo, *q.v.*), 98, 99, 116-19, 124, 128, 222; defeat at Matavai, 100, 101; requests Christian baptism, 115, 117; regains authority, 118-19; baptized, 121-2
Pomare III, 124-6
Pomare IV, Queen, 126, 128, 130, 135, 151, 152, 184, 222; signs pledge, 129; and Catholic priests, 137-8, 139, 140; and French ultimatum, 141-2; treaty with France, 142, 144; seeks British protection, 142-3, 145, 179, 180-1; and French intrigues, 146, 149-50, 154-7, 159-69, 180-2; submits to protectorate, 182; death of, 209
Pomare V, 209-11, 220, 223, 227-8
Pompidou, Georges, 263, 264
Porpoise, HMS, 95, 96
Portlock, Lieutenant Nathaniel, 76
Pouvanaa a Oopa, 262, 263
Pritchard, George (missionary), 128-9, 142, 143, 145-6, 156, 159, 187; seeks consulship, 130; attitude to Catholic missionaries, 136, 137, 138, 139; appointed Consul, 140; seeks British protection for Tahiti, 145, 146, 154-5, 159, 160-2; and French intrigues, 160-2, 163-7; arrested and deported, 169-70, 172-3, 174.

Providence, HMS, 76, 78-9
Puckey, James (missionary), 85
Puckey, William (missionary), 85, 90
Punaauia, 233
Purcell, William (*Bounty* carpenter), 52, 55, 56-7, 59, 60

Quintal, Matthew (*Bounty* seaman) 53, 54, 60, 62, 66, 111, 112

Raiatea island, 26, 40, 70, 119, 180, 182
Rarahu (in *Mariage de Loti*), 197-209
Rassemblement Democratique des Populations Tahitiennes, 254-260
Reine Blanche, La (French ship), 147, 150, 154, 162, 167
Resolution, HMS (Cook's ship), 31, 42-6, 51, 52
Resolution (*Bounty* mutineers' schooner), 67, 70, 71, 79
Rey, Henri, 265, 266
Reynolds, Sir Joshua, 34-5
Richerie, Gaultier de la, 186, 188, 189
Robertson, George (master of *Dolphin*), 11-19
Rodriguez, Maximo, 38, 40, 41
Ronciere, Count and Countess de la, 189, 190, 193, 195
Rotuma, 71
Rousseau, Jean-Jacques, 10, 23
Royal Admiral, 95
Russell, Captain Lord Edward, 139

Samuel, Mr. (*Bounty* clerk), 53, 60, 61
Sanders, George, 244
Sandwich, Lord, 32, 34, 35, 45
Sandwich Islands, 45
Sanford, Francis, 262-66
Scharnhorst (German raider), 239-41
Scherzer, Dr. Karl, 184
Scott, Lieutenant William, 95
Scott, William (missionary), 95, 100, 115, 116, 119
Sedgwick, Ellery, 246
Sever, Captain William, 46-7
Seymour, Admiral Sir George, 182
Shillibeer, Lieutenant John, 109-10
Simpson, Alexander (missionary), 122, 149
Simpson, George (*Bounty* quarter-master's mate), 52
Skinner, Richard (*Bounty* seaman), 53, 62, 66, 67, 69, 72

Titi (Gauguin's companion), 228, 230
Tofua, 73
Tone, Franchot, 247
Tonga islands, 58, 71, 94
Tootate, 65, 69
Topaz (American whaler), 105-7, 109
Tuamotu Archipelago, 185, 211
Tubuai, 62, 63, 64, 65-6, 85
Tucker, Captain J. J., 158, 162, 165, 167-8

Utomi, Chief, 148, 154

Vaitepiha Bay, 39, 41, 42, 43-4, 75
Valentine, James (*Bounty* seaman), 53, 56
Vancouver, Captain George, 73-5, 78
Vehiatua, Chief, 39
Venus (Bass's ship), 96 and *n.*
Venus (schooner), 101
Viaud, Julien (Pierre Loti), 196-209
Victoria, Queen, 142, 143, 145, 146, 166, 179, 180-1

Vindictive, HMS, 155, 168, 170, 172
Voltaire, F. M. Arouet de, 23

Wallis, Captain Samuel, 9, 10, 14, 18, 23, 25, 27, 28, 45
Waters, William (missionary), 95, 98
Watts, Lieutenant John, 46
Weatherhead, Captain Matthew, 75, 76-7, 78
Webber, John, 44, 46, 65
Wellington, Duke of, 173
Williams, John (*Bounty* seaman), 53, 55, 60, 62, 66, 111
Williams, John (missionary), 120, 121
Wilson, Charles (missionary), 95, 100, 115, 120
Wilson, Charles B., 146, 150, 151
Wilson, Captain James, 83, 84, 86, 87
Wilson, William, 84, 87

Youl, John (missionary), 95, 99
Young, Edward (*Bounty* midshipman), 52, 61, 62, 66, 111-12

Zelee (French gunboat), 240, 241

284